IDE-JETRO Series

The Institute of Developing Economies, Japan External Trade Organization (IDE-JETRO) series explores the economic issues faced in developing regions globally, providing new research and analysis of these economies, with the aim of creating a more comprehensive understanding of the issues and conditions they are experiencing. With a wide range of volumes covering key economic issues in developing economies, as well as examining the challenges faced as East Asia continues to integrate, the titles in this series are essential companions for academics and policymakers interested in cutting-edge research and analysis of developing economies.

More information about this series at
http://www.springer.com/series/14861

Contents

List of Figures

List of Tables

1

Introduction: New Sustainability Challenges for East Asia

Etsuyo Michida, John Humphrey, and Kaoru Nabeshima

Globalization has been central to the achievement of the East Asian miracle. Developing countries in Asia have achieved rapid economic growth, improved human welfare and equitable income distribution by allocating resources to productive sectors efficiently and, above all, by maintaining rapid export growth (World Bank 1993). Much of the story of globalization in the past 40 years has been about the emergence of the developing Asian economies as producers and exporters of manufactured products. The process

E. Michida (✉)
Institute of Developing Economies, Japan External Trade Organization (IDE-JETRO), Chiba, Japan
e-mail: etsuyo_michida@ide.go.jp

J. Humphrey,
University of Sussex, Brighton, UK
e-mail: Humphrey041@gmail.com

K. Nabeshima
Waseda University, Tokyo, Japan
e-mail: kknabeshima@waseda.jp

© The Author(s) 2017   **1**
E. Michida et al. (eds.), *Regulations and International Trade*,
IDE-JETRO Series, DOI 10.1007/978-3-319-55041-1_1

started with the Asian newly industrializing economies, took in the ASEAN-4 economies, and more recently has included some of the Greater Mekong sub-region economies, most notably Vietnam. Alongside the growth of manufactured exports, some East Asian economies have also increased their exports of agricultural products.

However, globalization presents new challenges for the rapidly growing economies of East Asia. One notable trend in global markets is the increasing importance of both public regulations and private standards as a condition of access to developed country markets. These regulations and standards have increased their scope (the range of issues covered has moved beyond consumer protection to include sustainability issues), their stringency, and their application of preventive controls to both domestic production and imported products. The latter place requirements on both the businesses and the regulatory structures of exporting countries to demonstrate in advance that the products exported to developed countries meet particular requirements related to consumer safety and environmental impact.

This collection of papers examines the impacts of public regulations and private standards in developed countries on exporting countries in developing Asia. It considers the impacts on trade between developing Asia and developed countries, the responses of regulatory authorities in developing Asia to the increasingly complex external environment, and the impacts on businesses in developing Asia as they respond to the new challenges. The papers focus particularly on EU regulations relating to chemicals and the recycling of electrical products (RoHS and REACH) and to standards in agriculture, particularly GlobalGAP. In addition to overview papers about trade and the regulatory environment, the collection includes a series of papers based on empirical studies in developing Asia that identify both the policy responses of these countries and the impacts on businesses of this changing regulatory environment.

The collection of papers in this book takes up the following questions across different chapters:

1. Why do developed countries introduce new regulatory policies and standards?
2. What are the motivations for businesses adopting private standards and what are the consequences for exports from developing Asia?

3. What are the processes through which new regulatory approaches are diffused to Asia?
4. How does the changing regulatory environment impact on country-level and firm-level competitiveness?
5. What are the lessons for regulatory policy in developing countries?

1.1 The Changing Regulatory Environment

This book focuses particularly on two aspects of the regulation of international trade that were virtually unknown 25 years ago. The first is food safety, where public regulations have become more stringent (e.g., with respect to limits on pesticide residues and measures to reduce the incidence of microbial contamination), and businesses in some developed countries have promoted the development and adoption of private standards for food safety as a means of meeting new regulatory obligations placed on them. The second area of interest is government-imposed product-related environmental regulations (PRERs), of which the EU's Restriction of Hazardous Substances (RoHS) regulation (which pertains to hazardous substances in electrical and electronic equipment) and its Regulation on Registration, Evaluation, Authorisation and Restriction of Chemicals (REACH) regulations (which pertain to the registration, evaluation, authorization and use restrictions for chemicals) are among the most important (Michida and Nabeshima 2012). In both cases, the new requirements place obligations on businesses putting products onto the market in the EU, which has affects not only on domestic producers, but also on businesses in countries exporting to that market.

For governments, one significant challenge arising from increased trade is to secure the benefits of this trade while at the same time maintaining adequate levels of protection for its citizens. For this, they need some degree of confidence that regulatory systems (at either the firm or public level) in exporting countries will provide an equivalent level of control to that achieved by (or at least sought from) domestic regulation. In addition to this, there is increasing concern about the global impacts of production and trade that affects all countries. To address this issue, a large number of treaties and programs have been developed over the past 20 years. Alongside global agreements, developed countries have also introduced controls within their national boundaries (and within the EU) and sought to extend best practices to other countries through new requirements for access to the national/regional market.

The second chapter, by Humphrey, on 'Regulation, standards, and risk management in the context of globalization' provides an overview of the motivations for new regulatory controls adopted in destination markets through an examination of the cases of forestry, horticulture and chemicals. It discusses the drivers for the introduction of these controls and how they are operationalized in ways that shape the activities of businesses located beyond the borders of the adopting countries.

In spite of the differences between the agriculture, chemicals and electrical/electronics sectors in the way that regulations and standards are being developed, Humphrey's chapter shows that there are some common features in their approaches to controls over traded goods:

1. New controls arise partly in response to changing perceptions of the sources of hazards and acceptable levels of risk. In the case of food safety, EU regulations on pesticide residues have been tightened up and new controls on food hygiene on farms and in processing establishments have been introduced in response to food safety scares. The REACH regulations on chemicals reflect a change in emphasis from allowing chemicals to be used until they are proven to be a risk to health or the environment to requiring businesses to show that products are not hazardous as a precondition for their introduction into the market.

2. In all three sectors, the new regulatory frameworks incorporate risk-based approaches. This requires risk assessment, risk management and risk communication.

3. A shift to preventive controls. Preventive controls are designed to prevent an incident occurring. Instead of depending upon inspection

as the means of control in the case of food safety, or identifying negative impacts of the chemicals following their use, these regulations and standards are designed to identify risks and prompt measures to eliminate them (or reduce them to an acceptable level) before harm occurs.

4. Private sector responsibility for ensuring conformance with the regulations and standards. For example, the REACH regulation means that 'importers and producers now will be responsible to collect data and evaluate toxicological and ecotoxicological effects of the chemical content of their products before putting them on the market' (Eklund and Karlsson 2010: 164).

5. A whole chain approach is adopted. Risks and controls are found along the chain, and effective management of risk may require communication and coordination along the chain. This means that the consequences of regulations spread along chains in exporting countries, encompassing not only direct exporters, but also their suppliers.

These regulations and standards have direct implications for what businesses and governments in exporting countries are required to achieve. For businesses, new regulations require, first, an understanding of the requirements of the export market. Second, businesses have to adopt certain procedures to comply with the regulations. In the case of food safety, this might mean applying food hygiene measures or establishing traceability systems. In the case of RoHS it might require the development of alternatives to the six hazardous substances whose use in electrical and electronics products is restricted by the regulation. Third, in order to demonstrate compliance with the regulations, businesses may need to record and document information about inputs, products or processes in order to show conformance to the regulations. Governments in exporting countries also have a role. They need to create domestic (and regional) regulatory frameworks and provide support for businesses. These issues are then explored in detail through studies of the impact of regulations on and in exporting countries.

1.2   Impacts on Developing Countries

The new wave of globalization has facilitated the access of developing country firms to global markets. As discussed by Baldwin (2011), businesses in developing countries can access to global markets through their participation in global value chains, undertaking activities that reflect their comparative advantage rather than making final products. Information and communications technology (ICT) allows firms to communicate with other firms that locate distantly in order to customize parts and accessories more easily. A firm slices up production stages and offshores the stages of parts, components and accessories according to the comparative advantage of different countries. This leads to increasing fragmentation of supply chains and a larger volume of intermediate goods trade. A study by the World Trade Organization (WTO) and Institute of Developing Economies, Japan External Trade Organization (IDE-JETRO) (2011) showed more than 50% of non-fuel merchandise trade was constituted by intermediate goods. Lower ICT costs change competition from the level of industrial sectors to the level of production stages (Baldwin 2011). In other words, international trade has shifted from the trade of goods toward trade in tasks (Grossman and Rossi-Hansberg 2008; WTO and IDE-JETRO 2011).

This has created new opportunities for developing countries. First, it has reduced entry barriers and allowed a specialization in tasks for which developing countries have a competitive advantage (e.g., labor-intensive assembly). Second, developing countries no longer require the whole set of supporting industries and services in order to participate in manufacturing for export. Third, through establishing links with more technologically advanced customers, developing country firms may be able to acquire new capabilities and gain access to advanced technologies and materials that cannot be procured domestically. As long as a firm remains in the supply chain, it continues to receive the support it needs for accessing export markets.

These opportunities are particularly important in the context of the changing scope for national industrial policy. Traditionally, industrial policy meant nurturing of domestic industry, usually coupled with significant trade barriers to protect the domestic market. Industrial strategy was based on the belief that in an initial stage, businesses could grow through supplying the needs of the domestic market. Once they had used this market to grow in size and acquire capabilities, then they would be able to start exporting to other markets. This conception of industrial strategy led many countries to adopt import substitution policies.

With the current stage of globalization, the idea that economic development is linked to industrialization remains unchanged. What has changed, however, is the notion of how industrialization should be achieved. With continuing efforts to liberalize trade and investment at the global level through the WTO and regionally through various agreements and initiatives, developing countries do not have many options for traditional industry policy sustained by trade restrictions. Instead, many developing countries see that plugging into global supply chains is one of the quickest ways to industrialize as exemplified by the experience of East Asian countries. This places greater emphasis on FDI as a way of securing resources for export-oriented development. At the same time, a new dimension of the industrial policy is the nurturing of regulation (and standards) compliance capabilities.

However, the new regulatory barriers make this task more difficult. The compliance responsibilities placed on businesses by the new regulations means that both businesses importing into developed countries and businesses exporting to these countries face greater risks in terms of direct losses arising from compliance failures or more diffuse losses in terms of reputation and brand image from such failures.

The complexity of modern supply chains increases these risks. Products passing through complex supply chains are very difficult to track across all the different stages of transformation, particularly when suppliers are located in different countries. Clear examples of the challenges are provided by the cases of microbial contamination and residues of agricultural chemicals for food safety and by chemicals and hazardous substances contained in products. In the case of processed shrimp produced in Vietnam and exported to large markets such as EU, USA and Japan, fingerlings come from China, feed is imported from Chile and antibiotics are produced in Canada. Shrimp is farmed in small plots owned by many different farmers. There may be traders collecting shrimp from different ponds to sell as a single batch to processing factories. Hygiene controls and effective cool chains are essential in processing and transport to prevent contamination and product degradation.

With increasing fragmentation and division of labor in the global economy, the ramifications of regulatory requirements extend down supply chains. Firms exporting directly to countries adopting new standards and regulations have to satisfy new legal requirements. Even firms not exporting directly can be affected by requirements by customers that are exporting to markets implementing new regulations. Various contributions to this volume highlight how domestic businesses in ASEAN countries have had to respond to new requirements placed on them by exporting companies and, in particular, multinational companies. Customers, both domestic and external, may also change their supply chain strategies in response to the risks of failing to meet new market requirements. For example, one large Japanese manufacturer of electrical and electronics products encountered a problem with hazardous materials that meant they were not compliant with EU regulations. To fix the problem, the manufacturer reduced the number of suppliers so that these could be monitored more easily and selected the suppliers that were most capable of meeting its requirements.

This creates new barriers for entry into these global value chains. Firms that are participating in global production networks need to be aware of the regulations and standards that prevail in importing countries. What is different from the past is that the regulations and standards adopted in importing countries are much more challenging, and this creates a gap between the export market requirements and the domestic regulations and capacities of developing countries. The discussion in the literature on regulatory responses in East Asia has so far specified some of the challenges facing governments and businesses in the region. The challenges by themselves do not provide information about how governments and businesses in East Asia will respond to these challenges. In fact, the responses are likely to be varied. Naiki's (2010) analysis of the response of the Japanese and East Asian governments to the REACH regulations shows a considerable diversity in responses. Similarly, one might expect businesses to respond to the new regulations that frame access to the EU market, but it is not clear which types of businesses are most successful in making the shift, their motivations for doing so and the resources they need to achieve compliance with the new obligations placed on them both by the regulations and by their customers. The papers in this volume bridge this evidence gap by providing empirically grounded analyses of the responses in Asia to public and private regulations and standards. It provides detailed empirical material from the ASEAN region about how the challenges faced by both public policy and businesses and the responses that have been made. Chapters 2–6 focus on the policy perspective, while Chapters 7–12 provide evidence of business impacts and responses through the use of business surveys in a number of ASEAN countries.

1.3   Policy Response to Export Market Regulation

Michida's chapter (Chapter 3) on 'Regulatory diffusion from the EU to Asia' focuses on the chemical regulation, RoHS, adopted by the EU. It considers the diffusion of the RoHS regulation to Asia and why governments in the region choose to adopt regulations similar to those introduced by the EU. It argues that the most important reasons for regulatory diffusion relate to supporting the export performance of economies in the region by enabling businesses to meet the requirements of export markets, by closing the gap between domestic and export market regulations, and by facilitating the management of supply chains in the domestic economy. Adoption of PRERs can also be motivated by the desire to control imports of unsafe products or to limit environmental degradation, but these motivations are markedly less important.

The importance of these different motivations varies across the region, particularly as some countries are more reliant on exports in general and exports to regulated markets such as the EU, in particular. This results in variations in adoption, and policy fragmentation within the ASEAN region as countries respond to the challenges in different ways, as well as heterogeneity with respect to the 'race to the top' in environmental management. The similar yet heterogeneous policies are creating complication in both regional and global trade. The chapter points out the need to have coordinated policy diffusion even though the processes occur in an *ad hoc* and voluntary manner. Moreover, there are countries that do not introduce regulations due to lack of capacity. A closer examination is needed so that these countries do not become pollution havens.

The study carried out by Ramungul (Chapter 4) on 'Adapting to EU chemical regulations: The experience of Thailand' looks specifically at the role of government in facilitating a response to the new regulatory challenges. It emphasizes the broad range of impacts on industry in Thailand of the RoHS directive and the fact that businesses underestimated the impact of the new regulation and had limited knowledge about its implications. In addition, the chapter highlights the difficulties both firms and government had in responding to the draft EU regulations because these lacked technical specifications. The chapter demonstrates how the government of Thailand promotes the collaboration between businesses through the ThaiRoHS. This enabled an effective industry-wide response to the new challenges.

The fifth chapter, by Michida and Nabeshima, on 'Diffusion of private food safety standard from Europe to Asia' examines the diffusion of standards for good agricultural practices (GAPs) in the ASEAN region. It takes up a number of themes that emerged in the previous chapters. It emphasizes that governments in the region view GAPs as important for access to export markets, for improving farming practices and as a means of facilitating intra-regional trade through standards harmonization. As in the case of chemicals, these motivations created heterogeneous responses across the region, and the paper highlights the different ways in which GAPs have been introduced across the region. The paper draws attention to the diversity of standards with respect to both the use of private and public initiatives and the extent to which standards introduced in the region are copies of standards prevailing in extra-regional markets or adaptations of them. The adaptation of private standards by government is seen as an industrial policy to keep market access to a large market. However, most of the adopted standards in Asia do not function as global standards. The chapter suggests that *ad hoc* adaptation of foreign private standards may lead to a mismatch with the country's philosophy, needs, and industrial structure.

The sixth and final chapter in the first part of the book, by Nabeshima 'Preliminary theoretical model for standard promotion from the government point of view', takes the argument offered in Chapter four one step further. It offers a theoretical model for the decisions to adopt foreign private standards by a government, taking into account their impacts on private sector, especially for exporters. The key driver of the model is the fixed costs associated with exports. The results suggest that the greater degree of difference between prevailing standards in two countries, the smaller the number of firms that will export. The chapter explores various scenarios and policy options in each situation.

Overall, these four chapters show that governments across the region have adopted a variety of different approaches to the issue of promoting good agricultural practices. In some cases they adopt leading global private standards in their entirety. In some cases they produce national variants of the standards, and in other cases they are more concerned to promote good practice through encouragement and education. The analysis shows that public policy can take to broad options. One is more based on market forces. In this instance, public policy will focus more on assisting firms to comply with regulations through training and perhaps introducing these regulations within the domestic context. Through these efforts, regulations and standards may converge into *de facto* harmonization. The other is to harmonize regulations and standards with other countries, to achieve *de jure* harmonization. In East Asia, it seems that countries are keener on pursuing de facto harmonization rather than *de jure* harmonization as a new addition to their industrial development policy.[1]

---

[1] This is similar to the pathways that East Asian countries have taken to regional trade integration efforts. The efforts to integrate regional trade within East Asia have taken the de facto route through liberalization of trade and investment, rather than taking the formal form such as free trade agreements. Only recently have these countries started to take a more formal approach.

1.4   Firm-Level Responses

It was argued earlier that the introduction of preventive controls in developing countries is particularly challenging for businesses. New capabilities are required to meet these requirements. How might businesses respond to pressures for compliance, and what resources will they be able to mobilize in order to meet the new regulations? How do responses differ according to size of firm and the level and nature of exposure to export markets? Part II of this book 'Impacts of environmental regulation on firms in Asia' examines how product regulations affect firm behavior and global supply chain structures. The analyses of all the chapters except Chapter 12 use unique firm survey data that IDE collected between 2011 and 2013 in Vietnam, Malaysia and Japan. Chapter 12 is based on data collected separately for the case of Thailand.

Michida, Ueki and Nabeshima's Chapter 7 on 'A snapshot view of PRER impacts on firms in Vietnam, Malaysia and Japan' introduces the section as a whole by providing an overview of the surveys conducted in the region. It outlines the research questions and how these were incorporated into the surveys in Vietnam, Malaysia and Japan. The initial results of the survey, presented in the chapter, reveal that firms facing tougher requirements for product quality worked intensively to comply with regulations while firms that have not faced new requirements or product rejections tend to overlook the needs to upgrade their capability. It can be hypothesized that responses may be reactive or proactive (Henson and Jaffee 2008). Reactive firms, as the name suggests, react to the changes after the fact. They will rely on information provided by the lead firm if they participate in a global production network. If they do not, they may not be aware of these changes at all. Proactive responses identify changes in regulations and standards through their efforts in regulatory and market intelligence to gather necessary information. By doing so, they can anticipate the change (or for large firms, influence the directions of change), and by the time these changes occur, they are ready. The survey also reveals that adapting to chemicals regulation leads firms to diversify material sourcing according to differences in the strictness of regulations in different markets. This may lead to the situation 'safer goods to regulated markets and less safe goods to less regulated markets'. Also, the tightness of supply chain control is shown to depend on both firms and countries. Many smaller firms are not aware of chemicals regulation overseas, and some policy is needed to provide information for firms that do not belong to supply chains to prepare for regulatory changes to keep market access. The analysis in Chapters 7–10 utilizes the data set presented in this chapter.

Chapter 8 by Ueki, Michida and Nabeshima, 'Transmission channels of requirements for chemicals in products to firms in Vietnam', examines how firms acquire the necessary knowledge and technologies to overcome obstacles to internationalization. This study investigates transmission channels of information on chemicals in products to firms in Vietnam. It takes up one of the themes that emerged in Chapters 2 and 5 by examining the interaction between public regulations and voluntary private standards and uses firm-level survey data to investigate hypotheses concerning how businesses manage chemical substances according to their value chain linkages, how much they export and the extent of their R&D capabilities. Although exporting firms may have direct links with foreign markets that introduce chemical-related regulations, exporting firms are not necessarily more likely to take measures necessary to comply with regulatory requirements than non-exporting firms. Non-direct exporting firms that are part of supply chains also take steps to comply with regulations. Much of the economics literature has examined differences between export and non-export firms. However, this chapter suggests the role of global value chains and indirect exports to facilitate export may also be of importance.

Chapters 9 and 10, by Otsuki and Honda, both focus on the impacts of EU chemical regulations – RoHS and REACH – on firms in Malaysia and Vietnam. The intent of the two chapters is to separate out the demand- and supply-side effects of technical regulations. Chapter 9 focuses on the cost impact of meeting standards, while Chapter 10 examines the impact of the foreign chemical safety regulations on the export performance of firms. Chapter 9 starts by emphasizing the broad range of industries affected by chemical regulations and the costs involved in demonstrating compliance. Through the use of the firm-level data set, and building on earlier work in this field, the chapter argues that there are substantial costs to businesses that take measures to meet new regulations. Chapter 9 found that compliance costs are lowered due to participation to global value chains in the case of REACH, but not in the case of RoHS.

Chapter 10 looks at chemical regulations that might impact on export performance. While compliance with regulations will raise costs, it might also signal improved product safety and quality and facilitate access to export markets. Firm-level survey data are used to estimate the effects of technical regulations on the entry of firms to export markets, the number of export markets entered and the amount of products exported. The chapter shows that compliance with RoHS and REACH increases the probability that firms will enter export markets, as it would demonstrate an overall level of competence and quality. However, it is also found that compliance decreases the number of export markets entered, possibly because compliant firms focus their efforts on the EU market: trade diversion from non-EU markets outweighs the signaling effect.

Chapter 11 on 'Diffusion of quality and environmental management systems through global value chains: cases of Malaysia and Vietnam' by Iguchi and Arimura also considers the signaling issue, but focuses on the relationship between product-related environmental regulations in chemicals (PRERCs) and the diffusion of ISO9001 and ISO14001. Using the same firm-level data sources on Vietnam and Malaysia, they consider the relationship between insertion into global value chains and the adoption of these ISO standards. Given that standards are a means by which businesses are able to obtain information about the capabilities and processes used in supplier firms, there is an expectation that adoption of the two standards will be higher among firms that export, directly or indirectly. Overall, the levels of ISO9001 adoption are greater than for ISO14001 across both countries.

The chapter shows that adoption of ISO9001 is higher among firms whose customers have made requests about addressing the chemical content of their products. Such certified companies are also more likely to be exporters. For ISO14001, the relationships are less clear-cut. In Vietnam, ISO14001 is associated with customer concerns about chemicals, but not in Malaysia. Conversely, exporting firms in Malaysia are more likely to adopt ISO14001, but not in Vietnam. It does, however, appear to be the case that firms that adopt ISO9001 are more likely to adopt ISO14001 subsequently. The overall implication is that the development of chemical regulations has not facilitated a flight to 'pollution havens' in developing countries, as these countries are also adopting environmental standards.

Ramungul in Chapter 12 on 'Challenges of EU chemical regulations: the case of Thai firms' discusses the responses of Thai firms during their transition to bring their products to comply with EU regulations through a study of survey results in Thailand. The data set for Vietnam, Malaysia and Japan provides data for one year but the data from Thailand covers three years, which enables an examination of dynamic changes by firms in response to regulation. It also shows that the differences in reaction depend on the positions of firms in supply chains. The chapter clearly shows that compliance was driven by customers, and middle-stream firms have been reactive to customers and regulatory requirements. Tightly connected supply chains help firms to comply with regulations.

Acknowledgments The editors have benefitted from comments made by seminar participants at the Public forum of the World Trade Organization (WTO) in 2015 andthe side event of the WTO 9th Ministerial Conference in Bali, at the Institute of Development Studies at the University of Sussex and the Universityof California, Berkeley. The editors would also like to express their appreciation for the valuable suggestions by David Vogel at the seminar in theUniversity of California, Berkeley, and for the insights into private standards in horticulture provided by Steve Homer.

References

Baldwin, R. (2011). *Trade and industrialisation after globalisation's 2nd unbundling: How building and joining a supply chain are different and why it matters.* Retrieved from Cambridge MA; National Bureau of Economic Research, http://www.nber.org/papers/w17716.

Eklund, B., & Karlsson, J. (2010). Assessing chemical risks: Evaluating products rather than substances, and the case of anti-fouling paints. In J. Eriksson, M. Gilek, & C. Rudén (Eds.), *Regulating chemical risks: European and global challenges* (pp. 163–176). London: Springer.

Grossman, G. M., & Rossi-Hansberg, E. (2008). Trading tasks: A simple theory of offshoring. *The American Economic Review, 98*(5), 1978–1997.

Henson, S., & Jaffee, S. (2008). Understanding developing country strategic responses to the enhancement of food safety standards. *The World Economy, 31*(4), 548–568.

Michida, E., & Nabeshima, K. (2012). *Role of supply chains in adopting product related environmental regulations: Case studies of Vietnam.* Retrieved from Chiba; Institute of Developing Economies, https://www.ide.go.jp/English/Publish/Download/Dp/343.html.

Naiki, Y. (2010). Assessing policy reach: Japan's chemical policy reform in response to the EU's REACH regulation. *Journal of Environmental Law, 22*(2), 171–195.

World Bank. (1993). *The East Asian miracle: Economic growth and public policy.* New York: Oxford University Press.

WTO & IDE-JETRO. (2011). *Trade patterns and global value chains in East Asia: From trade in goods to trade in tasks:* https://www.wto.org/english/res_e/booksp_e/stat_tradepat_globvalchains_e.pdf

Etsuyo Michida is an Associate Senior Research Fellow at Institute of Developing Economies, Japan External Trade Organization (IDE-JETRO) and was a Visiting Scholar at Haas School of Business, University of California, Berkeley from 2015 to 2017. Her research interest lies in trade and the environment with a special focus on developing countries. She has recently researched on the relationship between environmental regulation, firm behavior, and global supply chains. She holds a PhD in Economics from Graduate School of International Cooperation Studies, Kobe University.

John Humphrey was a Professorial Fellow at the Institute of Development Studies at the University of Sussex for many years and is currently a Visiting Professor at the School of Business, Management and Economics at the University of Sussex. He has researched and published extensively on global value chains, contributing both theoretical papers and the analysis, with particular attention paid to the global food industry. More recent work has focused on value chains and food standards. He has provided consultancy services to many international organizations on value chain issues.

Kaoru Nabeshima is an Associate Professor at the Graduate School of Asia-Pacific Studies, Waseda University. He holds a PhD in Economics from University of California-Davis, and a BA in Economics from Ohio Wesleyan

University. Prior to joining Graduate School of Asia-Pacific Studies, Waseda University in 2015, he worked for the Institute of Developing Economies, Japan External Trade Organization and the World Bank. Some of his publications include *Meeting Standards, Winning Markets: Regional Trade Standards Compliance Report East Asia 2013* (IDE-JETRO/UNIDO 2013), *Tiger Economies under Threat* (co-authored with Shahid Yusuf, 2009), and *Some Small Countries Do It Better: Rapid Growth and Its Causes in Singapore, Finland, and Ireland* (co-authored with Shahid Yusuf, 2012). His research interests lie in examining the relationship between regulations and international trade, the issue of middle income trap, and the innovation capabilities of firms in East Asia.

Part I

Regulatory Challenges Under Globalization

2

Regulation, Standards and Risk Management in the Context of Globalization

John Humphrey

2.1 Introduction

Increased interactions between national economies resulting from globalization create new regulatory challenges. Some of these challenges relate to removing obstacles to globalization, and in the area of trade in goods the World Trade Organization (WTO) has been successful in creating a framework for limiting barriers to trade. However, nation-states may also wish to manage globalization by developing rules that place restrictions on trade. Jacoby and Meunier suggest that the management of globalization has been a key element of EU policy over the past two decades:

> the concept of "managed globalisation," articulated explicitly as the central doctrine of EU trade policy since 1999 suggests that order and control should be restored to the process of globalization by framing it

J. Humphrey (✉)
University of Sussex, Brighton, UK
e-mail: Humphrey041@gmail.com

E. Michida et al. (eds.), *Regulations and International Trade*,
IDE-JETRO Series, DOI 10.1007/978-3-319-55041-1_2

21

with rules, obeying these rules, and empowering international organisations to make and implement these rules (Jacoby & Meunier, 2010: 304).

The mechanisms through which such rules are developed and enforced vary considerably. In their analysis of transnational regulatory arrangements, Keohane and Victor argue that transnational regulations run the gamut from "fully integrated institutions that impose regulation through comprehensive hierarchical rules" (which would be a description of WTO) to "highly fragmented collections of institutions with no identifiable core and weak or non-existent linkages between regime elements," with many variants in between (Keohane & Victor, 2011: 8). Specifically, they argue that regulatory arrangements that emerge out of interactions between a multiplicity of interdependent states and interests that change over time result in "regime complexes," which have been defined as "an array of partially overlapping and nonhierarchical institutions governing a particular issue-area" (Raustiala & Victor, 2004: 279).[1] These arrangements include both public regulations and private standards.[2]

This chapter is particularly concerned with how risk management has been incorporated into the regulation of trade. This chapter considers regulation in three sectors: forest protection, food safety and chemicals. In each of these areas, the management of globalization involves multilevel and multi-actor systems that lack comprehensive hierarchical rules. Alongside transnational public governance through a variety of institutions, transnational private governance also plays an important role in developing risk-management approaches to trade regulation. In addition, nation-states use bilateral arrangements to regulate trade—particularly restraints on market access and treaties that influence risk management in exporting countries. In the construction of these governance mechanisms, economic and political power matters. More powerful nations impose or negotiate rules and regulations, as do powerful businesses.

---

[1] Quoted in de Burca et al. (2013: 735).

[2] In this paper regulation is an activity will be applied to both public and private initiatives. When considering particular instruments, there will be reference to private standards (which do not have the force of law) and public regulations (which do).

Market access is an important weapon, for both governments and businesses. As a result, weaker agents—governments and businesses—are standards takers.

A lot of attention has been given in recent years to the impact of private standards on the economies of developing countries, in part because of the importance of private standards in agricultural and food exports and the importance of these sectors for the livelihoods of the poorest. In particular, the development of risk-based approaches in private standards has been seen to have particularly onerous consequences for poor producers (Fuchs et al. 2011; Graffham et al. 2007). However, public regulation, including the development of risk-based strategies, continues to develop, and understanding recent developments in this area will clarify the challenges facing developing countries in globalized trade.

2.2 Responding to the Challenges of Globalization

The regulatory challenges arising from globalization have received a lot of attention in recent years. Observers have frequently emphasized the growth of transnational private governance—regulatory initiatives that are designed move left, implemented and enforced by largely non-state actors:

> An increasing portion of business regulation emanates not from conventional state and inter-state institutions but from an array of private sector, civil society, multi-stakeholder and hybrid public-private institutions operating in a dynamic, transnational regulatory space. Accounting standards, fair trade labels, forestry certification schemes, labor rights monitoring, transparency standards, and many more: *transnational business governance* (TBG) has grown in scope and importance as production, consumption, and their impacts globalize and as states reconsider established modes of regulation (Eberlein et al. 2014: 1–2, stress in original).

In some areas, transnational private governance arises because governments do not wish to act, or are prevented from acting. Nevertheless, transnational private governance also addresses issues on which govern-ments do have the power to act. Food safety is an area where govern-ments have a long-standing and continuing commitment to regulation, but where private standards schemes have also proliferated. Why do private initiatives emerge in these areas?

Three reasons are commonly put forward to explain this. First, governments may themselves seek private involvement in standards development when they recognize a problem but defer to private sector expertise and outsource the creation and development of regulatory initiatives to private sector actors, as is seen with international financial regulation (Botzem, 2008) and with accounting and electrotechnical standards (Büthe & Mattli, 2011).

Second, the increasing complexity of value chains and the emergence of new risks create regulatory challenges that are beyond the capacity of estab-lished public controls. This is very evident in the food industry, which has become increasingly fragmented, not only in terms of geographical locations and trade, but also in terms of longer supply chains with greater numbers of actors involved in the movement of food from farm to fork. The use of established food safety controls such as border inspection is seen to be inadequate to face the new challenges. In this context, governments may seek to place more responsibility on businesses to ensure food safety, with private standards being one of the responses to the new obligations.

Third, it is argued that transnational public regulation is frequently impeded by differences in approaches between powerful global actors that make consensus impossible to achieve, preventing the creation of new hierarchical regimes. There are various instances of private standards arising as a response to public deadlock. The Greenhouse Gas (GHG) Protocol was developed when "Dissent among [developed countries] about the role of emissions trading, and thus, the possible *uses* of GHG emissions accounting standards took the issue of accounting methodologies off the agenda for inter-governmental cooperation" (Green, 2010: 2, emphasis in original). Similarly, Gulbrandsen (2014: 78) argues that the failure of inter-state initiatives accounts for emergence of the Forest Stewardship Council (FSC) and Marine Stewardship Council (MSC) initiatives. Bernstein and Cashore (2007) provide a similar argument in the case of private regimes for forest regulation. For chemicals, the Strategic Approach to International Chemicals

Management (SAICM) emerged in the context of the inability of leading nations to agree to a new binding agreement on chemicals because of their substantial differences in approach. The scope and financing of SAICM itself was also subject to lengthy negotiations and compromises, reflecting these differences (Perrez, 2006: 250–253).

The novelty of private regulation and private standards schemes[3] has created a lot of interest in the role of private actors in global regulation. This may reinforce a tendency to argue that private standards are gaining in importance, while public regulations and regulatory activities are in decline. Such a tendency is frequently linked to analyses of neoliberalism and expressed in ideas such as the privatization of governance and the decline of public regulatory capacity in the face of both globalization and the fragmentation of global power following the emergence of new actors on the global stage. Private regulation is certainly an expanding field, but it does not displace the public. Many public initiatives are being taken to manage globalization and achieve extraterritorial effects. Governments have developed a range of mechanisms that are risk-based and preventive and involve behind-the-border changes in exporting countries. These will be discussed in this paper. In other words, in spite of the extension of transnational private governance, national governments and intergovernmental organizations continue to be actively involved in regulation processes.

The European Union (EU), in particular, has made extensive interventions in areas such as trade in forest products (to be discussed later), the effectiveness of the "competent authorities" responsible for food safety in exporting countries, and the promotion of new transnational regulatory structures (e.g., SAICM for chemicals).[4] All of these initiatives

---

[3] The difference between a standard and a standards scheme is that a standard is a series of rules for behavior. A standards scheme also has rules, but they are complemented by monitoring and enforcement mechanisms that are designed to ensure compliance. For a discussion of the activities involved in the creation and operationalization of private standards, see Henson and Humphrey (2010, 2012).

[4] One of the drivers of these tendencies in the EU is the extension of the mechanisms for managing the internal market in the EU to relations with non-EU trading partners. Changes in food safety legislation, for example, were undertaken in response to the crisis in EU food safety and the recognition that variations in practice within the EU were not sustainable in the context of a single market.

seek to manage globalization. Such initiatives may be undertaken by public agents alone, but there are also interactions between public authorities and private agents, with public authorities working with and through private agents, or placing specific demands upon them.

This chapter will consider regulations concerned with controls over production and trade that are designed to impact upon the products imported from other countries and the processes by which they are produced. This section begins by considering two different ways in which the welfare of citizens in one country can be influenced by how products are produced in other countries. It follows by considering regulation as it applies to intrinsic and extrinsic product characteristics, and concludes with a consideration of how globalization impacts with differing levels of severity generate different regulatory strategies and different forms of implementation.

2.2.1 Global Impact Pathways

There are two ways in which production of goods in one country can have effects on citizens in another. The first is through trade. Globalization greatly increases the flow of products across national boundaries. Ideally, the level of safety of imported products should be no less than that of products produced domestically, but regulatory requirements and levels of regulatory capacity (specification, implementation and enforcement) vary from country to country. Therefore, increasing trade may result in increasing risks to citizens that arise from practices outside the jurisdiction of the consuming country. Food safety is an example of the challenges posed by (i) the sourcing of more products from a greater range of countries with different levels of development and food safety capabilities, (ii) the increasing complexity of trade (food products and food inputs may be traded and processed in multiple countries), and (iii) the recognition of new safety challenges (such as mad cow disease and microbial contamination). Governments and businesses have to decide how to keep these risks to acceptable levels by considering what types of controls might be introduced and the points along the value chain where they would be most effective. While much trade in food has, and continues to be, regulated predominantly through border inspections of products and paperwork, there are serious limitations to this approach.

The second type of regulatory challenges relates to the global impacts of production and trade. These include pollution, resource depletion and loss of biodiversity (e.g., the discussion in the study by van Waarden, 2012). They originate in particular places and at particular times, but their effects, taken in aggregate, have impacts on countries far removed from their origin. Depletion of resources or loss of biodiversity can have global impacts, creating a need for transnational initiatives to address them. Private standards that address, in one way or another, the issue of the management of common resources include the MSC, FSC and the Round table on Sustainable Palm Oil (RSPO). Similarly, chemical pollution, CFCs and GHG emissions have potentially serious consequences for human health and reproduction right across the world. Some, but not all, of these challenges are being addressed through both public regulations and private standards, as well as through intergovernmental agreements.

These issues can be addressed through a broad range of policy instruments. The direct impacts arising from trade can be most directly addressed through trade measures, and these appear increasingly to involve "behind-the-border" measures designed to solve problems at source rather than through border controls. To the extent that poor regulatory capability in exporting countries is a key issue, then the focus may switch to governments and regulation in exporting countries, rather than particular products, and if many exporting countries face the same challenges, then broad-based programs aiming at improving the productive and regulatory capacities of a number of countries might be the most effective response.

With respect to the global (indirect) impacts, one obvious solution would be a global one—global agreements to create collective responses to challenges such as resource depletion and environmental destruction. However, where such agreements are not forthcoming, action by both governments and consumers may try to shape activities in exporting countries through positive and negative sanctions. In particular, market access to larger economies is one of the major instruments that can be used to shape the behavior of exporting countries.

2.2.2 Choice of Regulatory Strategy

One frequent distinction made in relation to the regulation of the characteristics of products and the ways they are produced is that between product and process standards. Product standards lay out rules concerning the intrinsic characteristics of products. They define characteristics that are acceptable or unacceptable—in general or in particular circumstances (e.g., for particular usages). In terms of regulatory strategy, product standards are enforced through performance-based regulation (Coglianese & Lazer, 2003: 694) that is applied after the product has been made. Products that do not meet the standards for the uses for which they are intended may then be excluded from the market and placing them on the market is an illegal act. Enforcing a product standard requires some way of assessing the relevant product characteristics. Border inspection is one way of achieving this, as is approval by the authorities in exporting countries (e.g., through the use of SPS certificates).

Process standards can be used as a substitute for product standards. In this case, the overall objective of the standard is achieved through controlling the way products are made, transported and stored. This approach is most useful when the assessment of product characteristics through inspection is difficult to achieve. The case of microbial contamination in fresh fruit and vegetables is a good example of this strategy. Microbial contamination is difficult to detect through inspection because it can exist in small quantities that are very unevenly distributed within product lots. Random testing may not capture levels of contamination that could subsequently endanger consumers. Therefore, standards that identify the pathways through which products could become contaminated and introduce measures to eliminate these risks can be a more effective means of achieving food safety. The mechanisms for devising these rules are discussed later.

Process standards can also be developed as a means of promoting or enforcing particular ways of producing products that are valued for their own sake. The goal is not to produce a product with certain characteristics, but to implement processes that have desirable impacts. Examples include Fairtrade (for which the process objective is to improve the livelihoods of producers), environmental standards that aim to limit the negative environmental impacts of agricultural production (Rainforest Alliance, etc.), standards aimed at protection of forests (FSC, the PEFC[5] family of standards, RSPO and government initiatives such as the European Union's Voluntary Partnership Agreements for forestry) and standards relating to social impact (SA 8000, Ethical Trade Initiative, etc.).[6] In this case, the characteristics to be controlled are extrinsic to the product.

Such process standards can be managed in two different ways. First, there is what Coglianese and Lazer refer to as technology-based regulation, which specifies "technologies to be used or steps to be followed" (Coglianese & Lazer, 2003: 694). These mandate particular technologies or procedures that, if adopted, should lead to particular desirable outcomes. The standard itself identifies the problem and how it should be addressed. Examples would include the requirement for specific testing regimes and purity requirements for water used in agriculture.

Coglianese and Lazer identify a second approach to regulation, management-based regulation. In this form of process control, there is no attempt to specify a particular way of responding to potential hazards. Instead, businesses are obligated to produce "plans to comply with general criteria designed to promote the targeted social goal" (2003: 694).[7] A requirement for firms to introduce HACCP would be an example of management-based regulation. The requirement is not to introduce a particular

---

[5] Programme for the Endorsement of Forest Certification.

[6] Some standards schemes may combine a variety of product and process standards. Standards relating to good agricultural practices, for example, can be aimed simultaneously at impact issues such as protecting the environment and product issues such as food safety.

[7] The term "social goal" indicates that the goal of the regulation is to affect something which has consequences external to the enterprise. If all the costs and benefits of a firm's actions impacted clearly, directly and unambiguously on the firm, there would be no need for regulation.

procedure, but rather to show that risks have been identified and plans for eliminating or controlling them introduced. This approach is useful when the hazards facing enterprises vary considerably. It follows that if two factories have different levels of different hazards, their plans for containing them would be different.

2.2.3   The Severity of Risk

It was noted earlier that decisions about the introduction of private standards and public regulations are usually framed by considerations of costs and benefits. One consequence of this is that the way in which regulations are designed and implemented can vary substantially according to the level of risk to be addressed. The higher the perceived risk (and perceptions of risk will vary between agents), the greater the efforts to contain it, and the more likely it is that preventive strategies, often based on a risk management approach, will be employed.

This issue can be approached from the perspective of the presumption of innocence as opposed to the presumption of guilt. Border inspection regimes and tort law work on the basis of a presumption of innocence. In the EU, there is a legal obligation on food business operators not to place unsafe food on the market. However, imported products that are not inspected are assumed to comply with regulations, including the general obligation that food is safe. Many products that have not been inspected at the border are allowed to enter the country. In other words, there is a presumption of innocence. Action will only be taken if at some subsequent point in time a product is found not to be compliant.

The presumption of innocence may change to a "presumption of guilt" when the severity of the risk is higher and/or the risks of non-compliance with regulations are great. This applies to both public regulations and private standards schemes. In the case of private standards for food safety, for example, food processing establishments (and the products coming from them) are not considered compliant until they have shown themselves to be compliant through third-party certification. In this case, the presumption is one of guilt—in the absence of certification by a particular standards scheme, businesses that use that scheme will not accept that the establishment is compliant and will exclude it from their supply chains. No certification means no purchases.

Similarly, when products have the potential to create serious consequences—for plant or human health, the economy or long-term sustainability—public regulatory strategies will also tend to move toward a more interventionist approach based on the presumption of guilt. Regulatory practices in the case of high-risk foods, such as foods of animal origin, would be an example. In many countries meat processing is considered to be an activity that poses high risks for human health, and consequently food safety regulations focus on the origin of pathogens and contaminants: meat processing plants are required to implement hazard analysis and critical control point (HACCP) controls. HACCP systems are frequently backed up by on-site inspection by public inspectors. Governments may also impose specific controls in response to the identification of specific hazards that are considered both important for health and for which past experience indicates that there is a risk of contamination. The use of risk-based controls for fresh produce in the United States is discussed below.

2.3   Regulation in Food, Forestry and Chemicals

Standards and regulations vary according to the nature of the hazard that is to be controlled, the type of regulatory strategy to be employed and the severity of the risks involved. How do these factors influence the involvement of public and private actors? This question will be explored through the analysis of developments in regulation into three sectors: forest protection, food and food safety, and chemicals.

2.3.1 Forestry

The critical regulation issue in the forestry sector is the sustainable management of forests. In this context, sustainable management can refer to a broad range of issues, including sustainable forest production, protection of plant and animal life, forest rights for local populations, leisure activities, etc. These issues are seen to have impacts not only on localities and communities, but also more broadly. The destruction of tropical rainforests, in particular, leads to loss of biodiversity and the destruction of valuable habitats. Two private standards are important in forestry—the PEFC family of standards and the FSC. They compete for market share. Both standards work on the basis of certifying forests that are managed according to certain principles and then identify timber that has been sourced from such forests and operate traceability systems that enable this identification to be maintained as timber is processed and incorporated into a wide variety of products. While the two major schemes diverged initially and responded to different groups of stakeholders, there has been a convergence between the two standards in recent years, partly because governments have made clear their own preferences through their purchasing policies (Gulbrandsen, 2014: 79).

These private standards arose partly as a result of failures to reach globally binding agreements on forestry. The inter-governmental option failed to take off in the late 1980s and early 1990s, when proposals for a labeling system for sustainably-produced tropical timber, and later a binding UN Convention both met with resistance from some timber-exporting countries (Auld, 2014: 71–72; Overdevest & Zeitlin, 2014: 29). As Overdevest and Zeitlin note, the simple expedient of imposing unilateral trade restraints based on environmental considerations was also unavailable because of its incompatibility with WTO rules (Overdevest & Zeitlin, 2014: 30). The creation of the FSC in the 1990s was in part as a response of the failure of these initiatives. This process and the factors that led to the FSC are discussed by Auld (2014).

The biggest limitation of both schemes is their limited coverage in developing countries. One recent estimate of global coverage of forest sustainability standards puts the overall figure at 33% of the world's forests (Auld, 2014: 1), but Marx et al. (2012: 85–87) provide data for 2011 showing that coverage of the FSC forest management scheme in Africa, Latin America and Asia was under 10%. Given that protecting tropical rainforests was one of the main motivations for forest standards in the 1980s and 1990s, poor coverage of tropical forests is a major shortcoming.

In response to this challenge, governments have continued to intervene, not only within their own jurisdictions, but also in the management of forests in other countries. Legality Assurance Systems (LAS) or Legality Verification (LV) systems are being promoted by a number of governments, including those in developing countries that were unsympathetic (or hostile) to private certification (as discussed in Cashore & Stone, 2014). The legality assurance approach has also been promoted by the EU. While LAS have been offered by private sector certifiers, the coverage of the LAS approach has been considerably enhanced by the EU, which has negotiated with countries supplying tropical timber to extend the production and trade controlled by such schemes, redefine what is meant by "legal" and strengthen their monitoring and enforcement mechanisms. These schemes are designed to assure that exported timber conforms to the legal requirements of the exporting country. Illegal timber cannot be traded.

The Forest Law Enforcement, Governance and Trade (FLEGT) Action Plan, published by the EU in 2003, resulted in two initiatives. The first is the EU Timber Regulation (EUTR). This established assurance of legality as a requirement for placing timber (sourced from within the EU or elsewhere) on the EU market. This placed an obligation on organizations trading in timber to ensure that the supplies they used were legal (Forest Stewardship Council, 2013).

This uses market access as a means of enforcing regulations relating to forest management. It also puts part of the burden of ensuring legality on the private sector and foresees a role for private certification schemes. The European Commission's own guidance notes refer to "laying down the obligations of operators who place timber and timber products on the market" (The European Commission, 2013: 1), and operators are required to work with a due diligence system (DDS) to prevent illegal timber being placed on the market. Importers have a number of ways of meeting this due diligence requirement. The EUTR refers to "voluntary forest certification and timber legality verification schemes" in the context of the requirement for a DDS, but still puts the onus on private sector operators to "determine whether the scheme incorporates a standard that includes all the applicable legislation" (The European Commission, 2013: 15). An FSC document on the EUTR (Forest

Stewardship Council, 2013) provides an extensive discussion about the interaction between certification schemes and EUTR obligations.

This regulation is designed to have a considerable effect on the way exporting countries manage their own resources, and its impact is greatly increased through a second measure adopted by the EU, the FLEGT VPA. The VPAs are agreements that the EU has signed with a number of important timber exporting countries.[8] These address the legality issue from the supply side, focusing very directly on the challenges of extending the scope and effectiveness of controls over forestry in developing countries. In effect, the VPAs are designed to promote the development of national-level legality assurance schemes in timber exporting countries. Such schemes, if effective, would demonstrate that timber has been legally produced and acquired. As described by the Commission:

> "[VPAs] are bilateral agreements between the European Union (EU) and timber exporting countries, which aimed to improve forest sector governance and which ensure that the timber and timber products imported into the EU are produced in compliance with the laws and regulations of the partner countries. Under VPAs partner countries develop control systems to verify the legality of their timber exports to the EU. The EU provides support to establish or improve these control systems. Once ratified and implemented the VPA is legally binding on both parties, committing them to trading only in verified legal timber products" (The European Union and the Republic of Indonesia, 2011).

One of the incentives for agreeing to a partnership is that imports from a country with which the EU has signed a voluntary partnership agreements (VPA) are assumed to be compliant with the EUTR, and importers are under no further obligation is to prove legality (Fishman & Obidzinski, n.d.).

The implementation of legality assurance requires a range of actions to make it operational and effective. In one of the FLEGT briefing notes produced by the European Union and the Republic of Indonesia five

---

[8] By the end of 2011, these included Ghana, the Republic of Congo, the Central African Republic, Indonesia and Liberia (Overdevest & Zeitlin, 2014: 36).

different elements of a timber LAS are identified. These are summarized in Table 2.1, together with indications of the ways in which negotiations around VPAs can affect how an LAS is defined.

This approach offers some advantages compared with private standards schemes. Private schemes only apply to exports that are covered by the scheme. The VPAs go much further. As well as applying to all timber exported to the European Union, the goal of the VPAs is to subject *all* timber exports from partner countries to legality assurance. In the case of the EU Cameroon VPA, the treaty summary provided by the EU states: "The Agreement goes beyond the limited product coverage proposed in...'the FLEGT Regulation'...to cover trade in all timber products and, in doing so, commits Cameroon to building a system that will provide assurance to the EU that all forest products from Cameroon are legally harvested and produced and contributing positively and sustainably to Cameroon's growth."[9] Similarly, the briefing note on the EU Indonesia VPA states that "Indonesia has committed to using its Indonesian TLAS control systems to verify the legality of all exports of timber and timber products, regardless of the destination" (The European Union and the Republic of Indonesia, 2011: 12). Given that one of the weaknesses of both import control schemes and private certification is the relatively rapid growth of demand in emerging markets where government and consumer pressures for standards are lower, this extension of export controls is significant. The EU is using a combination of its market power as a major buyer of tropical timber products—in conjunction with concerns on the part of some exporting governments about sustainable forest management—to both extend the scope of its agreements beyond bilateral trade and play a part in the design of LAS in other countries. This is WTO compliant because the exporting countries are defining what they consider to be legal.

As with all process standards, the effectiveness of this approach depends on whether the controls in place would achieve the desired outcomes if functioning correctly, and the effectiveness of implementation of the controls. On the

---

[9] http://ec.europa.eu/world/agreements/prepareCreateTreatiesWorkspace/treatiesGeneralData.do?step=0&redirect=true&treatyId=8986&back=9341.

Table 2.1 Using Voluntary Partnership Agreements to define what legal and how legality is to be enforced

Legality assurance system requirements	How VPAs try to meet these requirements
A clear definition of what constitutes legally produced timber. This means specifying the legal framework and which laws apply.	The negotiation of the VPAs includes processes to define and strengthen the legal framework in the partner countries. Improvements in governance, law enforcement and transparency are part of the process (The European Union and the Republic of Indonesia 2011: 3). The definition of what is "legal" may include community rights, sustainable harvesting, protection of biodiversity, etc.
Compliance with the LAS and traceability system has to be verified through some system of audit/inspection.	VPAs develop or reinforce licensing systems based on audit and certification. Conformity Assessment Bodies are responsible for verifying compliance and issuing licenses for operators (The European Union and the Republic of Indonesia 2011: 13).
A traceability system that tracks timber products through the supply chain from origin to export.	The VPAs support the development of traceability systems. A FLEGT briefing note outlines what is required. The VPAs provide detailed agreements on traceability procedures, and traceability is verified by the Conformity Assessment Bodies.
Licenses have to be issued by some specified organization. This is an enforcement role.	VPAs are meant to strengthen governance and to provide mechanisms for enforcement.
Independent monitoring of the system is required in order to ensure its credibility.	VPAs include provisions for independent monitoring of the system. In the case of Indonesia, this includes giving civil society bodies the right to raise objections to certification or to make complaints about how forest businesses are operating. Comprehensive monitoring and periodic evaluation are built into the agreement (European Forest Institute n.d.; Fishman and Obidzinski n.d.).

Sources: Legality Assurance Scheme requirements, taken from European Commission (2007: 1)

first point, concerns have been raised about Indonesia's definition of legality, pointing to the fact that the definition of legality varies across four different types of forests, with controls for state-owned forests greater than for privately owned ones (European Forest Institute, n.d.: 1). On the second point, the overall goal of the VPA is clear:

> "The core of the VPA process is to define the set of laws and regulations that apply to the Indonesian forest sector ('the legality definition'), and to develop the control systems and verification procedures that ensure that all timber and timber products exported from Indonesia to the European Union are legal. This means that those products have been acquired, harvested, transported and exported in line with Indonesian laws and regulations" (The European Union and the Republic of Indonesia, 2011: 3).

But reservations have been raised about the complexity of the systems, the will and capacity of enforcement bodies and the politics of regulation. Fishman and Obidzinski note that there are many forests and many companies involved in forestry and timber, but in 2013 there were only 11 evaluators qualified to conduct legality verification (Fishman & Obidzinski, n.d.: 5–6). Further, these authors observe that the closeness and complexity of the relationships between the Conformity Assessment Bodies, the industry they are regulating and the government provides scope for regulatory capture. It remains to be seen whether these challenges will be mitigated through the monitoring processes provided within the VPA. In Indonesia, the VPA recognizes the role of civil society groups and individuals in pointing to problems, and there is also provision for "multi-stakeholder monitoring and evaluation working group," a periodic evaluation of the whole scheme and independent monitoring of licensed timber in the EU market (European Forest Institute, n.d.: 3).

2.3.2 Food Safety

This section considers the development of risk-based approaches to food safety, with a particular focus on the development of food regulations for fresh fruit and vegetables in the United States and the European Union.

The types of controls exercised over both domestic food production and imported food depend in part on the perceived risks arising from different types of food. The major focus of legislation in both regions has been on food processing establishments and food of animal origin. These are where the greatest risks occur and where food hygiene regulations are strictest.[10] In the United States all meat and poultry processing plants have had to develop pathogen reduction programs based on HACCP principles following the introduction by the USDA of the Pathogen Reduction/Hazard Analysis and Critical Control Point (PR/HACCP) regulation in 1996 (Ollinger et al. 2004). With such products, there is a "presumption of guilt," with producers and food processors having to demonstrate compliance with safety regulations.[11]

At the same time, there have been significant shifts in perceptions of the hazards that might arise from fresh fruit and vegetables, both in the USA and in the EU, leading to changes in both public regulations and private standards. The shift has been particularly marked in the United States. For a long time, the United States government was reluctant to impose controls on the production, harvesting and packing of fresh produce (fruit and vegetables). Rather than issuing mandatory rules and enforcing them, government agencies preferred to issue guidelines and provide tools that farmers could use voluntarily to check the safety of their farming systems (US Food and Drug Administration, 1998; USDA, 2009). Among the reasons put forward for taking this hands-off approach, two are highlighted by Calvin (2003). The first is the diversity of farming systems in the United States, which makes any country-wide system of good agricultural practices inefficient—standards applicable for one type of farming systems might be under- or over-specified for another. The second is that the scientific basis for strict controls was

---

[10] For food of animal origin, registration of processing plants, assessments of the competence of food safety authorities in exporting countries and the importer obligations create a much more stringent regime.

[11] These safety regulations for food of animal origin have been tightened in recent years, partly in response to food safety crises such as BSE (mad cow disease), which has led to greatly increased controls on live cattle and abattoirs.

lacking. According to Calvin, "guidelines do not outline specific testing and monitoring regimes because scientific data is lacking for establishing more specific guidelines" (2003: 77).[12]

Nevertheless, repeated outbreaks of foodborne illness arising from microbial contamination of domestically produced leafy greens (lettuce, spinach, etc.) and other fruits and vegetables did eventually change attitudes. In particular, a food illness outbreak in California in 2006 associated with E. coli O157:H7 in spinach led to over 100 people being hospitalized and 31 suffered from a serious complication associated with E. coli, haemolytic-uremic syndrome. It also led to a very substantial and prolonged decline in domestic spinach sales and the threat of import bans in Canada and elsewhere. In the EU, changing perceptions about the long-term threats to human health from excessive pesticide residues in fruit and vegetables led to a tightening of regulations in 2000 (The Commission of the European Communities, 2000), and repeated food safety scares in the EU in the 1990s (see Knowles et al. 2007: 46) led to the EU White Paper on food safety in 2000 and the subsequent establishment of the European Food Safety Authority (Caduff & Bernauer, 2006: 153–157).[13]

In neither area did the authorities respond to these challenges by immediately introducing preventive controls. But pressures on business did lead to the development of standards that achieved precisely this outcome. In the United States, the damage caused by the 2006 E. coli outbreak led shippers (the companies that processed and distributed products, but did not necessarily grow them) in the leafy greens sector, in collaboration with the California State government, to introduce the California Leafy Green Products Handler Marketing Agreement (LGMA) (LGMA, 2010). This introduced technology-based regulation as a strategy for minimizing the risks of microbial contamination. Good agricultural practices in areas such as water quality, water testing, worker hygiene and animal intrusion were prescribed and backed up by audit and certification by the California

---

[12] As will be seen subsequently, this approach to information requirements bears parallels with the requirements on the US Environmental Protection Agency (EPA) under the Toxic Substances Control Act (TSCA) to prove that chemicals are harmful before imposing restrictions.

[13] See also, Vincent (2004) and Vogel (2003).

Department of Agriculture. The adoption of the LGMA by shippers responsible for distributing 99% of California-produced leafy greens made compliance with its practices effectively mandatory for Californian farmers growing leafy greens.

In the EU, the most widely adopted standard for certification of farms growing fresh fruit and vegetables, GlobalGAP (known as EurepGAP until 2008) established preventive controls for food hygiene and pesticide residues.[14] This scheme was developed and adopted by large food retailers. While the initial motive was to secure compliance with the law rather than reassure consumers, it is noteworthy that its adoption was spurred in some countries by food scares that undermined consumer confidence in the safety of fresh fruit and vegetables, as was the case in Germany (Rodman, 2008). One initial driver for the development of this standard was the 1990 Food Safety Act in the UK. This introduced *strict liability* for food business operators. This means that they could not claim a warranty defense—in other words, a defense that they purchased the food in good faith with a warranty from the supplier, with the result that the supplier is responsible for any consequences of selling unsafe product. The Act allowed one line of defense for food business operators: they would not be found to have committed an offence if they could show that they had exercised "due diligence" in ensuring that the supply chain was delivering safe food (UK Government, 1990: Section 21, para. 1). GlobalGAP and other private standards relating to food, such as the British Retail Consortium's Global Standards (see http://www.brcglobalstandards.com/), are believed to provide a due diligence defense.

In both the United States and the EU, food safety challenges have led businesses to lead the way in establishing preventive controls through the use of private standards backed up by audit and certification schemes. GlobalGAP, like the LGMA, originally adopted an approach using technology-based regulation, with early versions of the standard (which is revised every 4–5 years) dictating very specific procedures to be adopted at farm level to eliminate food safety risks. More recent

---

[14] The scheme was later extended to a range of other agriculture and aquaculture products.

revisions have adopted a more management-based approach, requiring farms to develop credible assessments of risks to food safety, to implement plans to control for them and to take corrective action where necessary.

The role of government in this process is not straightforward. In the United States, continuing concerns about food safety eventually led to the FDA Food Safety Modernization Act (FSMA) being passed by Congress in 2010. The Act instructed the FDA to develop and introduce provisions for both increased use of preventive controls in food processing establishments and new, mandatory standards for the production and harvesting of "those types of fruits and vegetables that are raw agricultural commodities for which the Secretary [of Health And Human Services] has determined that such standards *minimize the risk of serious adverse health consequences or death*" (United States Congress, 2010: Section 105 (a)(1)(A), emphasis added). In other words, controls were needed because of unacceptable risks to human health arising from certain categories of fresh fruit and vegetables.

The rules subsequently introduced did mandate the introduction of a HACCP-based approach, with written food safety plans, monitoring, corrective actions and verification for food processing establishments. However, these establishments are not required to show compliance through certification. They are only required to provide documentation to the FDA showing that they have the required plans and processes in place, and it is far from clear how closely this documentation will be examined. Similarly, the extensive new rules proposed for regulating farm-level practices have explicitly ruled out the use of audit and certification for verifying compliance. The rules provide clear instructions and a legal obligation for farm to assess risks in their activities (e.g., through water testing and identification of animal intrusion) and take action when evidence of microbial contamination, or the risk of such contamination, is revealed. In spite of this, there still appears to be a presumption of innocence—no proof of compliance is required in advance of any inspection or identified contamination. The FDA does, however, expect that business pressures would lead to adoption of the rules. The 2013 proposed rule suggests that a combination of awareness raising and adoption by retailers of standards that will provide equivalent controls at farm level, such as the LGMA and existing USDA certification programs (US Food and Drug Administration, 2013: 391–392) will promote adoption, while simultaneously suggesting that inspections by public authorities will not be the primary basis for securing compliance.

In Europe, Regulation 178/2002, also known as the General Food Law, introduced an EU-wide approach to food safety incorporating a risk-based approach. The guiding principles, which were subsequently incorporated into subsequent regulations on food hygiene, put risk management at the center of this approach. It specified that the elimination or avoidance of risks to health requires risk assessment, risk management and risk communication (paragraph 17), and emphasized the centrality of the HACCP methodology for achieving this goal. At the same time, the General Food Law put food business operators at the heart of the food safety regime. Paragraph 30 of the preamble to the General Food Law legislation states that: "A food business operator is best placed to devise a safe system for supplying food and ensuring that the food it supplies is safe; thus, it should have primary legal responsibility for ensuring food safety" (The European Parliament and the Council of the European Union, 2002). Furthermore, "feed and food business operators at all stages of production, processing and distribution within the businesses under their control are responsible for ensuring that feed and food satisfy the requirements of feed and food law which are relevant to their activities" (The European Parliament and the Council of the European Union, 2004: preamble, para. 4).

How did these changes, which were primarily driven by concerns with tackling regulatory failures in domestic food industries, impact upon imports of food into the United States and the EU? In the United States, the new legislation did introduce specific obligations on food importers. The FDA Deputy Commissioner for Food, Michael Taylor, emphasized that importers would be made accountable for food imported into the United States, being obliged to verify that it was produced in accordance with US standards, or at an equivalent level of safety (Taylor, 2012). The proposed rule for importers issued by the FDA requires them to "develop, maintain, and follow an FSVP [Foreign Supplier Verification Program] that provides adequate assurances that your foreign supplier is producing the food in compliance with processes and procedures that provide at least the same level of public health protection as those required [for food establishments and for fresh produce safety in the United States]" (US Food and Drug Administration, 2014: 9). The proposed rule sets out three options for meeting this obligation: (1) for the importer to arrange for on-site audit and documentation of the foreign supplier by a "qualified auditor," as defined by the FDA; (2) to rely on FDA inspection of the foreign establishment; (3) for inspection by an officially recognized food safety authority in those countries whose food safety systems have been approved by the FDA. In this last case, the importer is still obliged to verify that the operation complies with the rules of the local food safety authority.

This is a significant increase in the obligations placed on importers, particularly with respect to food processing establishments. A presumption of innocence remains (as it does for the UK Food Safety Act), because it is not clear that importers have to provide proof of the effectiveness of the measures they are taking.[15] However, there would be severe penalties for not having a FSVP, and risk-averse importers would adopt one of the three options in order to meet their legal obligations. Given that the rules for food processing establishments appear to indicate that third-party certification provided by private standards-setting organizations may provide evidence of compliance with FDA requirements, importers might regard such certification as a convenient means of meeting their obligations.[16]

In the case of the EU, a literal reading of the regulations on food hygiene introduced in 2004 would suggest that with respect to food of non-animal origin (including fresh fruit and vegetables) food business operators in third countries are expected to comply with food hygiene

---

[15] As Coglianese and Lazer (2003: 699) point out, there are varying degrees of oversight associated with management-based regulation. This can range from no examination of the systems put into place up to detailed analysis of the steps taken to ensure conformance to legislation.

[16] The rule for food processing establishments does not endorse third-party certification, but it does state that "to the extent that scientific and technical information available from GFSI or another standard setting organization provides evidence that a control measure, combination of control measures, or the food safety plan as a whole is capable of effectively controlling the identified hazards, a facility may use such information to satisfy the validation requirements of the rule" (U.S. Food and Drug Administration, 2015: 56054).

regulations (European Commission, 2006: 14–15), and as a corollary, importers have a responsibility to ensure that there are sufficient food safety controls in place in the country of origin. The legislation states that: "Food and feed imported into the Community for placing on the market within the Community shall comply with the relevant requirements of food law or conditions recognized by the Community to be at least equivalent thereto or, where a specific agreement exists between the Community and the exporting country, with requirements contained therein" (The European Parliament and the Council of the European Union, 2002: Article 11).

But how difficult is this? There is the possibility that products imported from countries that have food safety controls validated by the EU would generally be accepted as being safe, with no obligations on businesses, but obligations on governments to show that the competent authorities for food safety are in fact competent. In fact, controls appear even less stringent than this. The EU guidance notes on food imports and hygiene regulations state that "with regard to food of non-animal origin, it is in many cases sufficient that exporting establishments in third countries are known to and accepted as suppliers by importers of food into the community" (European Commission, 2006: 10). A study by Neeliah et al. (2013) of exports of shrimp and fresh vegetables from Mauritius suggests that the controls facing fresh vegetable exporters are substantially less demanding than for those exporting fishery products. The exceptions to the presumption of innocence are products with known risks (such as nuts from countries with previous records of aflatoxin contamination), for which intensified border inspections are required, and for which improved access to the EU market is dependent upon preventive controls being introduced by governments and the exporting countries. A discussion of exporting country responses to aflatoxin restrictions and the types of preventive controls that might be adopted can be found in the study by Diaz Rios and Jaffee (2008).

Controls over fresh produce imports only increase after non-compliant products have been detected. In spite of this, the use of preventive controls by large food retail companies in some European countries has increased. As was noted previously, one reason for this is the overall legal requirement to place safe food on the market and the adoption of standards as a strategy for containing the risks from possible food safety lapses—risks to food retail businesses as much as to consumers. This can also be seen as a brand protection strategy by large retailers. In the UK, brand protection issues would have been exacerbated by the issue of due diligence.

In the fresh fruit and vegetables sector, then, governments have created legal frameworks that make businesses responsible for the safety of imported food that they might place on the market. Preventive measures are not obligatory and an assumption of innocence still prevails. Nevertheless, there are two ways in which the new food safety measures have impacts on exporting countries. The first is that governments may promote the adoption of new food safety standards in exporting countries because of the reduced controls placed on exports from countries that can demonstrate that their food safety systems are effective. Second, the responsibilities placed on businesses by the new regulations introduced in the past two decades, combined with the strategic role of large businesses for whom brand reputation is a significant and valuable commodity, have been sufficient to promote the development and adoption of controls, including private standards, that make the use of preventive methods into the production and processing of fresh fruit and vegetables a requirement for entry into some significant segments of export markets. As will be seen in subsequent papers in this volume, GlobalGAP has knock-on effects in other countries, and its relevance for producers in the ASEAN region is discussed in this book by Nabeshima and Michida.

2.3.3 Chemicals

The chemical industry is a global industry. Global trade in chemicals has expanded very rapidly in recent years, and there has been a considerable growth in chemical production and export by developing countries. The chemicals sector is also global in terms of its impacts, which have transboundary effects. These arise from trade in chemical substances and mixtures and from trade in products which incorporate chemicals, as well as from the release of chemicals into the environment and their spread around the world. With respect to the second effect, there are tens of thousands of chemical substances that are considered as dangerous for health or for the environment, and many substances are found in humans (including newborn infants) and in the oceans and uninhabited parts of the planet (Bengtsson, 2010: 183–184). Persistent, toxic chemicals that bioaccumulate are a particular concern because of the risks to the environment and to human and animal health.

Reflecting these risks, a large number of transnational agreements on chemicals management have been implemented. Some specific international conventions have been created to address some of these issues. As described by Selin (2013: 111–116), the global chemicals regime consists of a number of binding conventions (Basel on trade in international waste, Rotterdam on informed consent prior to trade and the Stockholm Convention on persistent organic pollutants).[17] Alongside these conventions, there are also many other transnational initiatives— "with upwards of 100 international agreements, programs and initiatives on chemical safety" (Bengtsson, 2010: 204). This is why Selin refers to a global chemicals regime: "Rather than organizing cooperation under an overarching framework convention, as in for example the cases of climate change, ozone depletion, and biodiversity, international legal and political efforts to address problems of hazardous chemicals are structured around a diverse set of legally independent treaties and programs" (Selin, 2013: 107).

In part, this diversity reflects divisions between the major powers about how to approach chemical safety (Bengtsson, 2010: 205). These divisions came out very clearly in the difficulties that arose in the negotiations that led to the creation of the SAICM. This pursues the goals set out by the World Summit on Sustainable Development in 2002—that "by the year 2020 chemical should be produced and used in ways that minimise significant adverse impacts on the environment and on human health" (Bengtsson, 2010: 188). However, the approach to be adopted by SAICM was the subject of intense negotiation, with disagreements about whether it should incorporate a legally binding

---

[17] See also the account by Simon (2012: 20–21) of these Conventions.

agreement and the use of the precautionary principle (Perrez, 2006: 250–252). As was noted in the case of forestry, the failure to achieve inter-governmental responses to global problems was a factor in creating transnational private governance initiatives. In the case of chemicals, the initiatives have been public and transnational, with the EU REACH program particularly important.

The main conventions on control of chemicals are targeted at particular substances and mixtures that have been identified as particularly hazardous for humans, animals and the environment. However, one of the challenges of chemical regulation is that among the many thousands of chemicals that are produced and used, information about their toxicity is lacking and also quite hard to establish. Here, national regulations on production, storage, use and recycling are more relevant. The traditional approach to chemical regulation worked on the basis of "acting only against proven effects" (Hansson & Rudén, 2010: 73), even though minimal information was available on the toxicity of many chemicals.[18] In other words, there was a presumption of innocence.

The shortcomings of this approach have been highlighted by critiques of the 1976 Toxic Substances Control Act (TSCA) in the United States. It has been characterized as ineffective in either "assessing the hazards of the great majority of chemicals" or "controlling those of greatest concern," or "motivating investment in . . . cleaner chemical technologies" (Schwarzman & Wilson, 2011: 103). The TSCA puts the emphasis on government (the Environmental Protection Agency) to provide scientific proof through a quantitative risk assessment that chemicals are dangerous before their production or use can be restricted, but it places no obligation on chemical companies to create or provide the information that might support a proper assessment. As has been argued forcefully by Sachs, "The default presumption of TSCA, therefore, is that the vast majority of chemicals can be freely marketed, even absent any toxicity testing, unless and until EPA can prove that they pose unreasonable risks" (Sachs, 2009: 1827).

---

[18] According to Hansson and Rudén, this lack of information extends even to the chemicals produced in the largest volumes (Hansson & Rudén, 2010: 72).

In the EU, the "presumption of innocence" stance held until the 1990s. Then, a series of chemical disasters pointed to the weakness of EU legislation. Just as food safety crises led to the White Paper on food safety in 2000, a review of EU chemicals regulation was launched in 1998 and a White Paper on chemical safety produced in 2001 (Hansen & Blainey, 2006: 270–271; Heyvaert, 2010: 219–220). This process culminated in the REACH Regulation in 2006. This legislation represented a paradigm shift in chemical regulation:

> "With the enactment of REACH in 2006, the EU launched a second generation of chemical regulation. The legislation is, in many respects, the 'anti-TSCA'—the transatlantic converse of the American regulatory regime. It fundamentally reshapes the €537 billion European chemical market and embodies a new paradigm in global chemicals management in which the burden of proof on chemical safety is shifted from government to industry for the most hazardous classes of chemicals" (Sachs, 2009: 1833).[19]

The presumption of innocence is replaced by a presumption of guilt. In order to gain access to the EU market, chemical companies need to provide data to show that products are safe. REACH places the onus on producers and importers of chemicals to provide the relevant data. The data required covers both hazards and risks. Hazards are the result of the intrinsic characteristics of a chemical, while data on risk "combines laboratory findings of hazard with analysis of actual human exposure to the compound. Risk, therefore, is the product of hazard and exposure" (Sachs, 2009: 1835–1863). This hazard and risk analysis requirement is usually summed up in the expression "no data, no market."

The data requirement is a fundamental element of chemicals risk management, as discussed by Bucht (2010).[20] It provides information about the hazardous properties of chemicals. This information is also transmitted along the value chain so that users of chemicals are properly informed about their properties. Chemical use information is also central to risk analysis, as this is

---

[19] Similar arguments are made by Schwarzman and Wilson (2011: 103–104).

[20] For an analysis of the content of the REACH legislation and what it is designed to achieve, see Karlsson (2010), Biedenkopf (2015) and Heyvaert (2010).

the basis for calculations of exposure (by workers, by consumers, etc.). This information then provides public institutions with a basis for decisions about how to regulate particular chemicals. The data requirement places new responsibilities on the private sector in the same way that private sector obligations and actions were generated by EU regulations on food safety and forestry. It is businesses that are required to provide information and to conduct risk assessments. At the same time, businesses are obliged to provide information for downstream uses of chemicals (Heyvaert, 2010: 223). This is a major departure compared to the TSCA and to regulatory approaches in Canada and Japan (Naiki, 2010). As Heyvaert notes, however, this does not mean that public authorities abandon their responsibility for chemical safety. REACH involved a strengthening and centralization of EU authority to enforce chemical regulations (2010: 224).

The overall goal of REACH is to achieve the safe production and use of chemicals in the EU. In order to achieve this, the EU has obliged chemical companies from many parts of the world to meet EU requirements with respect to information provision, compliance with restrictions on usage and investigation of possible substitutes. By shifting the burden of proof in one of the largest chemical markets in the world, the legislation promotes sharing of information about chemical hazards across many different countries. It also provides information that can be used by many authorities, public and non-public, and has encouraged harmonization and emulation. It provides a template for governments seeking to raise levels of control over chemicals, and a challenge to governments that do not.

The REACH legislation clearly uses access to the EU market to impose European norms and standards on other countries. Businesses in other countries have to change the way that they obtain and provide data on the safety of chemicals marketed in the EU, as discussed by subsequent chapters in this volume. Biedenkopf (2015: 122) shows that almost one-quarter of chemical dossiers provided by companies were submitted through the representative bodies appointed by foreign companies to make submissions. This figure does not include submissions by European subsidiaries of transnational companies, so the overall level of submissions by foreign companies would be even higher. This is the most direct way in which EU regulations impact on other countries, but just as VPAs in forestry are designed to affect trade with third countries, REACH will have broad impact through its influence on policy development in other countries. At the most basic level, this might arise through the use of the data generated by REACH to inform domestic decision-making. This is seen clearly in the case of the response in California: "In crafting its new chemicals policy, California is looking to Europe for regulatory models, chemical lists developed under EU directives and for potential hazard data that could become available under REACH" (Schwarzman & Wilson, 2011: 116).[21]

The response of other governments to EU regulations could vary considerably, as has been argued by Sachs (2009: 1847–1854)—ranging from opposition (including through the WTO)—not responding because the costs outweigh the benefits, harmonizing domestic regulations with REACH requirements and seeking transnational regulation as a means of providing an acceptable substitute for REACH.[22] The case of California indicates that government (in this case the State government) responses will partly be determined by their appetite for regulation, with the federal government in the USA taking a more oppositional stance. The choice of response(s) will also be influenced by the costs and benefits of incorporating REACH-like controls in the domestic market—how important is the export market in general and the EU market, how big a change will be required and what will be the costs? Exporting countries may decide to do nothing, leaving the response to private businesses, but even if this is considered to leave too much of a burden on the private sector and to potentially undermine competitiveness, the level to which domestic regulations are harmonized with REACH will vary. This comes out clearly in the analysis of the Japanese response to REACH provided by Naiki (2010). Japanese authorities have not replicated REACH in domestic legislation, although there are controls on production and use of chemicals that are more stringent than in the United States. The responses of other businesses and governments in Asia to REACH and RoHS regulations are discussed in subsequent papers in this volume.

---

[21] For further discussion of the use of the data on chemicals generated by REACH, see Biedenkopf (2015: 125–126).

[22] For countries closely tied to the EU market, such as the countries of the European Economic Area, there is no choice but to closely harmonise domestic regulations with those applying within the EU (Heyvaert, 2010: 230–231).

2.4 Conclusions

The literature on private standards has pointed to the limitations of government regulations in a globalized world, and there has been increasing recognition of the importance of business actors in regulating production and trade through the use of private standards. However, these trends should not obscure the continuing role of public regulations—not only in placing constraints and requirements on traded products, but also the potential of these regulations to directly impact upon production systems in exporting countries.

The analysis of the regulation of production and trade in the forestry, fresh fruit and vegetables and chemicals sectors shows that, first, preventive controls—controls that introduce obligations on producing and importing businesses that are designed to reduce or eliminate risks—can be developed and adopted by private companies or by a mixture of business and non-business actors. This is seen clearly in the private standards developed in the forestry and fresh produce sectors. Nevertheless, it is also apparent that the growth of private standards has, itself, been shaped by public interventions. In some cases, governments may actively promote private certification schemes when they recognize their role in providing effective preventive controls and offer private certification as one strategy for demonstrating compliance. In forestry and in fresh produce, the use of private standards is one of the options foreseen by legislation concerning import safety. In addition, private standards have also been developed by businesses in response to the legal environment created by national governments. These legal frameworks place obligations on businesses and expose them to certain risks arising from non-compliance, and private standards are then developed as a means of meeting the obligations and reducing risk exposure.

Second, it is clear that some governments—and in this paper the focus has been mostly on the EU—are able to use market access as a means of securing changes in exporting countries. In some cases, as with food safety, the changes may be aimed at improving the safety of products exported to the EU, but in other cases, the goal is much broader. In the case of forestry, one salient feature of the EU's VPAs is their intent to influence forest management through establishing legality norms that apply to all exports (including third countries) This concern with products that will not be imported into the country originating the regulation is a logical outcome of the recognition of the indirect harm that can arise from practices that, for example, undermine biodiversity or increase GHG emissions.

Third, it is clear that import controls sit alongside intergovernmental treaties, a broad range of global initiatives (such as SAICM) and bilateral agreements. There is a broad arsenal of attempts to manage globalization, and different sectors may benefit from different initiatives. Governments, too, may make different strategic choices about the use of instruments. Across the three sectors, there are marked differences in the nature of public interventions.

Fourth, the precise impact of preventive controls can vary considerably according to the way in which they are implemented. It was argued that the switch from a presumption of innocence to a presumption of guilt has a major impact on the challenges facing exporting countries and exporting businesses. How developing country governments and businesses respond to the challenges created by the increased use of preventive controls is the subject of the papers in this volume.

References

Auld, G. (2014). *Constructing private governance: The rise and evolution of forest, coffee, and fishery certification*. New York and London: Yale University Press.

Bengtsson, G. (2010). Global trends in chemicals management. In J. Eriksson, M. Gilek, & C. Rudén (Eds.), *Regulating chemical risks: European and global challenges* (pp. 179–214). London: Springer.

Bernstein, S., & Cashore, B. (2007). Can non-state global governance be legitimate? An analytical framework. *Regulation & Governance, 1*(4), 1–25. doi: 10.1111/j.1748-5991.2007.00021.x.

Biedenkopf, K. (2015). EU chemicals regulation: Extending its experimentalist REACH. In J. Zeitlin (Ed.), *Extending experimentalist governance? The European Union and transnational regulation* (pp. 107–136). Oxford: Oxford University Press.

Botzem, S. (2008). Transnational expert-driven standardisation: Accountancy governance from a professional point of view. In J.-C. Graz & A. Nölke

(Eds.), *Transnational private governance and its limits* (pp. 44–57). Abingdon and New York: Routledge.

Bucht, B. (2010). Capacity building for chemicals control: Legislation, institutions, public-private relationships. In J. Eriksson, M. Gilek, & C. Rudén (Eds.), *Regulating chemical risks: European and global challenges* (pp. 283–299). London: Springer.

Büthe, T., & Mattli, W. (2011). *The new global rulers: The privatisation of regulation in the world economy*. Princeton: Princeton University Press.

Caduff, L., & Bernauer, T. (2006). Managing risk and regulation in European food safety governance. *Review of Policy Research, 23*(1), 153–168. doi: 10.1111/j.1541-1338.2006.00190.x.

Calvin, L. (2003). Produce, food safety, and international trade: Response to U.S. foodborne illness outbreaks associated with imported produce. In J. Buzby (Ed.), *International trade and food safety: Economic theory and case studies* (pp. 74–96). Washington D.C.: United States Department of Agriculture, Economics Research Service.

Cashore, B., & Stone, M. (2014). Does California need Delaware? Explaining Indonesian, Chinese, and United States support for legality compliance of internationally traded products. *Regulation & Governance, 8*(1), 49–73. doi: 10.1111/rego.12053.

Coglianese, C., & Lazer, D. (2003). Management-based regulation: Prescribing private management to achieve public goals. *Law & Society Review, 37*(4), 691–730. doi: 10.1046/j.0023-9216.2003.03703001.x.

de Burca, G., Keohane, R., & Sabel, C. (2013). New modes of pluralist global governance. *New York University Journal of International Law and Politics, 45*(3), 723–786.

Diaz Rios, L., & Jaffee, S. (2008). *Barrier, catalyst, or distraction? Standards, competitiveness, and Africa's groundnut exports to Europe*. Retrieved from Washington DC; World Bank, http://siteresources.worldbank.org/INTARD/Resources/Making_the_Grade_ePDF2.pdf.

Eberlein, G. B., Abbott, K., Black, J., Meidinger, E., & Wood, S. (2014). Transnational business governance interactions: Conceptualisation and framework for analysis. *Regulation & Governance, 8*(1), 1–21. doi: 10.1111/rego.12030.

European Commission. (2006). *Guidance document: Key questions related to import requirements and the new rules on food hygiene and official food controls*. Retrieved from Brussels; European Commission, Health and Consumer Protection Directorate-General, http://ec.europa.eu/food/international/trade/interpretation_imports.pdf.

European Commission. (2007). *Legality assurance systems: Requirements for verification*. Retrieved from Brussels; European Commission, http://ec.europa.eu/europeaid/sites/devco/files/publication-flegt-briefing-note-series-2007-5-200703_en.pdf.

European Forest Institute. (n.d.). *Indonesia's timber legality verification system*. Retrieved from Joensuu, Finland; EFI, http://www.efi.int/files/attachments/euflegt/efi_newsroom_indonesia_legality_assurance_system_ed.pdf.

Fishman, A., & Obidzinski, K. (n.d.). *Verified legal? Ramifications of the EU Timber Regulation and Indonesia's Voluntary Partnership Agreement for the legality of Indonesian timber*. Retrieved from http://www.cifor.org/publications/pdf_files/Papers/PObidzinski1305.pdf.

Forest Stewardship Council. (2013). EU Timber Regulation, EUTR. Retrieved from http://www.fsc-uk.org/eu-timber-regulation-eutr.82.htm.

Fuchs, D., Kalfagianni, A., & Havinga, T. (2011). Actors in private food governance: The legitimacy of retail standards and multi-stakeholder initiatives with civil society participation. *Agriculture and Human Values*, 28(3), 353–367. doi: 10.1007/s10460-011-9310-5.

Graffham, A., Karehu, E., & MacGregor, J. (2007). *Impact of EurepGAP on smallscale vegetable growers in Kenya*. Retrieved from Greenwich; Natural Resources Institute, http://www.dfid.gov.uk/r4d/PDF/Outputs/EcoDev/60506fresh_insights_6_EurepGapKenya.pdf.

Green, J. (2010). Private standards in the climate regime: The greenhouse gas protocol. *Business and Politics*, 12(3), article 3. doi: 10.2202/1469-3569.1318.

Gulbrandsen, L. (2014). Dynamic governance interactions: Evolutionary effects of state responses to non-state certification programs. *Regulation & Governance*, 8(1), 74–92. doi: 10.1111/rego.12005.

Hansen, B., &Blainey, M. (2006). REACH: A step change in the management of chemicals. *RECIEL*, 15(3), 270–280. doi: 10.1111/j.1467-9388.2006.00527.x.

Hansson, S. O., & Rudén, C. (2010). REACH: What has been achieved and what needs to be done? In J. Eriksson, M. Gilek, & C. Rudén (Eds.), *Regulating chemicals risks: European and global challenges* (pp. 71–75). London: Springer.

Henson, S., & Humphrey, J. (2010). Understanding the complexities of private standards in global agri-food chains as they impact developing countries. *Journal of Development Studies*, 46(9), 1628–1646. doi: 10.1080/00220381003706494.

Henson, S., & Humphrey, J. (2012). Private standards in global agrifood chains. In A. Marx, M. Maertens, J. Swinnen, & J. Wouters (Eds.), *Private standards and global governance: Economic, legal and political perspectives* (pp. 98–113). Cheltenham: Edward Elgar.

Heyvaert, V. (2010). Regulating chemical risk: REACH in a global governance perspective. In J. Eriksson, M. Gilek, & C. Rudén (Eds.), *Regulating chemicals risks: European and global challenges* (pp. 217–237). London: Springer.

Jacoby, W., &Meunier, S. (2010). Europe and the management of globalisation. *Journal of European Public Policy, 17*(3), 299–317. doi:10.1080/13501761003662107.

Karlsson, M. (2010). The precautionary principle in EU and US chemicals policy: A comparison of industrial chemicals legislation. In J. Eriksson, M. Gilek, & C. Rudén (Eds.), *Regulating chemical risks: European and global challenges* (pp. 239–264). London: Springer.

Keohane, R., & Victor, D. (2011). The regime complex for climate change. *Perspectives on Politics, 9*(1), 7–23. doi: 10.1017/S1537592710004068.

Knowles, T., Moody, R., & McEachern, M. (2007). European food scares and their impact on EU food policy. *British Food Journal, 109*(1), 43–67. doi: 10.1108/00070700710718507.

LGMA. (2010). *California leafy green products handler marketing agreement: Audit checklist.* Retrieved from Sacramento; California Leafy Green Products Handler Marketing Agreement, http://www.caleafygreens.ca.gov/sites/default/files/Audit%20Checklist%20California%207-23-10.pdf.

Marx, A., Bécault, E., & Wouters, J. (2012). Private standards in forestry: Assessing the legitimacy and effectiveness of the Forest Stewardship Council. In A. Marx, M. Maertens, J. Swinnen, & J. Wouters (Eds.), *Private standards and global governance: Economic legal and political perspectives* (pp. 60–97). Cheltenham: Edward Elgar.

Naiki, Y. (2010). Assessing policy reach: Japan's chemical policy reform in response to the EU's REACH regulation. *Journal of Environmental Law, 22*(2), 171–195. doi: 10.1093/jel/eqq002.

Neeliah, S., Neeliah, H., & Goburdhun, D. (2013). Assessing the relevance of EU SPS measures on the food export sector: Evidence from a developing agri-food exporting country. *Food Policy, 41*, 53–62. doi: 10.1016/j.foodpol.2013.04.002.

Ollinger, M., Moore, D., & Chandran, R. (2004). *Meat and poultry plant's food safety investments: Survey findings*. Retrieved from Washington DC: United States Department of Agriculture, Economic Research Service, http://www.ers.usda.gov/publications/tb-technical-bulletin/tb1911.aspx.

Overdevest, C., & Zeitlin, J. (2014). Assembling an experimentalist regime: Transnational governance interactions in the forest sector. *Regulation & Governance, 8*(1), 22–48. doi: 10.1111/j.1748-5991.2012.01133.x.

Perez, F. X. (2006). The strategic approach to international chemicals management:Lost opportunity or foundation for a brave new world?. *RECIEL, 15*(3), 245–257. doi: 10.1111/j.1467-9388.2006.00528.x.

Raustiala, K., & Victor, D. (2004). The regime complex for the plant genetic resources. *International Organisation, 58*(2), 277–310. doi: 10.1017/S0020818304582036.

Rodman, N. (2008). *Private food safety standards and value chains: How does GLOBALG.A.P. change the sourcing strategies of German supermarkets?* (Diplomarbeit im Fach Wirtschafts- und Sozialgeographie), Cologne: Cologne University.

Sachs, N. (2009). Jumping the pond: Transnational Law and the future of chemical regulation. *Vanderbilt Law Review, 62*(6), 1817–1869.

Schwarzman, M., & Wilson, M. P. (2011). Reshaping chemicals policy on two sides of the Atlantic: The promise of improved sustainability through international collaboration. In D. Vogel & J. Swinnen (Eds.), *Transatlantic regulatory cooperation: The shifting roles of the EU, the US and California* (pp. 102–124). Cheltenham: Edward Elgar.

Selin, H. (2013). Global chemicals politics and policy. In R. Falkner (Ed.), *The handbook of global climate and environment policy* (pp. 107–123). London: John Wiley & Sons.

Simon, N. (2012). *Managing global chemicals governance: International organisations as interplay managers*. Paper prepared for Lund conference on Earth System Governance, Lund.

Taylor, M. (2012). *Ensuring produce safety in a global food system*. Speech made at the America Trades Produce meeting, Tubac, AZ.

The Commission of the European Communities. (2000). Commission Directive 2000/24/EC amending the Annexes to Council Directives 76/895/EEC, 86/362/EEC, 86/363/EEC and 90/642/EEC on the fixing of maximum levels for pesticide residues in and on cereals, foodstuffs of animal origin and certain products of plant origin, including fruit and vegetables respectively. *Official Journal of the European Communities*, L 107/28, 4 May

2000. Retrieved from http://eur-lex.europa.eu/legal-content/EN/TXT/PDF/?uri=CELEX:32000L0024&from=EN.

The European Commission. (2013). *Guidance document for the EU Timber Regulation*. Retrieved from http://ec.europa.eu/environment/forests/pdf/Final%20Guidance%20document.pdf.

The European Parliament and the Council of the European Union. (2002). Regulation (EC) No 178/2002 laying down the general principles and requirements of food law, establishing the European Food Safety Authority and laying down procedures in matters of food safety. *Official Journal of the European Communities, L 31/1*, 1 February 2002. Retrieved from http://eur-lex.europa.eu/legal-content/EN/TXT/PDF/?uri=CELEX:32002R0178&from=EN.

The European Parliament and the Council of the European Union. (2004). Corrigendum to Regulation (EC) No 882/2004 of the European Parliament and of the Council of 29 April 2004 on official controls performed to ensure the verification of compliance with feed and food law, animal health and animal welfare rules. *Official Journal of the European Union, L 191/1*, 28 May 2004. Retrieved from http://eur-lex.europa.eu/legal-content/EN/TXT/PDF/?uri=CELEX:32004R0882&from=EN.

The European Union and the Republic of Indonesia. (2011). *FLEGT Voluntary Partnership Agreement between Indonesia and the European Union*. Retrieved from Brussels; http://www.euflegt.efi.int/documents/10180/23029/FLEGT+Voluntary+Partnership+Agreement+Between+the+Republic+of+Indonesia+and+the+European+Union+-+Briefing+Note+May+2011/cfcd6026-55a9-4b7f-a28d-f147d9e6c9d5.

U.S. Food and Drug Administration. (1998). *Guidance for industry: Guide to minimise microbial food safety hazards for fresh fruits and vegetables*. Retrieved from Washington DC; U.S. Food and Drug Administration, http://www.fda.gov/downloads/Food/GuidanceComplianceRegulatoryInformation/GuidanceDocuments/ProduceandPlanProducts/UCM169112.pdf.

U.S. Food and Drug Administration. (2013). *Standards for the growing, harvesting, packing, and holding a produce for human consumption; proposed rule (corrected version)*.Retrieved from Washington DC; U.S. Food and Drug Administration, http://www.fda.gov/downloads/Food/GuidanceRegulation/ ... /UCM360734.pdf.

U.S. Food and Drug Administration. (2014). *Foreign supplier verification programs for importers of food for humans and animals*. Retrieved fromWashington DC; U.S. Food and Drug Administration, http://www.regulations.gov/#!documentDetail;D=FDA-2011-N-0143-0247.

U.S. Food and Drug Administration. (2015). *Current good manufacturing practices, hazard analysis, and risk-based preventive controls for human food; final rule.* Retrieved from Washington DC; U.S. Food and Drug Administration, http://www.regulations.gov/#!documentDetail;D=FDA-2011-N-0920-1979.

UK Government. (1990). *Food safety act.* Retrieved from http://www.legisla tion.gov.uk/ukpga/1990/16/enacted.

United States Congress. (2010). *FDA Food Safety Modernization Act.* Retrieved from Washington DC; 111th Congress, http://www.gpo.gov/fdsys/pkg/PLAW-111publ353/pdf/PLAW-111publ353.pdf.

USDA. (2009). *USDA good agricultural practices & good handling practice audit verification checklist.* Retrieved from Washington DC; United States Department of Agriculture, http://www.ams.usda.gov/AMSv1.0/getfile?dDocName=STELPRDC5091326.

van Waarden, F. (2012). Governing global commons: The public-private protection of fish and of forests. In A. Marx, M. Maertens, J. Swinnen, & J. Wouters (Eds.), *Private standards and global governance: Economic, legal and political perspectives* (pp. 15–59). Cheltenham: Edward Elgar.

Vincent, K. (2004). 'Mad Cows' and eurocrats – Community responses to the BSE crisis. *European Law Journal, 10*(5), 499–517. doi: 10.1111/j.1468-0386.2004.00228.x.

Vogel, D. (2003). *The politics of risk regulation in Europe and the United States.* Retrieved from Paris; Institut du Développement Durable et des Relations Internationales, http://www.iddri.org/Publications/Collections/Idees-pour-le-debat/id_0301_vogel.pdf.

John Humphrey was a professorial fellow at the Institute of Development Studies at the University of Sussex for many years and is currently a Visiting Professor at the School of Business, Management and Economics at the University of Sussex. He has researched and published extensively on global value chains, contributing both theoretical papers and empirical analysis, with particular attention paid to the global food industry. More recent work has focused on value chains and food standards. He has provided consultancy services to many international organizations on value chain issues.

3

Regulatory Diffusion from Europe to Asia

Etsuyo Michida

3.1 Introduction

Environmental regulation imposing requirements on product characteristics or production processes, which we call product- or process-related
environmental regulation (PRER), are increasing globally to protect
health, safety, and the environment. As Chapter 2 discusses, risk management under globalization is increasingly important, and PRERs have
been introduced to tackle the challenge. However, PRERs affect trade,
firm operations, and consumers, even outside the jurisdiction of the
regulations. The importance of PRERs is demonstrated by the World
Trade Organization (WTO) Technical Barriers to Trade (TBT)
Committee, to which member countries submit notifications about

E. Michida (✉)
Institute of Developing Economies, Japan External Trade Organization
(IDE-JETRO), Chiba, Japan
e-mail: etsuyo_michida@ide.go.jp

© The Author(s) 2017
E. Michida et al. (eds.), *Regulations and International Trade*,
IDE-JETRO Series, DOI 10.1007/978-3-319-55041-1_3

regulatory changes that significantly affect trade.[1] Half of the notifications to the committee between1995 and 2014 concern protecting human health and safety or the environment.[2]

The European Union (EU) has been the world's most influential economy in environmental policy since the 1990s (Keleman and Vogel 2010; Vogel 2012) and the EU enacted important PRERs in the 2000s. An influential EU PRER, the Restriction of Hazardous Substances (RoHS) Directive was issued in 2003 and restricts the use of hazardous substances, such as heavy metals and flame retardants, in electrical and electronic products.[3] The RoHS is intended to address at the source the problem of waste that contains hazardous substances and causes health problems or environmental degradation. The RoHS was implemented together with the Waste Electrical and Electronic Equipment (WEEE) Directive. The WEEE Directive controls hazardous substances in end-of-life products through collection or recycling so that the waste does not pollute the environment. The other EU PRER is the REACH,[4] which covers chemicals and a list of substances of very high concern contained in a wide variety of products. REACH was introduced to overcome some shortcomings of pre-REACH European chemicals policy such as complex legislation, lack of data, slow risk assessments of chemicals, and lack of innovation in developing safer chemicals (Biedenkopf and Park 2012, pp.782–791).[5]

PRERs introduced in an important market to manage risks involved in products have far-reaching effects on trade, especially in developing countries that now occupy a large portion of global value chains (GVCs) in manufacturing. Export-oriented developing countries are particularly aware that

---

[1] In the WTO TBT Committee, countries can raise concerns about economies that intend to introduce regulations.

[2] Of the 12,457 notifications from 1995 to 2014, 5961 notifications are on the protection of human health and safety and 1441 are on protection of the environment (WTO 2015, p. 12).

[3] RoHS Directive 2002/95/EC. It was revised by 2011/65/EU to RoHS 2.

[4] Regulation (EC) No 1907/2006 of the European Parliament and of the Council of 18 December 2006 concerning REACH, establishing a European Chemicals Agency.

[5] Beside RoHS and REACH, the End-of-Life Vehicles Directive was issued in 2000 and prohibits the use of certain heavy metals in motor vehicles. Directive 2000/53/EC of the European Parliament and of the Council of 18 September 2000 on end-of-life vehicles.

they are or will be affected by PRERs of other countries. If local firms do not meet PRERs, the firms cannot export to regulated markets, and the country's export competitiveness and economic growth are impaired. Moreover, some high-end markets in developed nations can be accessed only through supplying components or ingredients to multinationals' GVCs. Even for firms that do not export directly, participation in the GVC requires firms in developing countries to meet various PRERs. Firms may not be able to stay in the GVC if they do not satisfy PRER requirements and will lose their most important gateways to regulated markets. As the number of PRERs increases globally, Asian governments have actively responded by helping firms satisfy PRERs and by adopting PRERs in government policies by creating their own PRERs, resulting in policy diffusion.

The literature has extensively examined policy diffusion among the developed countries (e.g., Vogel 1995, Busch et al. 2005). The discussion in this chapter is closely linked to Vogel (1995), which discusses trade policy and the making of environmental or food regulatory policy. Vogel (2000) suggests that environmental regulation is being shaped more by forces outside nations through globalized trade using the case of developed countries. However, there is little in-depth discussion on policy diffusion to developing countries. This chapter extends the discussion presented by Vogel by including cases of policymaking in Asian developing countries and by adding new perspectives on the global supply web covering those countries and new related issues. This chapter[6] examines the motivations and implications of policy diffusion in developing Asian countries. Cases are shown where developing countries exhibit differences from developed countries, indicating that diffusion to developing countries requires additional attention. The following questions are examined.

1. Why are PRERs introduced in a pioneering country and diffused to other developed countries?
2. How do developing countries in Asia respond to PRERs?

---

[6] While this chapter focuses on diffusion of regulations, Chapter 5 examines diffusion of private standards.

3. Is Asia moving to a race-to-the-top or a race-to-the-bottom with diffused policies?
4. Does policy diffusion lead to policy fragmentation or harmonization?

This chapter focuses on PRERs, whereas previous political science literature has dealt with policy diffusion and convergence in the context of general environmental regulation. Environmental regulations on products and processes affect firms differently from other environmental regulations that control emissions or effluents at production sites. Mandatory emissions regulations on production sites do not affect other jurisdictions, although firms that invest and operate in a country with such regulations are subject to them. However, firms need to comply with PRERs irrespective of production locations. Even though some firms make small parts, such as screws or plating, and they are not fully aware which markets their products are destined for, they are remotely asked to comply with the EU regulations. This makes the mechanism of the PRER effects distinct from other environmental regulations on production sites and more relevant to developing countries, where many export products, both final and intermediate, are produced using cheap, abundant labor.

3.2 Innovative Policy and Diffusion in Developed Countries

Some studies offer insightful analyses for understanding the motives of a pioneer country for introducing stricter regulations. The first motivation lies in tackling a new environmental challenge through introducing innovative policy. Second, innovative policy tends to receive support from firms. A developed, greener country that has environmentally conscious voters tends to set stricter regulations as it is often easier for firms to comply with demanding regulation (Vogel 1995). Introducing stricter regulations sets business ground that makes firms with advanced environmental technology more competitive over competitors with lower environmental technology. Firms in developed regions have more advanced technology. Therefore, environmental regulation is beneficial for developed economies as the industrial policy of a large, influential economy under globalization.

Third, a large open economy has an incentive to impose strict regulatory standards because the compliance costs are shifted to foreign countries through international trade, and compliance can be enjoyed at a lower cost due to the increasing number of suppliers both within and outside the economy (Staiger and Sykes 2011).

A developed country usually pioneers an innovative policy. Innovative policy in the pioneer country can be diffused to both developed and developing countries. Policy diffusion is the process through which pioneering policy originating in one jurisdiction affects other jurisdictions, and the process happens without negotiated agreement (Biedenkopf 2012, p. 106). Although globalization reduces the role of sovereign nations and places more pressure on governments from international markets and multinational corporations, innovative policy that is created by a limited number of pioneering countries is adopted in other countries, resulting in policy diffusion (Jänicke 2005). One strand of the discussion on diffusion is centered on environmental policy introduced in some leader countries and diffused to other developed countries through learning processes to solve similar environmental problems. For developed countries, policy diffusion is more about diffusion of global norms of sustainable development (Jörgens 2003).[7]

3.3 Diffusion of the EU RoHS to Asia

Diffusion of regulations to less developed or less environmental friendly regions is not a new phenomenon. However, the mechanism and motives of diffusion are different from diffusion among developed countries. This section examines diffusion of the EU RoHS to Asia.[8]

---

[7] Diffusion does not have to result in introducing a similar policy, and responses to the innovative policy EU REACH differ across countries (Naiki 2010).

[8] Naiki (2010) examines how EU REACH, EU Chemical regulation did not diffuse to Japan. It shows that not all product regulations diffuse to other countries. REACH is chemical regulation and there are complex hierarchy of pre-existing chemical regulation in each country. This makes it hard for policymakers to adopt new regulation into their pre-existing regulatory system in a consistent manner even in the case that they wish to do so. One reason for EU RoHS to diffuse widely is that there was no existing regulations similar to EU RoHS in each country.

In Asian developing countries, the diffusion of regulations has not been driven by consumers demanding stronger health and environmental protection or by firms aiming to benefit from economies of scale by expanding regulatory areas to domestic markets.[9] Moreover, among the countries that have introduced RoHS-like policies, there are countries that are not ready to implement stricter environmental policy. Nevertheless, these countries impose product regulations or standards similar to those in a leading economy, and they do so voluntarily without international agreements or negotiations, leading to regulatory diffusion. Table 3.1 shows variants of EU RoHS policy in Asian countries.

Developing countries in Asia have policy priorities of economic development and poverty reduction. Implementing innovative environmental policy that deals with problems beyond urgent needs, such as air or water pollution that directly affect health, is not a priority. Even so, why do they follow EU regulations? Table 3.2 shows the factors involved in policy motivations for adopting a pioneering policy in developing countries. And following sections examine these factors.

3.3.1 IncreasingTrade Competitiveness

The most important factor for policy diffusion in Asia is the fragmentation of production and global supply chains. Production is fragmented by the manufacture of components in various countries, and the trading of components among countries to allow further processing or assembly (Kimura and Ando 2005). Production processes that are part of supply chains connected to the regulated market need to meet the regulatory requirements in order to keep market access. The mechanism that we observe for policy diffusion in Asia is similar to the California effect suggested by Vogel (1995). California effect refers that tighter regulatory standards have diffused to other

---

[9] See Chapter 4 for the lack of motives for environmental protection in Thailand.

Table 3.1 Diffusion of EU RoHS to Asia

Year of implementation	Country/Region	Name	Differences
2006/July	EU	RoHS Directive	
	Japan	JIS C0950 (J-Moss)	It is not restriction but labeling requirement when products contain regulated materials.
2007/January	California	Electric Waste Recycling Act of 2003	Scope of products is smaller.
2007/March	China	Administrative Measure on the Control of Pollution Caused by Electronic Information Products	Not only final products but also parts and materials are regulated. Household electrical equipment is not regulated. It is a labeling requirement for the first stage of implementation.
2008/January	South Korea	Act for Resource Recycling of Electrical and Electronic Equipment and Vehicles	It is a combined version of EU RoHS, WEEE, and ELV with a limited category of products.
2008/January	Norway	Prohibition on Certain Hazardous Substances in Consumer Products	
2009/Februrary	Thailand	TIS 2368-2551 (2008)	It is not regulation but standard.
2009/June	Turkey	Turkey RoHS	
2010/January	California	Assembly Bill No.1109 CHAPTER 534 the California Lighting Efficiency and Toxics Reduction Act	
2012/May	India	E-waste (Management and Handling) Rules, 2011	More focus is placed on WEEE. Information on components need to be described in product catalogue.
2012/December	Vietnam	Circular No.30/2011/TT-BCT	
2015–2016	Singapore	RoHS in Electrical and Electronic Equipment (EEE)	Regulation is limited to a smaller categories of EEE compared with EU RoHS. Related documents need to submit to the authority when products are imported.
2018/January	United Arab Emirates	RoHS in Electrical and Electronic Equipment	It requires product registration of the country authority.

Source: J-NET21 http://j-net21.smrj.go.jp/well/rohs/index.html

Table 3.2 Motivation of variant regulations

Motives	Countries/Region
1. Enhancing trade competitiveness	China, Japan, Thailand, Turkey, Vietnam
2. Coping with market failure	Japan, California, Thailand, Vietnam
3. Harmonizing domestic requirements	Thailand, Japan
4. Adopting policy innovation	Japan, California
5. Preventing environmental degradation	India, Singapore

jurisdictions. The California effect highlighted the relationship between environmental regulation and trade in policy diffusion. When countries with a large market enact product regulations, their trading partners are forced to meet those regulation to maintain their export market.

Although the California effect can occur within a country, a similar situation also occurs among countries through international trade. To maintain export competitiveness, Asian governments have introduced their own versions of EU PRERs to provide better information to small- and medium-sized enterprises (SMEs) and to encourage compliance with their domestic regulation in their own languages. Export competitiveness is the most important motivation for policy diffusion in Asia. It is a new type of industrial policy in the globalization era. In addition to PRERs, diffusion is observed in ISO standards. Prakash and Potoski (2006) showed that ISO 14001, which is a voluntary environmental process standard, is diffused from importing to exporting countries. Arimura et al. (2011) show that ISO14001 promotes diffusion of green supply chain management practices through customer demand.

A number of economic studies have addressed competitiveness, trade and welfare impact of regulations. Through international trade, domestic regulations alter the balance of competition among domestic and foreign manufacturers that sell goods in domestic markets. In an open economy with consumers who are unable to distinguish the quality of products, countries producing high-quality goods lose welfare and countries producing low-quality goods gain. When there is information asymmetry, introducing regulations or standards that regulate substandard products improves the welfare of countries that produce high-quality products (Bond 1984).

Regulations that affect trade without imposing a tariff are called non-tariff measures (NTMs). The effects of NTMs on trade have garnered increasing attention, partly because globalization has led to a significant growth in trade, and also because the relative importance of NTMs has increased as tariffs have been gradually reduced through multilateral and bilateral trade agreements (WTO 2013, p. 56). The effects of NTMs on trade are comparable with or larger than that of traditional tariffs (Kee et al. 2009). NTMs can be divided into those imposed on imports, those imposed on exports, and those imposed domestically (Staiger 2012). Domestic NTMs, especially regulations on products with regard to health, safety, and the environment, are TBTs in the WTO regime, and TBTs have come under increased scrutiny. When Asian governments recognize PRERs as TBTs, the governments attempt to lower the barriers for firms to export to regulated markets. One approach is to lower the cost of adopting regulations by introducing a similar policy without directly negotiating with a pioneering country.

PRERs of a country require manufacturers both inside and outside the jurisdiction to manage restricted substances used in products. PRERs may satisfy the WTO's requirements of equal treatment of domestic and foreign firms. Nonetheless, international disputes over domestic regulations arise partly because domestic regulations such as PRERs do not internalize foreign costs. The requirements affect both foreign final-product producers and parts or component producers, even though they are not directly subject to the domestic legal requirements. Negotiations for international agreements, such as free trade agreements and economic partnership agreements, on environmental policy provide a means for internalizing neglected foreign costs. Therefore, even in the absence of concerns over transboundary pollution, international agreements on environmental issues can offer welfare improvement at an international level (Ederington 2001). However, some governments may use loopholes when there are both negotiable and non-negotiable policies, and strategic interactions among countries have been examined in the literature (Copeland 1990). China, Japan, Thailand, Turkey and Vietnam are among the countries that have motivation linked to this approach.

3.3.2 Market Failures and Diffusion

PRERs can internalize market failures; when products cannot be differentiated based on quality, low-quality goods prevail in a market. A famous example is the market for lemons (Akerlof 1970). If chemicals contained in products are not visible and consumers cannot make choices related to product safety or environmental friendliness based on their preferences, low-quality products win out. Because information asymmetry leads to inefficiencies, regulations are introduced to internalize them by providing information to consumers or by restricting substandard products. The scope of regulation covers both domestically produced goods and imported goods.

Another reason that Asian countries have decided to adopt EU policy is concern over such market failures. Some small developing countries fear that their domestic markets are filled with substandard products that cannot be exported to regulated markets. If those developing countries have enough capacity to decide and implement appropriate PRERs within their jurisdiction, products that meet their own regulations should not do any harm. However, many developing countries do not have the capacity or finance to conduct scientific impact assessments of the effect of chemicals or hazardous substances on health and the environment. To avoid an inflow of products that are considered less safe in other jurisdictions, countries decide to introduce similar regulations.

The inflow of substandard products may harm the economy in two ways. First, hazardous substances contained in products are harmful to workers in the recycling sector and pollute the environment. The inflow of products containing hazardous substances may make a country without regulations a pollution haven unless the country introduces a suitable level of regulation. Second, if products that do not meet the EU PRERs cannot be differentiated from those that do, cross-contamination may occur so that the fraction of defective goods exported to the EU increases. Japan, California, and Vietnam have this motivation.

3.3.3 Harmonization of Requirements

A country like Turkey views regulations consistent with the EU's as being important policy for future possible integration into the EU economy. When introducing regulations, governments are fully aware of the importance of consistent regulations. This applies to most Asian countries that depend on exports in the manufacturing sector for economic development. Countries want to have regulations consistent with those of countries with which they have close manufacturing links. Regional economic integration helps governments make trade and environmental policy to accommodate the increase in trade and services.[10] However, Asian countries have attempted to balance national regulations or standards that are consistent with EU regulation with local regulations or standards that are better suited to the countries' situations. Providing domestically consistent standards and regulations helps SMEs understand and adopt the rules; participation in global supply chains is a key to SMEs' growth. Thailand, China, South Korea and Japan have many SMEs and are among these countries.

When the RoHS was initially implemented, electrical and electronics multinationals that exported to the EU developed their own thresholds of hazardous substances or had their own requirements for their suppliers to comply with RoHS. Consequently, their suppliers faced a variety of requests for meeting EU RoHS. Some firms were confused about the mandatory regulations governing exports to the EU. Other suppliers that have multiple customers need to meet multiple requirements, although all the requirements are intended to ensure compliance with the RoHS. To address this confusing situation, the Thai government issued public standards to clarify the actual requirements (see Chapter 6 for more details).

---

[10] For example, Kojima and Michida (2013) show how Asian governments use trade and environmental policies to manage the recycling trade.

In addition to harmonizing requirements to meet the RoHS, it is also necessary to harmonize data formats that are used to pass information about chemicals contained in products throughout supply chains in order to meet customers' requirements.[11] Because there are currently as many data formats as there are firms, customer firms provide their own forms for suppliers to submit chemical data. Copying the same information into different data sheets already requires considerable effort, especially for SMEs with a smaller number of employees. The Japanese government and an industrial association have taken action to harmonize data formats across industries and countries. This creates complications for adopting EU RoHS. Moreover, similar regulations have been introduced in Asia, which causes further complications. Harmonization of requirements was a motivation for Japan and Thailand.

3.3.4 Adopting Innovative Policy: Supply Chain Management

EU RoHS and REACH are innovative policies because they require firms to pass on information about hazardous substances throughout supply chains. This is because chemicals are not visible in products and can be identified only by testing or by information from the manufacturer. Without the information provided by the firms that choose and use the chemicals, it is difficult to detect the types and amounts of chemicals or hazardous substances contained in products. However, firms are often hesitant to provide chemical information as some of the information is linked to business secret. Without regulation, chemical information is passed from suppliers only on a voluntary basis and information may not be provided by a supplier because of business confidentiality. To create a supply management system, governments regard regulation as essential to ensure compliance.

---

[11] Japan began using the common format to share chemical data in 2015. https://chemsherpa.net/chemSHERPA/

3.3.5 Preventing Environmental Degradation

Some countries aim to prevent the inflow of substandard products, which harm consumers and the environment at the end of the product lifecycle. Countries are concerned about becoming a dumping ground for substandard end-of-life products. For example, California ensures that the waste generated by its large-scale consumption does not exceed its disposal capacity and it does not receive contaminated waste. India has become a major export destination for waste electrical and electronic products and is now concerned about becoming a final disposal site for products containing hazardous substances.

The following section presents country case studies to examine the motivations behind RoHS-like regulations in China, Japan, Thailand, South Korea and Vietnam.

3.4   Country Case Studies

3.4.1 China

China has become a major manufacturer and consumer of electrical and electronic products. In 2006, electrical devices accounted for about 23% of the country's total exports.[12] In light of China's dependence on this industry, the EU's WEEE Directive and RoHS have had a significant impact on the Chinese economy. Moreover, China was worried that many manufacturing firms would not be competitive enough and would lose out and exit the market soon after the regulations were introduced in the EU. In 2002, when the EU started discussing the WEEE and RoHS, China started its own regulatory process (JETRO 2007). China decided to establish regulations restricting hazardous substances to protect the environment, conserve resources, promote sustainable development in the electrical and electronic industries, and to improve the

---

[12] National bureau of Statistics of China. http://www.stats.gov.cn/tjsj/ndsj/2013/indexeh.htm accessed on July 8, 2014.

industries' competitiveness. An official in the then Ministry of Information Industry, who was responsible for creating the China RoHS, commented that because China had its own circumstances it could not adopt EU policy without modification, and that the country needed to set harmonized policies for development and environmental protection. The China RoHS was implemented in 2007. It requires firms to disclose information about hazardous substances voluntarily, and then obtain China Compulsory Certification for compliance. China set two stages for implementation of the RoHS. The first stage requires firms to disclose information and to label products; the second stage restricts substances and requires certification. Whereas the EU RoHS regulates final products in the market, the China RoHS regulates all products, including intermediate products. In China, the RoHS in all products is preferable for full compliance with EU RoHS. However, gradual implementation was adopted because of practical considerations for Chinese firms.[13]

3.4.2 India

Drafts of the India WEEE and RoHS were released in 2010 for public comment.[14] After revision in 2011, the e-waste (Management and Handling) rules[15] were implemented in 2012. Chapter 5 of the rules is equivalent to the EU RoHS. The rules are similar to a combination of the EU WEEE and RoHS and are aimed at tackling the problem of increasing e-waste, including domestically generated and imported secondhand waste. In particular, the surge of imports of used electrical or electronic products has caused environmental pollution when these products reach the end of their life cycle. Therefore, the primary objective of establishing the rules was to control e-waste.

---

[13] Nikkei Electronics April 19, 2007. "Policy maker for RoHS said on further details to be publicized in June" http://techon.nikkeibp.co.jp/article/NEWS/20070419/131199/.

[14] The revised draft can be obtained from http://moef.nic.in/downloads/public-information/Modified%20Draft%20E-waste.pdf.

[15] http://moef.nic.in/downloads/rules-and-regulations/1035e_eng.pdf.

3.4.3 Japan

In 2006, the year that the EU introduced its RoHS, Japan introduced J-Moss (Marking for Presence of the Specific Chemical Substances for Electrical and Electronic Equipment) in the Japanese Industrial Standards (JIS).[16] J-Moss is an industrial standard made mandatory by ministerial ordinances from the Ministry of Economy, Trade and Industry (METI). Manufacturers and importers are obliged to label products containing designated hazardous substances above threshold levels. In contrast to the EU RoHS, it is not mandatory to restrict the hazardous substances contained in products.[17] It requires firms to label whether products are compliant with the threshold of hazardous substances in products. No labeling is required for products containing substances below threshold levels. J-Moss is intended to disadvantage firms that do not meet the requirements without restricting the hazardous substances. This solves the asymmetry of information in the market. J-Moss is not designed to restrict hazardous substances in e-waste entering the waste stream because it does not restrict hazardous substances in products. However, labeling gives a signal for consumers to choose products containing less hazardous materials and is expected to work similarly as regulation. Moreover, Japan has an established e-waste collection system and hazardous substances in e-waste are not considered a major problem.[18]

In 2004, the National Development and Reform Commission of China and METI of Japan had a policy dialogue on recycling. Issues related to chemical regulations contained in products were raised and international cooperation was discussed.[19] In 2005, a working group called "Product 3R System Improvement"[20] was set up by METI to discuss how to adapt Japan's regulations to EU RoHS. While recognizing that China and the

---

[16] http://www.meti.go.jp/policy/recycle/main/3r_policy/policy/j-moss.html accessed on June 30, 2014.

[17] Personal computers, air conditioners, televisions, refrigerators, washing machines, microwave ovens, and clothes driers.

[18] Interview with a METI official in May 2014.

[19] http://www.meti.go.jp/committee/downloadfiles/g41005b60j.pdf.

[20] http://www.meti.go.jp/policy/recycle/main/admin_info/committee/h.html#kaigi_01.

United States were also planning to make adaptations for the EU RoHS, Japan examined possible adaptation measures considering its own situation. At that time, large Japanese manufacturing firms had already implemented measures to control hazardous substances contained in products, so that they could comply with the EU RoHS. There were four main motivations. The first was to promote reuse or recycling of parts and components by restricting hazardous substances, similarly to the EU. The second was to standardize labeling to inform the consumer about chemicals contained in electrical and electronic products, and to encourage the spread of environmentally friendly products. The third was to promote chemical management and adapt further to regulations throughout supply chains. For a final product to comply with regulations, component suppliers must coordinate and cooperate. The suppliers tend to be small firms with a limited capacity to comply with the regulations. Therefore, the fourth was to raise awareness and to promote compliance among SMEs. However, restriction of the substances was considered secondary to policy targets because pollution caused by the hazardous substances contained in electrical and electronic products was already controlled by recycling regulations. The labeling requirements alone were considered sufficient.[21]

3.4.4 Singapore

Singapore National Environment Agency gathered public opinions for Singapore RoHS-like regulation from January to February 2015. The main motivation of Singapore was to implement measures to reduce heavy metals in incineration ash and landfill through upstream control. Singapore is a small-state economy and incineration ash is used for landfill to extend the national land area. Soil contaminated with heavy metals will restrict future use of the reclaimed land. The proposed draft shows that they will regulate smaller categories of electrical and electronic products and adopt the EU RoHS exemption list. Although the EU

---

[21] Ministry of Economy, Trade and Industry, June 23, 2006, Documents for Chemicals in Product Information Sharing Working Group under Industrial Structure Chemical Meeting, Bio Risk Management Committee. SangyouKouzou Shingikai Kagaku. BaiobukaiRiskkanrisyouiinkai.

RoHS requires firms to prepare documents for when the authorities ask for submission, the Singapore RoHS asks firms to submit documents at the importation stage.

3.4.5 South Korea

The South Korea RoHS was developed considering the EU RoHS, EU WEEE, EU End of Life Vehicles (ELV) Directive, J-Moss, China RoHS, and California RoHS. The Act for Resource Recycling of Electrical and Electronic Equipment and Vehicles, promulgated in 2008 by President Decree No. 20480 and Ministry of Environment Ordinance No. 267, is a combination of EU RoHS, WEEE and ELV. The hazardous substances and their concentration limits listed in the Korean regulations are consistent with those in the EU RoHS and ELV. Furthermore, the regulations cover not only electrical and electronic final products but also parts and components, which is similar to the China RoHS. It applies to producers and importers of electrical and electronic products and vehicles. Compliance with the regulations limiting the concentrations of hazardous substances is mandatory, and if fraud is committed, a penalty is imposed.

Korea's regulations restrict hazardous substances as in the EU and Californian regulations. However, the Korea RoHS does not require labeling, as in China, and is consistent with the second stage of the China RoHS.

3.4.6 Thailand

Thailand has adapted to environmental product regulations through coordination between government and industrial organizations. Thailand introduced a Thai Industrial Standard that is similar to the EU RoHS and is often called the Thai RoHS. It is voluntary for firms to use the Thai RoHS and compliant firms that receive certification are allowed to label compliant products, benefitting compliant firms. An overview of the policy development related to the Thai RoHS is presented by Ramungul et al. (2013). The Thai government has been aware of RoHS since 2001, when the first and the second readings of the draft directive took place, and the Thai RoHS were introduced in 2009. The Thai RoHS were created because of pressure from the Federation of Thai Industry. Thailand has many suppliers of multinational firms, including those in the EU, USA, Japan and other countries. The report submitted to Asia-Pacific Economic Cooperation in 2008 by the Electrical and Electronics Institute[22] shows that the Thai RoHS was developed to harmonize product specifications and avoid the burden of multiple standards, to increase the number of local RoHS-compliant suppliers, and to provide industry with technical infrastructure for guiding acceptable practices and verifying product compliance. In addition, by establishing its own standards, Thailand aimed to avoid becoming a dumping ground for substandard products. The standard is voluntary and consumers may not be able to identify non-compliant products unless compliant products are labeled. Therefore, the Thai government chose to avoid unnecessary complications domestically and to maintain the competitiveness of industries. The targets of the legislation were domestic producers and importers.

3.4.7 Turkey

The EU—Turkey Customs Union was established in 1996, and the country started negotiation on accession to the EU in 2005. Against this backdrop, Turkey has attempted to harmonize its regulations with the EU.

3.4.8 Vietnam

Vietnam promulgated Circular No. 30/2011/TT-BCT[23] in 2001, and it was implemented in 2012. Vietnam restricts hazardous substances in products that enter the Vietnamese market, excluding

---

[22] "Thailand RoHS Development—Status Update" document submitted to the Asia-Pacific Economic Cooperation in 2008. 2008/SOM1/SCSC/TFTF/003.

[23] The English version can be downloaded from http://www.ecolex.org/ecolex/ledge/view/RecordDetails;DIDPFDSIjsessionid=41EA13916B86129D841AF0EE0584267F?id=LEX-FAOC107300&index=documents.

parts and components. The products covered by the legislation are the same as in the EU RoHS, which was implemented in 2006.[24] The regulations apply to organizations and individuals engaged in the manufacture, trade, or import of electrical and electronic products. Manufacturers and importers of electrical or electronic products are required to compile and disclose information about regulated chemicals. Vietnamese manufacturers and importers, who were unaccustomed to the regulation of chemicals in products, were not well prepared, so the Vietnam RoHS was intended to prevent substandard products flowing into the country's domestic market.

3.4.9 California, United States

In contrast, to the regulations in Asian economies, which mainly focused on easing the effect of trade on the manufacturing sector, the California RoHS is more focused on avoiding becoming an e-waste disposal site because the state, which has a large consumer market, has experienced a surge in e-waste. The California RoHS was implemented in 2007, and it required the Department of Toxic Substances Control to adopt regulations prohibiting regulated electronic devices from being sold or offered for sale in California if the device is prohibited in the EU by the EU RoHS.[25] The California RoHS was directly linked to the EU RoHS to avoid California from becoming a pollution haven for products diverted from EU markets. In contrast to the EU RoHS and the regulations in other countries,the regulations apply to devices with CRT or LCD displays. This partly reflects the increasing difficulty of offering disposal sites for e-waste including CRTs.

---

[24] EU RoHS was revised in 2012 and the products covered were expanded.

[25] https://dtsc.ca.gov/HazardousWaste/rohs.cfm.

3.5   A Race-to-the-Top or Pollution Havens?

Policy diffusion could result in either a race to the top, which makes countries' policies more stringent, or a race to the bottom, which makes other country policies' more lax. A race to the bottom can occur as countries try to attract firms by intentionally setting lower environmental standards (Woods 2006;Konisky 2007 for the interstate case in the United States). If a race to the bottom occurs, there is a concern that developing countries with weaker environmental regulations may become pollution havens as pollution-intensive industries move from developed to developing countries where compliance costs are lower (Mani and Wheeler1998).

Vogel (1995) argues that for product regulation, diffusion leads to a race to the top rather than to a race to the bottom. After a wealthy country imposes stringent standards, regulatory competition among its trading partners that intend to export to the regulated market leads them to set similar or higher standards. Race-to-the-top diffusion is explained as being driven by actors—consumers, producers and governments. When similar regulations are introduced domestically, producers in an exporting country that have already met regulations in their export markets can sell compliant products to both the export markets and the domestic market. Because the producers can exploit economies of scale as well as competitiveness over firms that produce non-compliant products, some companies demand higher standards to be introduced for domestic markets. Moreover, in an exporting country, consumers or environmental organizations may demand similar standards for products sold in the domestic market. Therefore, producers and consumers in an exporting country have incentives to adopt regulations. A government tends to support this producer or consumer demand. Hale and Urpelainen (2015) focus on the roles of producers, governments, and technology diffusion to explain policy diffusion.

Some Asian countries have developed mandatory regulations similar to the EU to restrict hazardous substances. Although major manufacturing countries have introduced RoHS-like regulations, there are other countries that have not yet done so, including Indonesia, Cambodia, and Laos (by the time of 2015). This is because industrial agglomerations have not yet developed in the electrical and electronic product sectors of these countries; therefore, the governments do not see a need to regulate. Furthermore, some governments do not have the capacity to examine and implement regulations. This leads to a partial regulatory race to the top. A questionnaire survey showed that around 50% of Vietnamese firms and 40% of Malaysian firms use different chemicals depending on the destination markets (see Chapter 7). This implies that products containing restricted chemicals are destined for countries without regulations, creating a pollution haven for substandard product waste in countries without regulation.

3.6   Policy Fragmentation

Policy diffusion may lead to policy convergence regionally or globally (Jörgens 2003). Policy convergence leads to a better global equilibrium if problems such as global warming and the depletion of the ozone layer are tackled by international convention. Global emissions are reduced when more nations introduce similar policy-by-policy convergence. However, for product regulation, policy diffusion without hierarchy leads to policy fragmentation. The RoHS diffusion to Asia discussed in this chapter demonstrates that policy diffusion with various modifications to the original policy creates variants and causes complications for producers.

There are diverse motivations behind regulatory diffusion from the EU to Asia. Although manufacturing activities along supply chains take place globally, regulations are formulated in individual countries to reflect their specific motivation and circumstances. Governments attempt to modify the policies that correspond to the EU policies to suit domestic conditions; however, this creates complexity for manufacturers that have global supply chains.

Although RoHS-like environmental regulations in different countries are similar, they are slightly different in terms of targeted products, reporting requirements, monitoring, labeling, and other areas. When firms are required to place specific labeling on products or to meet specific requirements for products, economies of scale in the production of a single product that can be sold to many countries cannot be exploited.

International policy diffusion creates policy fragmentation and firms must comply with multiple countries' regulations. The life cycle of products—from procurement of materials, production of parts and components, assembly, distribution, consumption, recycling, to disposal of end-of-life products—takes place along globally dispersed value chains, whereas product regulations are formulated and implemented within jurisdictions reflecting each country's situation (WTO 2012). Therefore, regulatory diffusion creates complexities for business activities and has a significant effect on firms. No platform has been developed for coordinating PRERs. The TBT Committee of the WTO offers a venue for countries that introduce NTMs to inform other members and for countries that may be affected to raise concerns.

3.7   Conclusion

When innovative product regulations are introduced in an important economy to protect consumers and the environment, the regulations have prompted other countries to learn and have diffused voluntarily without international agreements. Our case studies on countries' policy reveal that the main motives behind the adaptation of regulations in Asian countries fall into the following categories: maintaining export competitiveness, preventing the inflow of hazardous materials to protect health and the environment, harmonizing domestic private requirements that are created by firms to adapt to PRERs, adopting policy innovation, and preventing the environmental degradation. In Asian versions of PRERs, there is a weaker motivation to protect health, safety, and the environment, although this is the main motive in the pioneering policy.

"Policy diffusion has made Asian regulation stricter, creating a race to the top, which has benefitted health, safety, and the environment in developing countries. However, as the policies have been designed to maximize trade benefit rather than to protect the environment, the policies and their implementation offer limited benefits to health and the environment compared with the pioneering policy. In addition, from a regional perspective, regulatory diffusion creates only a partial race to the top because some countries do not introduce and implement PRER owing to a lack of policy capacity.

From a trade perspective, diffusion through adaptation of policies may not be efficient, although policy diffusion partly creates policy convergence. Creating similar versions of regulations has caused policy fragmentation, which makes smooth trade over the global supply web around world more difficult. Under globalization, the manufacture of parts and components depends on the competitive advantages of each country, and a product is rarely completed within a single country; rather products consist of parts and components manufactured in many different countries. An increase in regulatory complexity may hamper trade and put SMEs that have smaller capacity to understand the regulatory environment abroad at a disadvantage. Policy diffusion in the Asian context may do more harm than good unless international coordination over policy diffusion is properly managed.

Problems related to chemicals in products have been raised as an emerging global policy issue in the Strategic Approach to International Chemicals Management, a policy framework for promoting chemical safety globally under the International Conference on Chemicals Management. To achieve global environmental governance on chemicals, it is desirable to coordinate the fragmented environmental policies at a global level, because duplication of regulations across countries disrupts transnational economic activity. To achieve coordination, it is necessary to examine the current situation and to elucidate policy motivations. Examining why and how non-EU developing governments introduce regulations and standards similar to those in the EU will help future policy coordination.

Acknowledgment This work was supported by JSPS KAKENHI Grant Number 15K00675.

References

Akerlof, G. (1970). The market for lemons: Quality uncertainty and the market mechanism. *Quarterly Journal of Economics, 84*(3), 488–500. http://dx.doi.org/10.2307/1879431.

Arimura, T. H., Darnall, N., & Katayama, H. (2011). Is ISO 14001 a gateway to more advanced voluntary action? The case of green supply chain management. *Journal of Environmental Economics and Management, 61*(2), 170–182. http://dx.doi.org/10.1016/j.jeem.2010.11.003.

Biedenkopf, K. (2012). Environmental leadership through the diffusion of pioneering policy. In R. G. Deborah (Ed.), *Environmental leadership: A reference handbook* (pp.105–112). Washington D.C.: SAGE.

Biedenkopf, K., & Park, D. Y. (2012). A toxic issue? Leadership in comprehensive chemicals management. In R. G. Deborah (Eds.), *Environmental leadership: A reference handbook* (pp.782–794). Washington D.C.: SAGE.

Bond, E. W. (1984). International trade with uncertain product quality. *Southern Economic Journal, 51*(1), 196–207. http://dx.doi.org/10.2307/1058332.

Busch, P. O., Jörgens, H., & Tews, K. (2005). The global diffusion of regulatory instruments: The making of a new international environmental regime. *The Annals of the American Academy of Political and Social Science, 598*(1), 146–167. http://dx.doi.org/10.1177/0002716204272355.

Copeland, B. R. (1990). Strategic interaction among nations: negotiable and non-negotiable trade barriers. *Canadian Journal of Economics23*(1), 84–108. http://dx.doi.org/10.2307/135521.

Ederington, J. (2001). International coordination of trade and domestic policies. *The American Economic Review, 91*(5), 1580–1593. http://dx.doi.org/10.1257/aer.91.5.1580.

Hale, T., & Urpelainen, J. (2015). When and how can unilateral policies promote the international diffusion of environmental policies and clean technology? *Journal of Theoretical Politics, 27*(2), 177–205. doi:10.1177/0951629813518128.

Jänicke, M. (2005). Trend setters in environmental policy: The character and role of pioneer countries. *European Environment, 15*(2), 129–142. http://dx.doi.org/10.1002/eet.375.

JETRO. (2007). Point kaisetsu, China RoHS (Explanatory note on China RoHS). Retrieved from Japan: http://www.jetro.go.jp/jfile/report/05001394/05001394_004_BUP_0.pdf.

Jörgens, H. (2003). *Governance by diffusion: Implementing global norms through cross-national imitation and learning* (FFU-Report 07-2003). Berlin, Germany. Retrieved from https://papers.ssrn.com/sol3/papers.cfm?abstract_id=652942.

Kelemen, R. D., & Vogel, D. (2010). Trading places: The role of the United States and the European Union in international environmental politics. *Comparative Political Studies, 43*(4), 427–456. http://dx.doi.org/10.1177/0010414009355265.

Kimura, F., & Ando, M. (2005). Two-dimensional fragmentation in East Asia: Conceptual framework and empirics. *International Review of Economics & Finance, 14*(3), 317–348. http://dx.doi.org/10.1016/j.iref.2004.12.005.

Kojima, M., & Michida, E. (Eds.). (2013). *International trade in recyclable and hazardous waste in Asia*. Edward Elgar Publishing.

Konisky, D. M. (2007). Regulatory competition and environmental enforcement: Is there a race to the bottom? *American Journal of Political Science, 51*(4), 853–872. http://dx.doi.org/10.1111/j.1540-5907.2007.00285.x.

Looi Kee, H., Nicita, A., & Olarreaga, M. (2009). Estimating trade restrictiveness indices. *The Economic Journal, 119*(534), 172–199. http://dx.doi.org/10.1111/j.1468-0297.2008.02209.x.

Mani, M., & Wheeler, D. (1998). In search of pollution havens? Dirty industry in the world economy, 1960 to 1995. *The Journal of Environment & Development, 7*(3), 215–247. doi:10.1177/107049659800700302.

Naiki, Y. (2010). Assessing policy reach: Japan's chemical policy reform in response to the EU's REACH regulation. *Journal of Environmental Law, 22*(2), 171–195. http://dx.doi.org/10.1093/jel/eqq002.

Prakash, A., & Potoski, M. (2006). Racing to the bottom? Trade, environmental governance, and ISO 14001. *American Journal of Political Science, 50*(2), 350–364. http://dx.doi.org/10.1111/j.1540-5907.2006.00188.x.

Ramungul, N., Michida E., & Nabeshima K. (2013). *Impact of product-related environmental regulations/voluntary requirements on Thai firms*. (IDE Discussion Paper No. 383). Chiba: Institute of Developing Economies.

Staiger, R. W. (2012). Non-tariff measures and the WTO. World Trade Organization, Economic Research and Statistics Division. Retrieved from Geneva: https://www.wto.org/english/res_e/reser_e/ersd201201_e.pdf.

Staiger, R. W., & Sykes, A. O. (2011). International trade, national treatment, and domestic regulation. *The Journal of Legal Studies, 40*(1), 149–203. http://dx.doi.org/10.1086/658402.

Vogel, D. (1995). *Trading up: Consumer and environmental regulation in a global economy*. Cambridge: Harvard University Press.

Vogel, D. (2000). Environmental regulation and economic integration. *Journal of International Economic Law, 3*(2), 265–279. http://dx.doi.org/10.1093/jiel/3.2.265.

Vogel, D. (2012). *The politics of precaution: Regulating health, safety, and environmental risks in Europe and the United States*. Princeton: Princeton University Press.

Woods, N. D. (2006). Interstate competition and environmental regulation: A test of the race-to-the-bottom thesis. *Social Science Quarterly, 87*(1), 174–189. http://dx.doi.org/10.1111/j.0038-4941.2006.00375.x.

WTO. (2012). *World trade report 2012.* Retrieved from Geneva: http://www.wto.org/english/res_e/ . . . /world_trade_report12_e.pdf.

WTO. (2013). WTO annual report2013. Retrieved from Geneva: http://www.wto.org/english/res_e/publications_e/anrep14_e.htm.

WTO. (2015). *Twenty-first annual review of the implementation and operation of the Tbt agreement.* /G/TBT/38.

Etsuyo Michida is an Associate Senior Research Fellow at Institute of Developing Economies, Japan External Trade Organization (IDE-JETRO) and was a Visiting Scholar at Haas School of Business, University of California, Berkeley from 2015 to 2017. Her research interest lies in trade and the environment with a special focus on developing countries. She has recently researched on the relationship between environmental regulation, firm behavior, and global supply chains. She holds a PhD in Economics from Graduate School of International Cooperation Studies, Kobe University.

4

Adapting to EU Chemical Regulations: The Experience of Thailand

Nudjarin Ramungul

4.1 Introduction

The electrical and electronic equipment (EEE) industry and the automotive industry are important to the Thai economy. In 2014, the country's top three export products were from these sectors and accounted for about 42% of total export value. These industries have created more than 1 million jobs, with large enterprises providing about

This paper summarizes the efforts made by the National Metal and Materials Technology Center (MTEC) and its partners to support Thai industries to adapt to products' environmental and chemical safety legislations during 2002 to 2012. However, the views and opinions expressed in this paper are strictly those of the author and should not be purported to represent the views of MTEC.

N. Ramungul (✉)
National Metal and Materials Technology Center, National Science,
Pathum Thani, Thailand
e-mail: nudjarr@mtec.or.th

© The Author(s) 2017   **85**
E. Michida et al. (eds.), *Regulations and International Trade*,
IDE-JETRO Series, DOI 10.1007/978-3-319-55041-1_4

half of them. The shift of market regulations toward technical require-ments, especially those related to substances contained in products, will undoubtedly affect the Thai economy.

In the past decade, Thailand has extended its supply-chain network, becoming a factory for the world. Most of the country's factories (>90%) are operated by parts and components makers who supply their products along local and global supply chains to assemblers. Thailand is also a major supplier of finished products such as air conditioners, refrigera-tors, and automobiles. Considering the complexity of the EEE and automotive supply chains, the challenges facing these industries include not only exporting the finished products to overseas markets such as Europe but also supplying goods to firms along the supply chain which may or may not know the final destinations of their products.

This chapter presents some of the measures taken by the National Metal and Materials Technology Center (MTEC) and its partners during 2002–2012 to support the Thai EEE and automotive industries in trans-forming their production practices to produce products that comply with modern environmental and chemical safety (ECS) regulations, particularly regulations like the European Restriction of certain Hazardous Substances (RoHS) in EEE Directive (European Parliament 2003a) and the Regulation on Registration, Evaluation, Authorisation and Restriction of Chemicals (REACH) (European Parliament 2006). ECS regulations have many implications. This chapter focuses on only the part of ECS regula-tions related to chemical substances within manufactured products. MTEC, a national research center that specializes in materials technology, provided technical assistance to support Thai industries in adjusting their practices in order to eliminate hazardous substances from products and processes and to achieve greater sustainability.

4.2   Adopting EU RoHS

Actions related to RoHS in Thailand date back to 2002 when the Department of Foreign Trade in the Ministry of Commerce formed a strategic subcommittee to monitor drafts of the EU WEEE Directive

(European Parliament 2003b) and RoHS and to provide policy recommendation to the government. Unfortunately, this subcommittee was disbanded during government restructuring under the Administrative Reorganization Act, BE 2545 (2002). Nevertheless, the subcommittee's initial work planted seeds in several specialized institutions, including MTEC (Fig. 4.1).

To clarify the subcommittee's initial concerns on the status of the EEE industry in relation to the provisions mandated by RoHS, MTEC conducted a preliminary survey to assess the state of the industry in February 2002. This initial survey results together with responses from interviews with top executives led MTEC to realize that the Thai EEE industry had underestimated the implications of RoHS. The reasons for this were identified as a lack of understanding of materials technology and the extended producer responsibility concept.

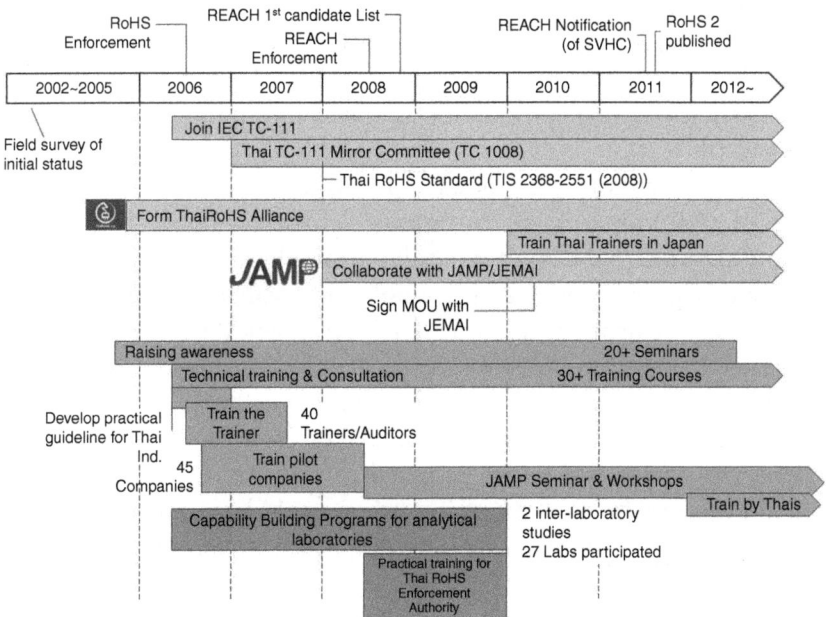

Fig. 4.1 Summary of key activities during 2002–2012 (*Source*: Author generated)

The EEE industry relies on a variety of materials to produce products with cutting-edge performance. Materials used in the industry are often modified to achieve desirable characteristics. Many firms, particularly those that supply parts or provide manufacturing services in the supply chain, used modified materials without fully understanding the content or purpose of each modifier. The industry's lack of awareness of the complexities of materials led to underestimation of the adjustment process, and hence, underestimation of the time required before their products could become RoHS-compliant. In particular, firms did not recognize that prohibited substances could already be incorporated in their products even though they did not use the substances.

Therefore, before any real actions could begin, during 2003–2004, MTEC launched a series of seminars under the theme "Ecomaterials" to provide basic knowledge on hazardous substances in materials and products and the impacts of these substances on the adjustment to become providers of RoHS-compliant products. The leaders in the industry began to worry after realizing that (i) the directive was intended to control the content of restricted substances in products not emissions from factories, (ii) the materials they used were in fact not pure, and (iii) the restricted substances were incorporated into products for technical reasons.

The actual adjustment process in Thailand started around the second half of 2003, mostly via mandates by multinational corporations (MNCs). Most MNCs set a deadline for phasing out the restricted substances, generally no later than mid-2005, which was one year before RoHS enforcement began. Different MNCs took different approaches. In general, however, most subsidiaries of MNCs were required to adjust their materials management system, and to realign and re-qualify all suppliers in order to ensure proper RoHS compliance. All producers along the supply chain were expected to provide satisfactory proof of compliance or else non-compliant orders would be terminated.

The original version of RoHS did not include technical specifications. Notably, it did not specify permissible maximum concentration values, standard test methods that it would recognize, or a means for verifying declarations of conformity by producers. Without official criteria, proof of compliance became the most troublesome issue for both vendors and purchasers. Purchasers tended to protect themselves by imposing strict measures while gathering as much information from suppliers as possible. These actions overloaded the supply chain with complex technical questions and requirements. More importantly, most brand-name customers set their own standards, which generally required suppliers to provide proof of compliance by means of analytical testing.

Actual practices related to analytical testing of supplied materials and parts as required by purchasing firms during this period had several technical problems. First, requests were very rigid and MNCs' guidelines had to be strictly followed. Suppliers were required to provide analytical results for all restricted substances even if they were irrelevant, for example, analytical results to prove the absence of PBBs and PBDEs in metals or ceramics,[1] and analytical results to prove the absence of mercury in aluminum alloys.[2] Second, the analytical testing methods specified were often not suitable for the types of substances and the required detection level; for example, "ICP certificates" were required for all six restricted substances covered by RoHS in all supplied materials and products.[3] Third, although standard test methods existed for certain heavy metals and brominated flame retardants (e.g., EPA test methods), they were developed and validated for wastewater and sludge samples. There were no standard test methods available for determining the levels of the six restricted substances in EEE materials and products, which are more difficult to analyze. Fourth, though capable of testing toxic pollutants in environmental samples, laboratory technicians were unfamiliar with analysis of the target substances in engineering materials, and at the time, few suitable certified reference materials (e.g., printed circuit board

---

[1] Polybrominated biphenyls (PBBs) and polybrominated diphenyl ethers (PBDEs) are polymers used as flame retardants in plastics. Metals and ceramics do not require flame retardants and are typically produced by high-temperature processes exceeding the decomposition temperatures of PBBs and PBDEs.

[2] Mercury and aluminum are incompatible materials. Mercury will constantly destroy the natural protective layer of the aluminum, leading aluminum to rust very rapidly. Since this reaction does not consume mercury, it will continue until either aluminum is completely destroyed or mercury evaporates out entirely.

[3] Inductively coupled plasma (ICP) is used for analyzing trace elements (e.g., the elements Cd and Pb) but would be inappropriate for identifying and quantifying the restricted polymers.

with certified concentrations of lead and cadmium, or polystyrene with certified concentrations of PBB and PBDE) were available for laboratories to verify their performance.

At the same time, Thai industries were losing their competitive advantage to competitors with lower labor costs. RoHS-compliant products offered a solution to this problem. To produce such products efficiently, RoHS compliance must be a quality item that firms aimed to control and improve. Like other quality items, RoHS compliance should be confirmed via quality assurance systems. MTEC, therefore, established the Trace Element Analysis Lab to serve as a contact point for companies that needed assistance. MTEC published a book (National Metal and Materials Technology Center 2004) and organized short courses in "Materials and Impurities in Electrical and Electronic Components." The objectives of these activities were to provide basic background information about materials and to convince firms to adopt RoHS compliance as a new quality item.

4.2.1 ThaiRoHS Alliance

The efforts of Thai producers to comply with RoHS requirements up to then had not been coordinated, with companies regarding each other more as competitors rather than as allies. The status of the adjustment process in Thailand around mid-2004 is illustrated in Fig. 4.2. This state of affairs put the heaviest burden of proof on the weakest link in the supply chain. It had become clear to most stakeholders that the unorganized approach only put unnecessary burdens on all parties and did not necessarily guarantee that products would always be free of the restricted substances. At the fourth "Ecomaterials" seminar organized by MTEC in collaboration with the Federation of Thai Industry (FTI), the Electrical and Electronics Institute (EEI), the Pollution Control Department, and the Department of Industrial Works, on September 16, 2004, over 340 participants from more than 130 companies agreed on the need for all stakeholders to cooperate in establishing necessary structures to improve the ability of the country to address RoHS requirements and to increase the competitiveness of Thai products. As

Fig. 4.2 Status of Thai EEE industry in 2004
(*Source*: Ramungul, N. (2004))

a result, the ThaiRoHS Alliance was formed, which is an informal group of representatives from manufacturers, research institutes, testing laboratories, equipment providers, and private and government organizations. These various players came forward and shared their knowledge and expertise to help establish the necessary support platform for improving the industry's ability to handle the new market regulations.

The first task for the ThaiRoHS Alliance was to identify the root of the problems and formulate an action plan to ease the situation. Through the alliance's activities, it was realized that the biggest challenge for most Thai producers was not finding alternative materials but rather finding competent suppliers, establishing a cost-effective materials control program, finding ways to verify and guarantee compliance, and building up experience to master new processes.

The alliance laid out three important goals:

(i) Find consensus on testing methods
(ii) Find consensus on acceptable requirements and guidelines for establishing compliance (declaration of compliance)
(iii) Help one another to bolster the competency of laboratories

4.2.2 Supports from the European Delegation to Thailand

In 2005, MTEC received funding from the European Delegation to Thailand through the Small Project Facility program to implement two capacity-building projects: the TREE-Green Project ("A practical guideline to become RoHS/ELV compliance producers and preparation for the Energy using Products (EuP) directive") in collaboration with FTI, EEI, and the Institute for Small and Medium Enterprise Development; and the PRO-TREE Project ("Capacity build up for the determination of levels of regulated substances in electrical, electronic and automotive parts") in collaboration with FTI.

4.2.2.1 TREE-Green Project

The TREE-Green Project planned to implement actions in two areas: (i) formulating an integrated package for producers that wished to become a hazardous substance-free (HS-free) product provider and (ii) arranging for appropriate preparations for the upcoming Energy using Products (EuP) Directive (European Parliament 2005). The main activities implemented under the TREE-Green Project are summarized in Fig. 4.3.

In activity 1, MTEC established a website (www.ThaiRoHS.org) to become an anchor point for Thai companies that wanted to learn more about relevant directives and about the recommended approaches to adjusting their practices to become HS-free producers. During the one-year duration of the project, about 250 documents were published on the website and accessed more than 150,000 times. The download center had about 190 documents that were downloaded more than 50,000 times.

Note that the role of the website was not just information dissemination. It also served as a consultation platform for producers that had technical problems and/or difficulties understanding the directive. Figure 4.4 shows some of the topics discussed in the website's discussion forum.

Activity 2 of the TREE-Green Project aimed to stimulate meaningful collaboration and to strengthen the ThaiRoHS Alliance such that it

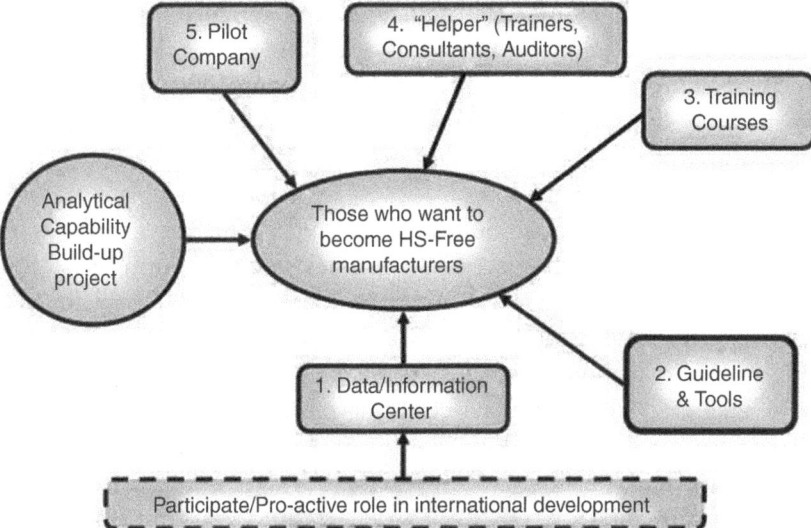

Fig. 4.3 Activities under the TREE-Green project
(*Source*: Author generated)

1. Is there any way we can reduce CRM problem?

2. I heard that there will be Interlab on XRF

3. Some questions about RoHS; Restricted substances and packaging;

4. Homogeneous materials

5. RoHS test method? Accuracy of EDXRF, ICP method

6. Cd and EEE; Need help on SoC; RoHS and PCB

7. Definition of Green product?

8. Frequency of analytical testing under ELV directive?, ELV Exemption?

9. Does Japan control exports of EEE? Korean RoHS & Packaging directive?

10. Which products are covered by REACH?

Fig. 4.4 Examples of topic under discussion in www.ThaiRoHS.org forum
(*Source*: Thai RoHS.org)

could contribute to practical guidelines and templates for companies that wished to fulfill requirements for RoHS and the End-of Life Vehicles Directive (ELV) (European Parliament 2000). This development carefully considered industry needs in order to provide all necessary components in one package so that it would be ready for any company to implement.

Through the collaboration of ThaiRoHS Alliance members, the project came up with practical guidelines for other firms to follow. The key concepts and elements recommended in the guidelines are shown in Fig. 4.5. Details of the guidelines' recommendations pertaining to quality assurance systems are shown in Fig. 4.6.

These guidelines were tested in a pilot experiment that closely resembled a real setting. Finally, after making suitable adjustments to reflect the practical situation, the guidelines were published as a handbook (Ramungul, N. et al. 2007) bundled with seven companion books and pamphlets and a DVD containing information.

The practical guidelines proved to be an effective tool for helping industry comply with RoHS and ELV. They served as a starting point as well as a manual for companies that planned to become HS-free product providers. The guidelines became an invaluable resource for firms that wanted to adjust their practices toward HS-free products. Most questions related to the adjustment process were answered with recommendations for best practices. In particular, the guidelines directed readers to consider practices that were more sustainable. Instead of ad hoc change, the guidelines focused on systematic adjustment. The whole production system must be revised, starting from management perspectives. Project participants strongly believed that by using this approach, companies could handle not just RoHS and ELV, but similar regulations as well.

The success of this valuable work was realized only because of collaborative efforts of the target group, the ThaiRoHS Alliance devoted nearly 400 person-days to completing this work.

The practical guidelines, however, could not be disseminated fast enough to cope with the urgency of the situation. To ensure widespread acceptance and effective knowledge transfer, the TREE-Green Project implemented three activities: properly designed training courses; training of the trainers/helpers; and practical training for pilot companies.

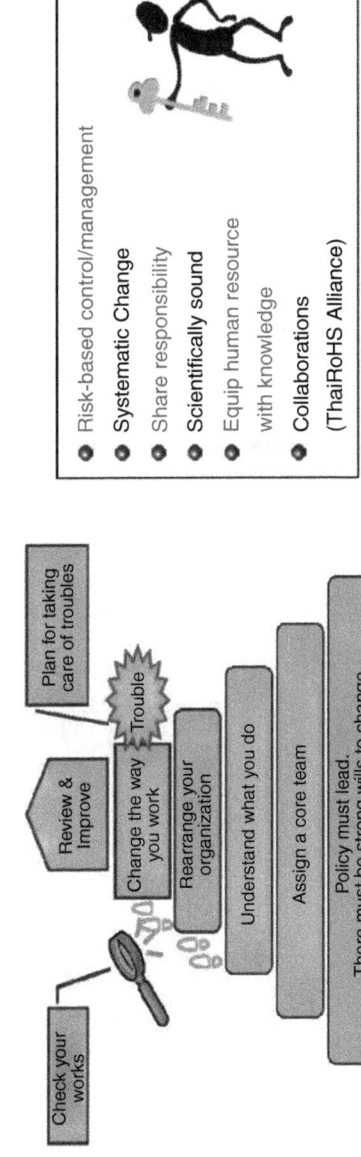

Fig. 4.5 A schematic diagram showing the concept and key elements for adjustment
(*Source*: Author generated)

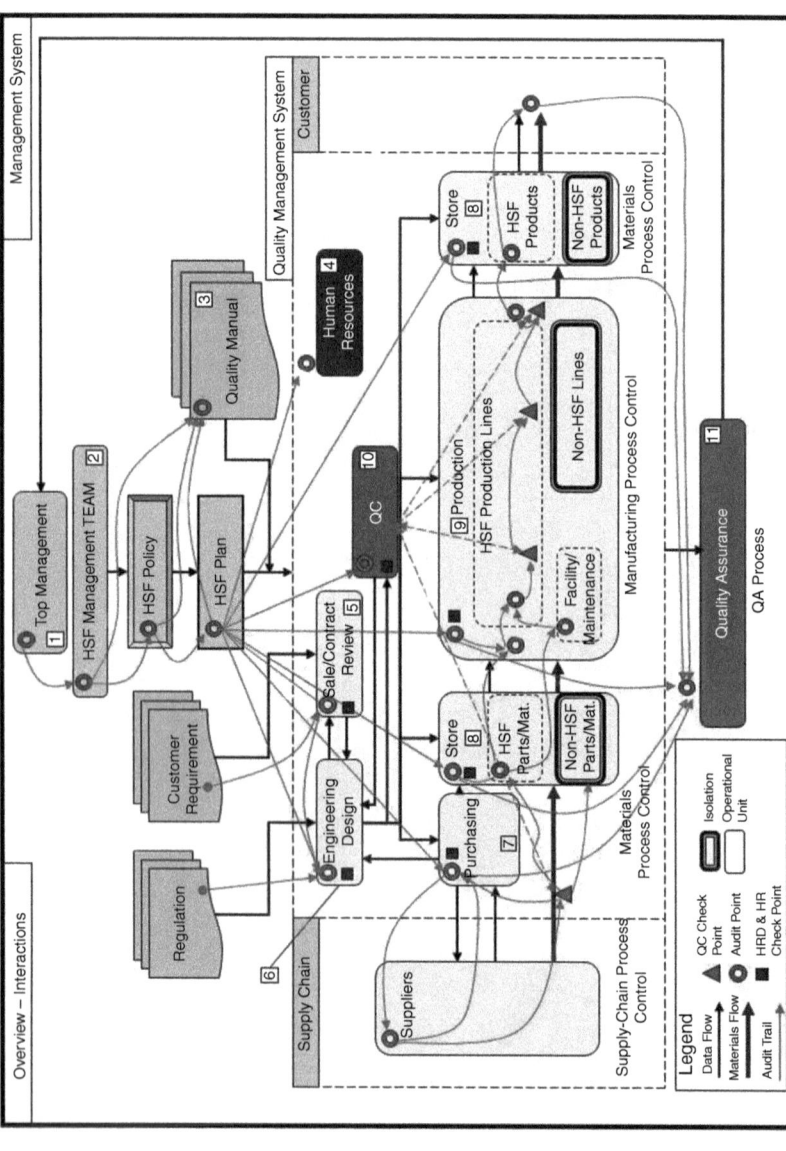

Fig. 4.6 Diagram shows recommended linkages between different operations in a restricted substances management system (*Source*: Ramungul, N. et al. (2007))

Specifically, the project formed a working group consisting of 15 organizations to evaluate industrial needs and design appropriate training courses to provide trainees with basic knowledge and guide them to develop a suitable restricted substances management system. Then, the project offered advanced training for trainers, auditors, and consultants. Trainers helped companies get started and brought them up to speed, consultants helped guide the company, and auditors checked whether systems were properly implemented. Finally, the trained personnel gave back the project by working with designated pilot companies and helping them develop a proper management system in later guideline training courses.

These three activities proved to be very useful in the long run. The training courses were in high demand. MTEC offered public training courses along these lines until 2012. The trainers and auditors also spread their knowledge by training their co-workers and suppliers. Some helpers also offered similar training courses as well as consultation services. The pilot companies could pass audits by important customers and could knowledgably handle inconsistent requests from both local and overseas customers. Interestingly, because of these types of actions by suppliers, pilot companies reported that their customers were surprised and quite satisfied. Firms also reported that these new capacities helped in attracting more customers.

4.2.2.2 Pro-TREE Project

The Pro-TREE Project aimed to improve the analytical capabilities of the Thai EEE and automotive industries so that they could meet obligations imposed by the EU RoHS and ELV with confidence. This project had two challenging objectives: to enhance the capability of relevant business operators in screening and verification testing to meet the requirements imposed by RoHS and ELV and to build a platform to encourage the exchange of knowledge and experiences in implementing and verifying standard test procedures for substances of concern among relevant operators. After discussion with relevant stakeholders, the project came up with the six developmental elements as shown in Fig. 4.7.

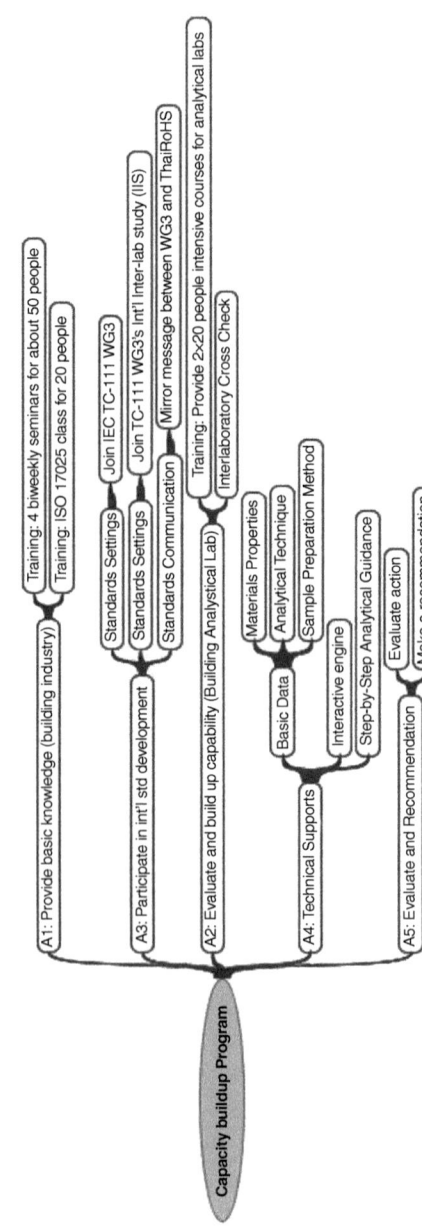

Fig. 4.7 Key elements of the Pro-TREE project

(*Source*: Author generated)

During the starting period of this project, RoHS and ELV started to make a large impact on the industry. The most urgent problems were attributed to misunderstanding. Among many points of confusion, trace element analysis was characterized as the weakest area, where the concern parties operated based on "personal feelings" because they did not have sufficient understanding of the field. This created an urgent demand for the project to give correct information to the target group and provide them with proper knowledge to help them understand the situation and make the right decisions on issues related to trace elements analysis. A series of training courses on issues related to analytical testing and the requirements of RoHS were offered. In particular, the project offered nine basic training courses on different analytical techniques that could be used for trace elements analysis, one basic course on engineering materials, and one course on ISO 17025. In all, the project provided training to many participants, more than five times the number in the proposed work plan. These efforts were later found to be worthwhile as daily inquiries on issues rooted in misunderstandings were gradually replaced by more technical problems.

The absence of standard test methods at the time led to the development of standards by customers. Though such standards can be useful in specific areas, here they proved to be burdensome for suppliers. After discussion with stakeholders, it was generally agreed that Thailand should not aggravate the problem by developing yet another standard. The project then joined international standard development in this area, namely, development of IEC TC-111. Three project members were nominated by the Thai government to serve in IEC TC-111 working group 3 (WG3), the working group responsible for developing standard test methods for the determination of the restricted substances in EEE products. With financial support from the project, these experts could actively participate in the working group meetings, provide the working group with opinions from the perspective of Thai industries, participate in working group activities, and convey messages and information from WG3 to Thai stakeholders for better understanding and proper preparation. This participation also enabled the project to join IEC Interlaboratory Study-II (IIS-2) to evaluate the effectiveness of the draft standard IEC 62321/1CD. Experience gained from participation in IEC IIS-2 was shared with other laboratories in Thailand via seminars and discussion forums. Moreover, the lessons learned from joining IEC IIS-2 activities were utilized in the design of Interlaboratory Crosscheck Study (ILS) activities.

To allow laboratories to assess and compare their competencies in determining the levels of the six restricted substances under RoHS and to allow the project to evaluate the effectiveness of the draft IEC 62321 standard, the project initiated a three-stage ILS, with each stage designed to target one important factor. Over 700 test specimens were prepared for this study. Twenty-four laboratories participated (23 in Thailand and 1 in Singapore). More than 600 test specimens were distributed to participating laboratories for analysis according to test methods outlined in the draft IEC 62321/1CDV standard.

All participating laboratories contributed nearly 5,000 analytical data points, producing a wealth of information for the project. The most critical piece of information was that the uncertainty in RoHS/ELV analytical results could be very high and it increased drastically with the complexity of both the test method and the sample under test. The project attempted to identify some obvious causes to address the situation. Among the many sources of uncertainty, the project identified lack of control of analytical procedures and complexity of the sample under test as specific problems. Some "global problems" stemmed from a lack of important components for reliable analytical tests, such as certified reference materials and analytical methods. Nevertheless, with proper knowledge of important issues, including the components of the samples, the materials under test, and analytical techniques, together with good laboratory practices, most sources of uncertainty could be well controlled. This information was fed back to participating laboratories with comments on important performance issues to allow them to make improvements. Unclear issues and signs of problems were discussed in more detail in a discussion forum where participating laboratories discussed their practices, identified causes of problems, and proposed ways to control or prevent them in the analysis of real samples.

Instead of being competitors, commercial laboratories collaborated in fruitful discussion and offered to share resources such as certified reference materials to bring up one another's competency level. Proactive support from test equipment manufacturers also helped achieve more reliable results from in-house laboratories.

The ILS activity was very successful both in boosting the confidence of laboratories and in fostering an atmosphere of collaboration so that laboratories could help one another. This activity was in high demand because it was the only means available at the time for the laboratories to check their performances. In 2009, after the initial ILS funding ceased, MTEC offered another ILS to satisfy demand from stakeholders. This ILS-2009 was also completed successfully.

4.2.3 RoHS V2

In 2011, the European Commission published RoHS Version 2 (V2) (European Parliament 2011), which was to replace the first version in 2013. RoHS V2 contained many more technical provisions than the original RoHS. In particular, this version specified an acceptable compliance scheme as well as the roles of each business operator. The new directive also dictated the establishment of a harmonized standard for demonstrating compliance.

Since the provisions for the demonstration and declaration of compliance indicated in RoHS V2 were in line with the management practices promoted in Thailand to cope with the original RoHS, there was relatively little capacity-building work to be done to bring firms into compliance with RoHS V2. Through the established data/information platform and the monitoring channel for firms' regulations and requirements, messages and suggested action items were disseminated while RoHS V2 was in the draft stage, which was followed by a couple of rounds of seminars to summarize the changes when the final version was published. Firms needed only to review their management systems, verify that their practices could meet specific requirements, and ensure that all the required documents were available.

In March 2015, the European Commission added four new restricted substances (DEHP, BBP, DBP, and DIBP)[4] (European Parliament 2015) to the list of restricted substances under RoHS V2. Again, since there were appropriate systems in place that were ready to handle the changes in the regulation, only a little work had to be done.

---

[4] DEHP: bis(2-ethylhexyl) phthalate; BBP: benzyl butyl phthalate; DBP: dibutyl phthalate; DIBP: diisobutyl phthalate.

4.3   Adopting EU REACH

In 2006, EU published yet another high-impact regulation known as REACH. This regulation is highly complex. It aims to ensure that risks associated with the use of chemicals are known and provisions for their safe use are appropriately addressed. REACH is a risk-based regulation. Its underlying concept was not clearly understood by relevant parties in Thailand at the time. The majority of REACH provisions place obligations on manufacturers of chemical substances and mixtures. Producers of articles, on the other hand, are expected to fulfill obligations in two areas: one related to a group of substances contained in the so-called candidate list of substances of very high concern (SVHC-C[5]), and the other related to substances whose use is restricted. In particular, a supplier of articles is obligated to provide the recipient of articles with sufficient information if an article contains an SVHC-C at a concentration above 0.1% by weight.[6] Producers and importers of articles are also obligated to notify the European Chemical Agency (ECHA) if an article contains an SVHC-C at a concentration above 0.1% by weight and the substance is present in quantities totaling over 1 metric ton per producer/importer per year. The duty to communicate information on a substance in articles is mandated the moment the substance is included in the candidate list posted on ECHA website,[7] while the duty to notify the agency must be fulfilled within six months after the inclusion of the substance in the candidate list.

REACH and RoHS are closely related but they are not entirely alike. This fact posed the first challenge to Thai firms. They not only had to make sure that they understood the differences between REACH and RoHS so that they could make appropriate adjustments, but also had to be able to relay the information to their customers and suppliers and ensure that all parties had a correct understanding.

---

[5] Chemical substances that meet criteria laid down by REACH for substances of very high concern (SVHC) *and* were later selected according to REACH mandates to include in the candidate list of substances of very high concern.

[6] Based on the ruling by the European Court of Justice on Case C-106/14 handed down on September 10, 2015.

[7] http://echa.europa.eu/web/guest/candidate-list-table.

The second challenge of REACH was rooted in the nature of the requirements pertaining to the candidate list of SVHCs. It is a "living list" and is expected to be updated to include more substances every six months until all SVHCs are completely addressed. The use of these substances is not restricted but their presence in articles over the threshold must be communicated to the recipients of the articles. Most substances on the candidate list are unfamiliar substances to most firms except those that use or produce them. Unlike restricted substances under RoHS and ELV, these substances may or may not be relevant to the EEE and automotive industries. In theory, REACH imposes no obligation on producers if their products contain no substances on the candidate list. In practice, with limited knowledge about substances on the candidate list, both suppliers and purchasers had limited means to weed out irrelevant substances. Although the practical guidelines to become an RoHS-compliant producer could be adapted to add regulated substances and materials data into the quality assurance system, it was clear that adjusting firms' practices alone would not be effective enough to cope with this difference. Nevertheless, as when adapting to RoHS, firms along the supply chain needed to work together to come up with a suitable solution to fulfill the REACH SVHC obligations. It was possible that this task could be accomplished through the ThaiRoHS Alliance network. Unfortunately, since there were many substances to control and communicate, and the transmission of relevant data had to be in formats that customers could accept, an effective tool was needed for the management and transfer of substances data. This task was beyond the capacity of supply-chain firms or the ThaiRoHS Alliance.

To address this difficulty, MTEC collaborated and later signed a memorandum of understanding with the Japan Environmental Management Association for Industry (JEMAI) to cooperate in the development and spread of the Joint Article Management Promotion-consortium (JAMP) data collection and transfer tools. This collaboration allowed MTEC and JEMAI to conduct seminars and hands-on work-shops on JAMP tools in Thailand for five years. The collaboration also included provisions to train Thai JAMP trainers in Japan and opportunities to observe practices at Japanese factories. This activity resulted in 50 trainers who later gave back to the project by becoming trainers both for public seminars and workshop and for their supply-chain firms.

Joining international organizations and adopting JAMP tools helped ease the situation but could not solve the problem entirely. Through JAMP trainings and JAMP tools, Thai firms could adjust their practices to ensure data integrity. However, the data transfer format and any extensions of the data requested depended on the receiver of the data, that is, MNC brand-owners. The different natures of the products have made it impossible, at least for now, to establish a single system or solution that works for every industry. Data requirements and, hence, data collection strategies, for long-life products such as automotive parts are not the same as those for short-life products such as IT products. Supply-chain firms, particularly upstream firms, supply their products to different industries. They have to communicate the same information on substances in many formats that are not quite compatible with one another. Customers in the automotive industry require International Material Data System data. Some MNC customers, particularly, Japanese firms, require JAMP data. Others, particularly medical device companies, require BOM Check data. Other product sectors, such as furniture and toys, have no preference because they are the data requester. They could choose to accept any data available to them or choose a data communication system that fit their needs. The task of data communication can be burdensome if it has to be done repeatedly every 6 months. It is important to note that this burden is not shared with firms inside the EU since REACH already mandates the flow of the relevant data to producers of articles.

4.4   Conclusion

Thailand had spent years of effort to help its industries adjust their practices to better cope with modern ECS regulations. The support that MTEC provided to Thai firms, especially small- and medium-sized enterprises (SMEs) and supply-chain firms, in adapting their practices in a timely manner was successful for the following reasons:

1. Early efforts by the subcommittee in 2002 that engaged specialized institutes to help address the problem.

2. Collaborative efforts of ThaiRoHS Alliance members, which helped not only in addressing the right problems but also in using the right approaches.
3. Sufficient and timely funding from the European Delegation to Thailand to support initial capacity-building programs.
4. Continued support from the Thai government to see the work through.
5. Collaborative efforts from JEMAI/JAMP to ensure mutual understanding between Japanese firms and Thai supply-chain firms and to equip firms with appropriate data transfer tools to cope with SVHC under REACH.

Although regulations like RoHS and ELV could be addressed locally, dealing with SVHCs under REACH is beyond the ability of most firms in Thailand, which are predominantly SMEs. Because of the growing length of the candidate list of SVHCs and inconsistent industry data collection practices, compliance with REACH is becoming far too complex and beyond the capability of SMEs which have weak bargaining power and few resources. With low production volumes, SMEs are obliged to bear a very high burden in relation to their output. To manage chemical substances information and transfer the data along long and increasingly complicated supply chains, a common mechanism must be established. This task can only be accomplished through international collaboration to establish an appropriate platform to handle the massive flow of chemical safety data generated under REACH.

References

European Commission. (2015). Commission Delegated Directive (EU) 2012/863 of 31 March 2015 amending Annex II to Directive 2011/65/EU of the European Parliament and of the Council as regards the list of restricted substances.

European Parliament. (2000). Directive 2000/53/EC of the European Parliament and of the Council on end-of life vehicles. Retrieved from http://eur-lex.europa.eu/LexUriServ/LexUriServ.do?uri=CONSLEG:2000L0053:20050701:EN:PDF.

European Parliament. (2003a). Directive 2002/95/EC of the European Parliament and of the Council on the Restriction of the Use of Certain Hazardous Substances in Electrical and Electronic Equipment

European Parliament. (2003b). Directive 2002/96/EC of the European Parliament and of the European Council on Waste of Electrical and Electronic Equipment

European Parliament. (2005). Directive 2005/32/EC of the European Parliament and of the Council on establishing a framework for the setting of ecodesign requirements forenergy-using products and Council Directive 92/42/EEC and Directives 96/57/EC and 2000/55/EC of the European Parliament and of the Council.

European Parliament. (2006). Regulation (EC) No 1907/2006 of the European Parliament and of the Council of 18 December 2006 concerning the Registration, Evaluation, Authorization and Restriction of Chemicals (REACH).

European Parliament. (2011). Directive 2011/65/EU of the European Parliament and of the Council on the restriction of the use of certain hazardous substances in electrical and electronic equipment.

National Metal and Materials Technology Center. (2004). *Basic knowledge on substances in products (In Thai)*. Patumtani, Thailand: National Metal and Materials Technology Center.

Ramungul, N. (2004). Status of RoHS Adjustment in Thailand: report to UNCTAD Consultative Task Force (CTF) on Environmental Requirements and Market Access for Developing Countries. *1st Meeting of the Consultative Task Force (CTF) on Environmental Requirements and Market Access for Developing Countries*, Geneva, 5–6 November 2004.http://unctad.org/en/pages/MeetingsArchive.aspx?meetingid=9930.

Ramungul, N., Wongwuttikultorn, P., Tiyapatanaputi S., & TREE Green Project working group. (2007). *Guideline for the adjustment to become a hazardous substances free producer (In Thai)*. Patumtani, Thailand: National Metal and Materials Technology Center.

Nudjarin Ramungul is a Research Specialist and Director of Environment Research Unit at National Metal and Materials Technology Center, Thailand. She received her PhD degree in Electrical Engineering from Rensselaer Polytechnic Institute, NY, USA in 1998. She started working on WEEE and RoHS directives since 2002. She initiated several research projects aimed to gain in-depth understanding of Thai firms and to provide them with appropriate technical supports. Her works led to the initiation of ThaiRoHS alliance and the subsequent multi-stakeholders collaborative works that helped Thai EEE and automotive firms cope with global waves of substances in products regulations.

5

Diffusion of Private Food Standards from the European Union to Asia

Etsuyo Michida and Kaoru Nabeshima

5.1 Introduction

Domestic policy is increasingly influenced by other countries' policy because of globalization (Meseguer 2005; Jänicke 2005). This influence also extends to private practices that require certification or streamlined processes for business. As discussed in Chapter 2, private standards and standard schemes have been developed to supplement public regulations in developed countries.

This chapter focuses on good agricultural practices (GAPs), particularly one of the most influential private standard schemes called GLOBALG.A.

E. Michida (✉)
Institute of Developing Economies, Japan External Trade Organization (IDE-JETRO), Chiba, Japan
e-mail: etsuyo_michida@ide.go.jp

K. Nabeshima
Waseda University, Tokyo, Japan
e-mail: kknabeshima@waseda.jp

© The Author(s) 2017   **107**
E. Michida et al. (eds.), *Regulations and International Trade*,
IDE-JETRO Series, DOI 10.1007/978-3-319-55041-1_5

P.[1] and its diffusion to Asia. The main motive of Asian countries to adopt GLOBALG.A.P. is to maintain access to the European Union (EU) market. Trade-motivated diffusion of private practices is similar in mechanism to the diffusion of the EU regulations of hazardous substances discussed in Chapter 3. However, this chapter deals with diffusion of a private voluntary standard scheme instead of mandatory public regulation. What is interesting is that a *private* initiative in a pioneering country now can be imitated in *public* initiatives in Asia. Follower countries have different policy settings and business environments from the pioneering country. Moreover, the private standard scheme that Asian countries took as a model for diffused schemes was created with different motives from those of the Asian public sectors.

GLOBALG.A.P. is a specific implementation of GAPs. GAP is a general term referring to a collection of best practices in agriculture; there are many types of GAPs all over the world. The Food and Agriculture Organization (FAO) promotes GAPs that are adapted for the local environment (FAO 2004). GAP codes have also been developed in many countries by various stakeholders in both the public and private sectors, including governments, farmers' associations, food industry associations, retailers and non-governmental organizations (NGOs). The definition of GAP differs from place to place, depending on local issues, resources and constraints. In the EU, GAPs were adopted by farms to fulfil government subsidy requirements, whereas in Japan, they were promoted as a voluntary system to improve farming practices such as risk management and efficiency. The large number of GAPs is described by FAO[2] and a multiplicity of GAPs and varying motivations are mentioned. There are many types of GAPs, but it should be noted how GLOBALG.A.P., which is enforced by third-party certification, has spread to Asia, albeit unevenly.[3]

---

[1] How an entity meets standards is via one of the three methods: self-evaluation, supplier audit, or third-party certification. A standard scheme is typically associated with the third form: third-party certification.

[2] FAO GAP Page, http://www.fao.org/prods/gap/.

[3] For any kind of standards, there are three different ways to assess compliance. The first is self-assessment, where the practitioners assess their own actions. Promotion and adaption of best practices typically falls into this category. The second is assessment by the buyer. In a business setting, this is often used in the form of supplier audits by the buyer. The third type is third-party

GLOBALG.A.P. was started in 1997 as a third-party certification scheme called EUREPGAP to ensure safety of agricultural products, and was led by British retailers and supermarkets[4,5]. GLOBALG.A.P. applies to production on farms to ensure the safety of food produce and promote sustainable agriculture in economical and efficient ways, while protecting the environment, worker health, and animal welfare. GLOBALG.A.P. was developed to facilitate the procurement by retailers of fresh produce that met their requirements from all over the world. Therefore, GLOBALG.A.P. is intended to be a standard scheme that can be used to select qualified producers, who must obtain third-party certification as proof of their adherence to the standards. There were two different factors behind the creation of GLOBALG.A.P. First was globalization; British retailers wished to apply a similar quality assurance standard to both domestic produce and imported produce to allow them to manage global supply chains for supplying safe imported and domestically grown food to consumers. Second, the introduction of the Food Safety Act of 1990 in the UK imposed strict liability on retailers for the safety of the food they placed on the market, and only allowing food businesses to escape liability if they could show that they had exercised due diligence along their supply chains (Loader and Hobbs 1999; Van Der Grijp et al. 2005).[6] In other words, firms became responsible for the safety and quality of the food they sold and could not transfer legal responsibility to their suppliers (Jaffee and Masakure 2005). The Act coincided with the effort by the EU to move towards a single market, which included the harmonization of EU regulations, in particular the maximum residue levels for pesticides in fresh produce (Humphrey 2008). It foreshadowed subsequent legislation on food safety in the EU after 2000 (see Chapter 2). Part of the motivation

---

certification schemes, where the assessment is done by an independent entity, often a well-established certification agency. ISO certification falls into this category and Chapter 11 deals with ISO certifications.

[4] GLOBALG.A.P. homepage http://www.globalgap.org/uk_en/who-we-are/about-us/history/index.html, accessed on 24 November 2015.

[5] For instance, in a sample of firms in Peru studied by Schuster and Maertens (2015), GLOBALG.A.P. certification was the main private standard adopted by the Peruvian asparagus industry, accounting for 34% of the standards adopted. HACCP and BRC are the top two standards adopted in food processing establishments in the Peruvian asparagus industry.

[6] For more on the history of GLOBALG.A.P., please see (Van Der Grijp et al. 2005).

behind the creation of GLOBALG.A.P. is the effects of globalization that Asian countries also face. However, it is also motivated by the legal requirements imposed on large retailers being specific to Europe and there being no counterpart requirements in Asia.

This chapter discusses the diffusion of a private standard scheme, GLOBALG.A.P., to Asian countries and examines the variations in diffusion and motivation. Cases of variant GAPs are presented to examine the issue further. The following questions are explored. Why do Asian governments adapt private initiatives of other countries and regions? How do differences in motivations and country-specific conditions lead to variants of GLOBALG.A.P.? Do local GAPs that emulate GLOBALG.A.P. achieve their goals in Asia? Previous literature has not discussed the diffusion of private standards from the perspective of developing countries. This chapter attempts to fill the gap in understanding the diffusion mechanism.

The rest of this chapter is organized as follows. Section 5.2 examines determinants of GLOBALG.A.P. diffusion. Diffusion in this chapter includes both diffusion resulting from the spread of firms obtaining GLOBALG.A.P. certification and diffusion resulting from the spread of local GAP creation based on GLOBALG.A.P. Section 5.3 discusses the modes and motivation of GLOBALG.A.P. diffusion with cases from Asian countries. Section 5.5 examines the implications of local GAP diffusion, and the discussion is summarized in the Conclusion.

5.2   Determinants for Diffusion of GLOBALG.A.P.

Of the many variant GAPs, why did GLOBALG.A.P., which is a private standard scheme with third-party certification, diffuse to Asia? Mandatory regulation and a private standard scheme that requires third-party certification have different characteristics, although they have similar mechanisms affecting firms across borders. Governments introduce food safety regulations to protect citizen's health from various food threats such as pesticide residues and microbial contamination. The private sector, especially large retailers, also aims to comply with mandatory regulations and to provide safe food to consumers by reducing associated risk through managing global value chains. Global value chains from farm to fork are becoming increasingly complex under globalization. To manage complicated supply chains, the private sectors in developed regions, especially in Europe, have introduced private standards and standard schemes to manage their suppliers around the globe (see Chapter 2).

Compliance with the food safety regulations of importing countries is required for agricultural products and for food producers exporting to regulated countries. Failure to comply with regulations of destination markets may lead to product rejection at borders (UNIDO 2010 and 2015 for global border rejection analysis, Institute of Developing Economies, Japan External Trade Organization (IDE-JETRO) and UNIDO 2013 for Asian border rejection analysis).

A fundamental difference between public regulations and private standards lies in the weight of scientific evidence. Public regulations must be based on scientific evidence (Henson and Humphrey 2009).[7] In many areas, this is required to stand the test of World Trade Organization (WTO) disputes. In contrast, private standards can be created without needing to provide a scientific justification. Thus, creating a regulation typically requires stringent proof of causality, whereas private standards do not. Thus, the validity of claims made in regulations and private standards are based on different thresholds of rigor and causality. In this case, adopting a foreign private standard as a domestic regulation must be considered cautiously and evaluated. Making such a private standard a voluntary public standard is permissible without large alterations, although differences in local conditions must be considered carefully. For private standards diffused to Asia, different motivations lead to different adaptations.

Chapter 3 discusses regulatory diffusion from the EU to Asia. For mandatory regulations, failure of compliance results in the rejection of produce by authorities at borders and sometimes non-compliant producers are listed publicly. Failure tarnishes the brand image of producers

---

[7] This is especially true if such regulations are seen as impediments to international trade. Because all countries in East Asia are members of the WTO, Technical Barriers to Trade (TBT), and Sanitary and Phytosanitary (SPS) agreements require that such measures be based on scientific evidence.

and can damage future business. Unlike these public, mandatory regulations, private standards are not legally binding. However, for producers, meeting the requirements specified in private standards and obtaining certification of the standards if required is a prerequisite for gaining access to these buyers, for example, many supermarkets in northern Europe.[8] Therefore, both public mandatory regulation and private voluntary standards or standard schemes affect producers similarly in developing countries (ITC 2011; Henson and Humphrey 2010, 2012; Henson et al. 2011; Humphrey 2012). Consequently, the effect of the diffusion of GLOBALG.A.P. is as strong as that of the diffusion of mandatory regulation.

5.3   Modes and Motives in the Diffusion of GLOBALG.A.P.

In Asia, the private sector and governments have been involved in adapting and creating their versions of standards that are similar to foreign private standards. For East Asian countries, the diffusion of GLOBALG.A.P. can be categorized into the following four modes based on actors, actions, and motivations. Different combinations of actors, actions, and motivations in each country lead to the emergence of variants of GLOBALG.A.P. Categories for adoption styles and actors are show in Table 5.1.

5.3.1 Mode 1: Certified by GLOBALG.A.P.

In mode 1, firms or producers are motivated to obtain GLOBALG.A.P. certification because they are required by their customers to do so, or they see the potential to maintain or expand their business in the EU or other relevant markets by obtaining GLOBALG.A.P. certification. This category of motivation has been examined in previous literature. Many studies have examined the effect of private standards, including

---

[8] See Chapter 2 by Humphrey for standard and standard scheme.

Table 5.1 Four modes of diffusion

	Main actor: private	Main actor: public
Foreign standards not modified	Mode 1: Straightforward adoption of foreign private standard schemes by the private sector.	Mode 2: Straightforward adoption of foreign private standards by the public sector
Foreign standards modified	Mode 3: Creation of similar standards by the domestic private sector based on foreign private standards. a. As a supplier code of conduct audited by the customer. b. As third-party certification (either as a competing scheme or as a stepping stone for global standards).	Mode 4: Creation of similar standards by the government based on foreign private standards.

Source: Author created

GLOBALG.A.P., in developing countries. Herzfeld et al. (2011) identified the conditions in countries that encourage diffusion of private standards, such as GLOBALG.A.P., and they found that previous trade relationships, per-capita GDP, and the size of the country are positively related to the number of farmers being certified by GLOBALG.A.P. They also found that developing countries with more established export horticulture sectors tend to be certified by GLOBALG.A.P.[9,10] Kersting and Wollni (2012) show the adaptation process of the GLOBALG.A.P. in Thailand and discuss the main motivation for those who have received GLOBALG.A.P. certification in Thailand, namely to maintain access to the market and follow the buyers' requirements.

---

[9] Even though GLOBALG.A.P. certification may increase export sales, organic certification may provide a higher return. In the case of pineapple producers in Ghana, organic certification created more value for farmers (Kleemann et al. 2014).

[10] For GLOBALG.A.P. applied to certified lychee exports from Madagascar, see Subervie and Vagneron (2013).

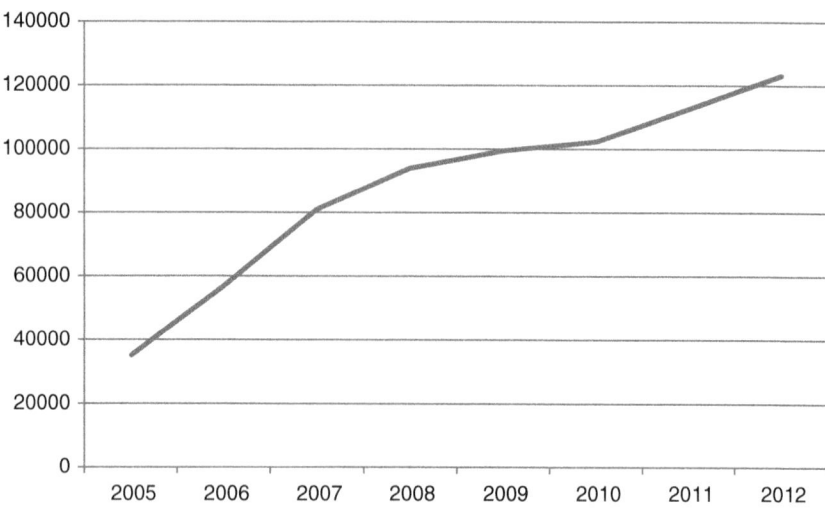

Fig. 5.1 Number of GLOBALG.A.P.-certified producers

Source: GlobalG.A.P. annual reports

The number of GLOBALG.A.P.-certified producers is increasing globally, reaching more than 120,000 in 2012 (Fig. 5.1). The number of producers certified in East Asia is also increasing. There are more than 200 producers certified in China, Korea, Thailand, and Vietnam (Table 5.2).

Table 5.2 Number of GLOBALG.A.P.-certified farms in selected East Asian countries, 2009–2012

	2009	2010	2011	2012
China	272	254	280	292
Indonesia	3	6	4	3
Japan	66	88	20	122
Korea	1	46	7	259
Malaysia	18	21	7	9
Philippines	1	5	5	5
Taiwan	54	65	3	0
Thailand	923	595	263	277
Vietnam	66	305	258	204

Source: GlobalG.A.P. annual reports

5.3.2 Mode 2: Use of GLOBALG.A.P. for Trade Promotion and Restriction

Mode 2 is using GLOBALG.A.P. as an instrument of trade promotion or restrictive measures. If a country adopts a foreign private standard as it is and makes it a private standard, this could increase trade between countries. If the private standard is widely adopted, it may also lead to an expansion in exports. Aligning the regulations with widely used private standards in the foreign market can make it easier for domestic firms to access foreign markets.[11] However, this mode can also be used to restrict trade. Indonesia is an example of mode 2, where the government uses GLOBALG.A.P. as part of their trade restrictions. In 2003, the Indonesian Ministry of Agriculture issued an import regulation[12] stating that to obtain import approval for horticultural products, importers must provide land and plantation registration information or a GAP certificate, among other requirements. The Indonesian government uses GLOBALG.A.P. to protect their domestic market, and the policy is applied to fresh produce that is subject to import quotas. The required GAP certificate is not restricted to GLOBALG.A.P., but GLOBALG.A.P. certification satisfies their requirements. Currently, JGAP, a third-party scheme GAP created by the Japanese private sector, also fulfils the Indonesian requirements as long as there are additional communications with the regulators.[13]

5.4 Motives Behind Creating Domestic Versions of GAPs (Modes 3 and 4)

Although the number of GLOBALG.A.P.-certified producers (mode 1) in East Asia is increasing, GLOBALG.A.P.-like private or public standards were also created and spread across Asia during the early 2000s (Table 5.3). The

---

[11] There are questions about the legitimacy of this approach. Even if it promotes trade, regulations could be set without the participation of domestic citizens.

[12] Peraturan Menteri Pertanian Nomor 47/Pementan/OT.140/4/2013.

[13] According to the interviews by JETRO Indonesia on 21 January 2015, but the situation may change.

Table 5.3 Selected list of GLOBALG.A.P.-like standards in East Asia

GAPs in Asia	Country/Region	Year	Public/Private, and Certification body
EurepGAP/ GLOBALG.A.P.	EU	1997/ 2007	Private: Third-party certification with scheme approved by accreditation body
AEON A-Q	Japan	2002	Private: Two-party certification for only their own suppliers
Q GAP	Thailand	2004	Public: Department of Agriculture
Co-op GAP	Japan	2004	Private: Created by Japanese Consumers' Cooperative Unions, Two-party certification
China GAP	China	2005	Private: Third-party certification
SALM(Agriculture), SPLAM(Livestock) SALT(Aquaculture)	Malaysia	2005	Public: Department of Agriculture, national standard
Phil GAP	Philippines	2005	Public: Department of Agriculture
GAP VF	Singapore	2005	Public: Horticulture Technology Department, Agri-Food and Veterinary Authority of Singapore audits and certifies.
ASEAN GAP	ASEAN	2006	Public: Guideline for national GAP standards in ASEAN countries
JGAP	Japan	2006	Private: Third-party certification
Korea GAP	South Korea	2006	Public: the Ministry of Agriculture, Food and Rural Affairs (MAFRA), National Agricultural Products Quality Management Services offers certification.
Thai GAP	Thailand	2007	Private: Third-party certification

Table 5.3 (continued)

GAPs in Asia	Country/ Region	Year	Public/Private, and Certification body
VietGAP	Vietnam	2008	Public: Vietnam Certification Centre (QUACERT), national certification body under the Ministry of Science and Technology offers certification.
Indo-GAP	Indonesia	2009	Public: Province Agro department
Cambodia GAP	Cambodia	2010	Public: the Ministry of Agriculture, Forestry and Fisheries
Lao GAP	Lao People's Democratic Republic	2011	Public: Department of Agriculture, Ministry of Agriculture and Forestry does inspection and certification of GAP for workers health, safety and welfare module.
MyGAP	Malaysia	2013	Public: Minister of Agriculture and Agro-based Industry
Brunei GAP	Brunei	2013	Public: Certified according to Brunei Certification Manual
IndGAP	India	2014	Public/Private: Voluntary labelling

Source: Author created

documents specifying control points and compliance criteria issued by EUREPGAP and GLOBALG.A.P. have had strong effects on Asian GAPs. Asian GAPs, both public and private, explicitly refer to either EUREPGAP or GLOBALG.A.P. as a model during their development processes. Standard adapters have various motives in adapting GLOBALG.A.P. by creating own versions. Depending on the motives, the original standard scheme is modified or simplified according to the geographical and economic circumstances of the countries. Table 5.4 shows the actors of GLOBALG.A.P. diffusion and motivations for modes 3 and 4.

Table 5.4 Actors of GLOBALG.A.P. diffusion and motivations for modes 3 and 4

Motivation/ developer		To serve as a stepping stone for global standards	To improve domestic practices	To harmonize domestic/ regional standards
Mode 3	Developed Countries		AEON A-Q	JGAP
	Developing Countries	Thai GAP		
Mode 4	Developed Countries		Prefectural GAPs in Japan	
	Developing Countries	IndGAP, VietGAP, MyGAP	Q GAP, SALM GAP VF PhilGAP, ChinaGAP, IndoGAP	ASEAN GAP

Source: Authors

The first motivation for a standard adapter is related to external market access. Private standard schemes that require third-party certification are developed in major countries and they affect producers outside the countries through trade, similar to product regulations. To maintain access to the market requiring a specific certification, public or private sectors decide to create a national standard or standard scheme similar to GLOBALG.A.P., so that farmers can upgrade more easily to GLOBALG.A.P. after adopting local GAPs.

The second motivation is to improve domestic farming practices by emulating GLOBALG.A.P. standards. Governments, associations, or retailers may wish to implement measures to improve the safety of the domestic food supply, while simultaneously ensuring that small-scale farmers can meet GAPs. In this case, certification may not be required and the overall level of stringency can be lower. It is more important to have simpler, cheaper local GAPs so that more farmers can adopt the practices.

The third motivation is to harmonize existing domestic and regional standards. Asian countries face problems with multiple domestic standards for food safety. These standards were set by different layers of government or by governments in different geographical areas. The standards are often not benchmarked with each other and are complicated for farmers. Local GAPs are expected to play a role in harmonizing and standardizing domestic regulations. Similarly, at the regional level, the motivation is to harmonize national GAPs. Although the standards in local GAPs are taken from GLOBALG.A.P., the methods for monitoring and the certification mechanism for local GAPs are different from those of GLOBALG.A.P.

5.4.1 Mode 3 a, b

The motivations behind creating domestic standards by either the private or public sectors are a mixture of all the motivations discussed above. The first motivation is to offer localized, simpler standards that help upgrade domestic farming practices to improve domestic competitiveness and safe food supply. The second is harmonizing domestic standards. The third is to offer a stepping-stone for GLOBALG.A.P. certification for trade purposes. The combination of actors and motivations creates variants among local GAPs in Asia.

AEON A-Q and JGAP in Japan are categorized as mode 3 because they are developed by private sector companies and are modelled on GLOBALG. A.P. AEON A-Q is categorized as mode 3a and was intended to improve suppliers' farming practices. AEON A-Q was developed by the Japanese retailer AEON as a supplier code of conduct for primary products. Therefore, audits are conducted by AEON. AEON and other retailers took the requirements and conditions from GLOBALG.A.P., but formulated them as a supplier code of conduct, audited by the retailers (second-party audit). The code could also be used as a form of self-assessment, treating the standard as a set of best practices. These three different assessment mechanisms lead to different levels of credibility and generality.[14]

---

[14] In Japan, many different local GAPs were introduced because initially GAPs were introduced as a best practice scheme, rather than as a standards scheme to ensure a certain level of food safety uniformly across the country. This means that GAPs in Japan are not standardized. There is much confusion in Japan, where many equate GAP with GLOBALG.A.P. and JGAP, when in fact the GAPs that are present in Japan are mainly best practices (with self-assessment), whereas GLOBALG.A.P. and JGAP are standards schemes that require verification by a third party.

JGAP is categorized as mode 3b. JGAP was initiated by farmers who were required to obtain GLOBALG.A.P. certification to export to EU. Because farmers found it too technical to be certified by GLOBALG.A.P., one reaction was to develop a localized and simpler standard scheme similar to GLOBALG.A.P. The experience of obtaining GLOBALG.A.P. certification suggested that a local version of GLOBALG.A.P. in Japan was needed for farmers to understand the requirements more easily. This led to the creation of JGAP. JGAP was created as a third-party certification scheme and was expected to be a stepping-stone for GLOBALG.A.P. The initial aim of JGAP was to be benchmarked against GLOBALG.A.P. to maintain equivalence between these two standards schemes. However, benchmarking between GLOBALG.A.P. and JGAP was not successful. JGAP plays another role in offering a domestic certification scheme for producers selling only for domestic markets. It is easier for local suppliers to adopt a local GAP written in a local language as opposed to understanding and satisfying private foreign standards.[15] Modifications to GLOBALG.A.P. are also provided. For example, the water usage requirements are less stringent in the Japanese standards than in GLOBALG.A.P. because there are fewer water shortage problems in Japan than in many European countries. In contrast, the JGAP requires farmers to store fertilizer properly to avoid accidental explosions and to satisfy specific regulations in Japan. The certification costs for JGAP are lower than for GLOBALG.A.P. so it is more accessible for smaller farmers. These modifications were made because many farmers operate only in the domestic market and do not export. Another motivation for JGAP is to streamline haphazard regulations concerning agriculture, food safety, and the environment introduced by various levels of government. Similarly, ThaiGAP, developed by the Thai Chamber of Commerce, is also categorized as mode 3b because it aims to align with GLOBALG.A.P.

---

[15] To accommodate these needs, GLOBALG.A.P. establishes national technical working groups. The groups can develop national standards equivalent to GLOBALG.A.P. that are then benchmarked to GLOBALG.A.P. in a process organized by GLOBALG.A.P. that is subject to the approval of its members and is accepted by international buyers.

5.4.2 Mode 4

In mode 4, a government or a government-related organization sets up local GAPs modelled on GLOBALG.A.P. Asian governments also try to manage these GAPs with differing motives. Some GAPs aim to be benchmarked to GLOBALG.A.P., whereas others position themselves as a stepping-stone through offering simplified standards and certification. For instance, with VietGAP, the Vietnamese government, together with the local fresh produce association, saw the importance of meeting the GLOBALG.A.P. standard because of their experience in the EU market as export-oriented producers. To assist domestic farmers in obtaining GLOBALG.A.P. certification, the government took the lead in establishing VietGAP in 2008.[16] VietGAP functions as a bridging standard to GLOBALG.A.P. or other standards for local producers. In 2013, the Vietnamese Ministry of Agriculture and Rural Development announced that it aims to upgrade VietGAP for vegetables, fruits, and tea, by using GLOBALG.A.P. as a benchmark after 2015. For foreign buyers who are concerned with sustainability, VietGAP is considered as a stepping-stone for certification by bodies such as the Aquaculture Stewardship Council (Nabeshima et al. 2015). For other foreign buyers, VietGAP may be sufficient for their business. The reason that Vietnam's approach is categorized as mode 4 rather than as mode 3 is that the agricultural sector in Vietnam has traditionally been led by the government and the Vietnam government decided to introduce VietGAP as a government standard because government initiatives are more effective than private initiatives (Nabeshima et al. 2015).

MyGAP, a certification scheme introduced in 2013 by the Malaysian Ministry of Agriculture and Agro-based Industry is intended to be recognized in international markets by combining the pre-existing Malaysian Farm Certification Scheme for Good Agricultural Practices (SALM), Livestock Farm Practices Scheme, and the Malaysian Aquaculture Farm Certification Scheme.[17] IndoGAP, developed in 2009 by the Indonesian

---

[16] Source: http://www.quacert.gov.vn/en/good-agriculture-practice.nd185/vietgap-standard.i88. html accessed on 26 January 2015.

[17] From the Minister of Agriculture and Agro-based Industry website: http://www.moa.gov.my/en/mygap, accessed 4 January 2016.

Department of Agriculture,[18] aims to improve agricultural practices and the competitiveness of the agricultural sector.

ASEAN GAP is a standard guideline in an era of freer regional trade within ASEAN that aims to improve trade competitiveness and harmonize countries' standards. Because there have been multiple GAPs in ASEAN, such as those in the Philippines, Malaysia, Thailand, and Singapore, ASEAN GAP is intended to help harmonize GAP programs within the ASEAN region. ASEAN GAP was developed with the assistance of the Australian government and AusAID. The document states that ASEAN GAP is referred to EUREPGAP and other standards. PhilGAP was also introduced by the Department of Agriculture of the Philippines.[19] It aims to achieve full alignment with ASEAN GAP. Before 2013, PhilGAP only had a food safety module. PhilGAP is fully subsidized by the government and no fee is required to obtain a certificate, which is issued by the Department of Agriculture. GAP-VF was developed by the Agri-Food & Veterinary Authority of Singapore and its main focus is on improving local farming practices.

Latecomer GAP standards introduced in other ASEAN countries are more closely linked to ASEAN GAP than to GLOBALG.A.P. Based on ASEAN GAP, Cambodia started a GAP program in 2010,[20] Laos in 2011,[21] and Brunei in 2013. The diffusion is no longer directly affected by a foreign private standard, but rather by a regional guideline that is affected by the foreign private standard. The GAP standards in ASEAN countries following ASEAN GAP guidelines are not convergent because local GAPs reflect each country's context more closely.

---

[18] Peraturan Menteri Pertanian No. 48/Permentan/OT.140/10/2009

[19] With Administrative order no.25, series of 2005 of the Department of Agriculture

[20] Ministerial Decision No. 099, Ministry of Agriculture Forestry and Fisheries, 3 October2010

[21] Decision of the Minister of Agriculture and Forestry No 0115/MAF, 27 January 2011 for food safety, Decision of the Minister on Good Agriculture Practices for Environmental Management Standard No. 0538/MAF, Decision of the Minister on Good Agriculture Practices for Produce Quality Management Standard No. 0539/MAF.

5.5 Effect of local GAP

Variations of motivations have resulted in the creation of varieties of local GAP standards around the Asian region. A variety of local GAPs may provide easier access to information and requirements for local producers and function as best practices. However, if a local GAP is created as a simpler and cheaper version as a stepping-stone for GLOBALG.A.P. questions are raised about how appropriate the standard is. Many local GAPs require some kind of monitoring mechanisms, yet they do not function as global standards because certification and monitoring mechanisms are different from GLOBALG.A.P. Although some local GAPs are intended to be benchmarked with GLOBALG.A.P., so far most of these local GAPs, except one version of ChinaGAP and ThaiGAP, are not recognized as equivalent to GLOBALG.A.P (see Lei 2015 for ChinaGAP). Is creating local GAPs helpful if it does not improve access to the EU market? Moreover, creating various GAPs without benchmarking with them in the region may create yet another layer of complexity for regional trade. Local GAPs that are aimed at making it easier for firms to obtain GLOBALG.A.P. to maintain market access in advanced countries can now become standards that are recognized only in the domestic market, hindering regional trade. As long as there is a promising (large) domestic market that provides the demand for certification, such a local GAP scheme can survive and play a role in strengthening food safety and enhancing sustainable agriculture practices. In addition, local standards can be used as a stepping stone to more stringent foreign standards.

The creation of many local GAPs in Asia is driven by the public sector. If the private sector in a large country has sufficient capacity, domestic certification schemes can emerge.[22] However, the private sector is still weak at this stage in Asia. This is one of the main reasons why governments in Asia are actively involved in the diffusion of certain private standards. Governments see that local GAPs based on GLOBALG.A.P. can achieve

---

[22] For this to happen, strong leadership is needed. In the EU, where the retail sector is highly concentrated, this was provided by retailers.

two desirable objectives simultaneously. One is to improve the safety of the domestic food supply, and the other is export promotion. They believe that adapting foreign private standards that are suitably localized to reflect local conditions can build domestic capacity and lead to an expansion in exports. To some extent, governments in developing countries are increasingly seeing these private standards as impediments to trade and diffusing these standards domestically is one way to counter trade restrictions. In a way, creating local GAPs is seen as an industrial policy.

5.6   Conclusion

With rapid globalization, many governments, even in developed countries, are finding that they are not well equipped to implement coherent and effective regulations. Increasingly, domestic policies are influenced more by the actions of other countries, because of the financial capacity, knowledge, and jurisdictional coverage of governments. First, many governments have limited fiscal resources with which to introduce, administer, and enforce regulations. With limited resources, governments must be selective in what kind of regulations they introduce and how they enforce them. Second, the organization of production has become more complex compared with the past, with global supply chains spanning many different countries. Many governments, at least in advanced countries, tend to feel that business operations are becoming more complex, and that new issues require specialized knowledge, which many governments lack. Moreover, business activities are beyond any one country's jurisdiction. Therefore, to some extent, they must rely on the private sector to regulate itself. This is not to say that governments have all given up on regulating the business activities of the private sector. On the contrary, governments are still active in setting regulations. However, there is only so much that a government can do, which is the third point. Globalization and the emergence of global supply chains mean that a large portion of production activities is now conducted abroad, outside the jurisdiction of the government at the point of consumption. Unless these governments engage in bilateral, plurilateral, or multilateral agreements, cross-border issues can be difficult to resolve.

In these circumstances, private standards (or public standards modelled after private standards) can play a role in streamlining activities throughout the supply chain.[23]

Within this context, many local GAPs based on GLOBALG.A.P. have been introduced in Asia, often as public policies. The question is whether and how the government should use these (foreign) private standards in the domestic context. As mentioned earlier, four modes of diffusion are possible with varying degrees of government involvement. Among these, governments in East Asia are mostly taking approaches categorized as mode 4, or the introduction of public standards with or without a certification scheme as a method to diffuse a third-party GAP certification scheme, especially GLOBALG.A.P. This can help domestic farms adopt practices to supply safer food through a standardized method and can help to harmonize various practices, standards, and regulations within a country. This approach also helps local farmers to improve their farming practices to meet export quality standards and contributes to the ultimate goal of obtaining GLOBALG.A.P. certification. In contrast, local GAP schemes that are not benchmarked as equivalent to GLOBALG.A.P. cannot be used as a way to access the global market. There are two options for this kind of public standards.

For developing countries, participation in global supply chains is leading to the diffusion of knowledge about these private standards in the private sector and in the public sector. Governments in developing countries are interested in foreign private standards because they can increase exports or act as trade barriers. In addition, given the general lack of capacity of governments in developing countries, they may use these private standards as shortcuts towards strengthening their standards and perhaps their regulations. However, the governments in developing countries would be well advised to evaluate these private

---

[23] Harmonizing regulations is difficult. Even if public regulations are based on scientific evidence, how such scientific evidence is framed can create different regulatory regimes. The situation in the EU and the US illustrates this clearly. The EU generally takes a precautionary approach. In this regulatory philosophy, scientific evidence must establish the absence of harm. In contrast, the US takes a reactive approach. Scientific evidence required is to show that positive harm will be caused. It is often harder to establish that something is safe than it is to establish that something is dangerous. Depending on the philosophy of the regulatory approach, regulations aimed at a similar goal may still have different levels of strictness.

standards to ensure that adopting or adapting these standards will fit their goals. In addition, governments in developing countries must be mindful of the assumptions on which these private standards are based. These assumptions include the regulatory philosophy (precautionary or reactionary); industrial structure (how concentrated certain industries are); citizens' preferences; scientific and measurement infrastructure; and the general quality of the governance, including the rule of law, among many other issues.

Therefore, governments in developing countries face a dilemma. It could be that the best course of action is to allow these private standards to be private. Governments could take no action or only limited action to encourage the diffusion of these private standards and leave much of the decision-making to the private sector. However, given that capabilities within the private sector in developing countries vary more widely than in developed countries, leaving everything to the private sector could widen the gap between good performers (often correlated with large size and export status) and poor performers (often smaller domestically oriented farms/firms). Thus, the industry will split into export and non-export sectors with the non-export sector lagging behind. The government has an interest in raising the quality of the lower performing group.

In addition to industrial and export motives, governments may also have a genuine interest in using these standards to improve domestic conditions. One advantage of private standards is that the cost of enforcement is borne by the private sector. For a government with limited fiscal resources, reliance on private standards may be a cost-effective way of introducing some public regulations. In addition, the parameters of the private standard are set elsewhere, meaning they are free from the typical rent-seeking activities domestically, and this may provide an easier avenue for domestic reform.

However, reliance on private standards as a substitute for domestic standards and regulations could lead to a mismatch among the regulatory philosophy, the preferences of citizens, domestic industrial structures, and quality assurance infrastructure. Whether the adoption of private standards is a reasonable and desirable action to be taken by the government must be critically evaluated on a case-by-case basis.

References

FAO. (2004). *Good agriculture practices: A working concept*. FAO GAP Working Paper. Food and Agriculture Organization (FAO). Rome.

Henson, S., & John, H. (2009). The Impact of Private Food Safety Standards on the Food Chain and on the Public Standard-Setting Process. *FAO and WHO*. www.fao.org/3/a-i1132e.pdf

Henson, S., & John, H. (2010). Understanding the complexities of private standards in global agri-food chains as they impact developing countries. *The Journal of Development Studies, 46*(9), 1628–1646.

Henson, S., Oliver, M., & John, C. (2011). Do fresh produce exporters in Sub-Saharan Africa benefit from GLOBALGAP certification? *World Development, 39*(3), 375–386.

Henson, S., & Humphrey, J. (2012). Private standards in global agri-food chains. In Marx, A., Maertens, M., & Swinnen, J. F. (Eds.), *Private standards and global governance: Economic, legal and political perspectives*, 98–113. Edward Elgar Publishing.

Herzfeld, T., Drescher, L. S., & Grebitus, C. (2011). Cross-national adoption of private food quality standards. *Food Policy, 36*(3), 401–411. http://dx.doi.org/10.1016/j.foodpol.2011.03.006.

Humphrey, J. (2008). *Privates standards, small farmers and donor policy: EUREPGAP in Kenya*. IDS Working Paper. Institute of Development Studies, the University of Sussex. Brighton, UK.

Humphrey, J. (2012). Convergence of US and EU production practice under the new FDA food safety modernization act. *The World Economy, 35*(8), 994–1005.

ITC. (2011). *The impacts of private standards on global value chains: Literature review series on the impacts of private standards - Part I*. Geneva: International Trade Centre.

Jaffee, S., & Masakure, O. (2005). Strategic use of private standards to enhance international competitiveness: Vegetable exports from Kenya and elsewhere. *Food Policy, 30*(3), 316–333. http://dx.doi.org/10.1016/j.foodpol.2005.05.009.

Jänicke, M. (2005). Trend-setters in environmental policy: The character and role of pioneer countries. *Environmental Policy and Governance, 15*(2), 129–142.

Kersting, S., & Wollni, M.. (2012). New institutional arrangements and standard adoption: Evidence from small-scale fruit and vegetable farmers in Thailand. *Food Policy, 37*(4), 452–462. http://dx.doi.org/10.1016/j.foodpol.2012.04.005.

Kleemann, L., Abdulai, A., &Buss, M. (2014). Certification and access to export markets: Adoption and return on investment of organic-certified pineapple farming in Ghana. *World Development, 64*(0), 79–92. http://dx.doi.org/10.1016/j.worlddev.2014.05.005.

Lei, L. (2015). *A closer look at diffusion of ChinaGAP*. IDE Discussion Paper 501, Institute of Developing Economies, Japan External Trade Organization, Chiba, Japan.

Loader, R., & Jill, E. H. (1999). Strategic responses to food safety legislation. *Food Policy, 24*(6), 685–706.

Meseguer, C. (2005). Policy learning, policy diffusion, and the making of a new order. *The Annals of the American Academy of Political and Social Science, 598*(1), 67–82.

Nabeshima, K., Etsuyo, M., Aya, S., & Vu H. N. (2015). *Emergence of Asian GAPs and its relationship to global G.A.P.* IDE Discussion Paper 507, Institute of Developing Economies, Japan External Trade Organization, Chiba, Japan.

Schuster, M., & Maertens, M. (2015). The impact of private food standards on developing countries' export performance: An analysis of asparagus firms in Peru. *World Development, 66*(0), 208–221. http://dx.doi.org/10.1016/j.worlddev.2014.08.019.

Subervie, J., & Vagneron, I. (2013). A drop of water in the Indian Ocean? The impact of GlobalGap certification on lychee farmers in Madagascar. *World Development, 50*(0), 57–73. http://dx.doi.org/10.1016/j.worlddev.2013.05.002.

Van Der Grijp, N. M., Marsden, T., & Cavalcanti, J. S. B. (2005). European retailers as agents of change towards sustainability: The case of fruit production in Brazil. *Environmental Sciences, 2*(1), 31–46. 10.1080/15693430512331333384.

Etsuyo Michida is an Associate Senior Research Fellow at Institute of Developing Economies, Japan External Trade Organization (IDE-JETRO) and was a Visiting Scholar at Haas School of Business, University of California, Berkeley from 2015 to 2017. Her research interest lies in trade and the environment with a special focus on developing countries.She has recently researched on the relationship between environmental regulation, firm behavior, and global supply chains. She holds a PhD in Economics from Graduate School of International Cooperation Studies, Kobe University.

Kaoru Nabeshima is an Associate Professor at the Graduate School of Asia-Pacific Studies, Waseda University. He holds a PhD in Economics from

University of California-Davis, and a BA in Economics from Ohio Wesleyan University. Prior to joining Graduate School of Asia-Pacific Studies, Waseda University in 2015, he worked for the Institute of Developing Economies, Japan External Trade Organization and the World Bank. Some of his publications include *Meeting Standards, Winning Markets: Regional Trade Standards Compliance Report East Asia 2013* (IDE-JETRO/UNIDO 2013), *Tiger Economies under Threat* (co-authored with Shahid Yusuf, 2009), and *Some Small Countries Do It Better: Rapid Growth and Its Causes in Singapore, Finland, and Ireland* (co-authored with Shahid Yusuf, 2012). His research interests lie in examining the relationship between regulations and international trade, the issue of middle income trap, and the innovation capabilities of firms in East Asia.

6

Preliminary Theoretical Model for Standard Promotion from the Perspective of Governments

Kaoru Nabeshima

6.1 Introduction

This chapter explores a theoretical model of private standard[1] diffusion from country to country and examines the policy options available for the domestic government. A foreign private standard typically diffuses to other countries through trade links. Even though a private standard is a *voluntary* standard, the request coming from the buyer to comply with a particular private standard is as binding as public *mandatory* regulations

---

[1] This includes international standards, such as ISO, and other standards created by private companies, regardless of whether they are made public and those created by non-governmental organizations.

K. Nabeshima (✉)
Waseda University, Tokyo, Japan
e-mail: kknabeshima@waseda.jp

© The Author(s) 2017   **131**
E. Michida et al. (eds.), *Regulations and International Trade*,
IDE-JETRO Series, DOI 10.1007/978-3-319-55041-1_6

from the company's point of view.[2] Furthermore, in recent years, some governments, especially in East Asia, are actively importing these foreign private standards and using them as part of public *voluntary* standards and *mandatory* regulations. The motivation behind their eagerness to incorporate foreign private standards in their public policies appears to stem from the desire to increase exports. The underlying assumption is that if standards and regulations are harmonized with major importing countries, then their exports will increase.

Based on how private standards have diffused to other countries as described in Chapter 5, the ways in which foreign private standards are adopted can be categorized into the following four modes with varying degrees of government involvement.

1. Adoption of foreign private standards by the private sector.
2. Adoption of foreign private standards by the public sector.
3. Creation of similar standards by the domestic private sector based on foreign private standards

    a. as a supplier audit
    b. as a third party.

4. Creation of similar standards by the government based on foreign private standards.

In mode 1, a domestic private company decides to adopt foreign private standards because this creates export opportunities. In this case, the initiation and expansion of exports and subsequent increase in profits is a sufficient incentive for a domestic company to adopt private standards.[3]

---

[2] Although typically, non-compliance with public regulations leads to a punishment, there is no such mechanism for non-compliance with private standards, except for losing sales, which is a sufficient incentive for a private company.

[3] Most empirical research focuses on this case. For agricultural products, see Henson et al. (2011), Jaffee and Masakure (2005), Subervie and Vagneron (2013) on the effect of GLOBALG.A.P. certification on exports from developing countries, and Kleemann et al. (2014) on organic certification. For manufactured products, see Chen et al. (2014), Honda (2012), Michida et al. (2014), Michida et al. (2014a, 2014b), Otsuki et al. (2014), Ramungul et al. (2013).

The government is not involved in this, although sometimes a government provides subsidies for a company wishing to adopt foreign private standards.

In mode 2, the government adopts foreign private standards as it incorporates them into their public policies. Even though this is rare, it has been used in California and Indonesia.[4]

In mode 3, the domestic private sector imitates foreign private standards and introduces domestic versions of the standard. The domestic private standards can be benchmarked against the original foreign private standard, although they do not have to be.[5] The government is not actively engaged in this mode; they have the choice to encourage or discourage the development of domestic private standards, which are a modified version of the original.

In mode 4, the government takes the initiative to adapt foreign private standards and create modified domestic public standards or regulations.

The main difference between modes 1 and 2 and modes 3 and 4 is whether the foreign private standards are modified or not. In modes 1 and 2, foreign private standards are taken as they are. In modes 3 and 4, foreign private standards are modified to the extent that they are different from the original. To establish equivalencies between the domestic and foreign standards, benchmarking must be performed by the foreign private standard owners or by a benchmarking entity.[6]

---

[4] For example, Indonesia is including certification for some good agricultural practices (a specific private standard, GLOBALG.A.P.) to obtain licenses to import certain agricultural products (Nabeshima et al. 2015). In addition, California in the United States of America is including the European Union's Restrictions on Hazardous Substance (RoHS) directive as a part of their environmental policy (See Chapter 3).

[5] Standards a and b may be different. However, they can be benchmarked with each other to establish equivalency, so that both standards lead to equivalent outcomes. This is similar to the mutual recognition agreement between governments, although it is different from harmonization where the content of the standards is the same.

[6] Benchmarking can be done by the standard owner or by another entity. For instance, GLOBALG.A.P. (a private standard created by major European retailers aimed at primary product production) benchmarks other private standards. Global Food Safety Initiatives (GFSI) by the Global Consumer Forum also benchmarks different standards related to food safety. Under GFSI, GLOBALG.A.P. and other standards are recognized as approved standard schemes. GFSI does not own any standards, but focuses on benchmarking activities.

Below, we develop a simple theoretical model to analyze the effect of different modes of private standard diffusion to assess the effect on the number of companies in a particular sector. Our focus is on a particular industrial sector rather than on the economy as a whole because the type of private standards that we are interested in tends to be industry-specific.

6.2   Model

Below we construct a simple theoretical model to illustrate the effect of fixed cost on the number of companies producing for the domestic market and for the foreign market (exports). First, we consider the autarky situation as a baseline and consider the situation where two countries trade with different scenarios. In the next section, these analyses are linked to the diffusion modes mentioned above.

6.2.1 Basic Set-up

The basic set-up follows the monopolistic competition model proposed by Krugman (1979) with a standard constant elasticity of substitution utility function. Initially, we consider a closed economy. There are N differentiated goods where $0 < i < N$. We have a representative consumer in this model.

$$U = \left(\sum_{i=1}^{N} x_i^{\frac{\sigma-1}{\sigma}} \right)^{\frac{\sigma}{\sigma-1}} \tag{1}$$

where $0 < \sigma < 1$

subject to $S = \sum_{i=1}^{N} p_i x_i$

U is the utility of the representative consumer, x is individual good, σ is the elasticity of substitution, i is index for the good, and p is the price for the good. The utility function is chosen to maintain the analytical tractability. The consumer will maximize the utility function specified in equation (1) with the budget constraint, S, which is the expenditure on this particular commodity group. We assume that consumers are all identical. Solving this maximization problem will yield the demand function for each x_i.

We assume that each company produces a variety of products, and has a simple cost function of

$$TC = F_0 + cx_i \tag{2}$$

where $F_0 > 0, c > 0$

F_0 is a fixed cost associated with production. In this formulation, we use a constant marginal cost of c. We assume that companies are identical. The industry is characterized as a monopolistic competition. For each type of goods, each producer acts as a monopolist. There is an additional assumption of free entry and exit. This results in the profit of each company to be driven down to zero, which enables us to determine the number of products and companies.

Because the company is acting as a monopolist, the price it will charge will depend on the elasticity and marginal cost as

$$p_i = \left(\frac{\sigma}{\sigma - 1}\right)c \tag{3}$$

The profit that a company earns is

$$\pi_i = p_i x_i - TC = \left(\frac{\sigma}{\sigma - 1}\right)cx_i - F_0 - cx_i$$
$$= \left(\frac{1}{\sigma - 1}\right)cx_i - F_0 = 0 \tag{4}$$

Solving for x_i yields

$$x_i = \frac{(\sigma - 1)F_0}{c} \tag{5}$$

Spending on these goods must equal the aggregate industry spending, so

$$S = \sum_{i=1}^{N} p_i x_i$$

$$S = \sum_{i=1}^{N} p_i x_i = N \times \left(\frac{\sigma}{\sigma - 1}\right) c \times \frac{(\sigma - 1)F_0}{c} = N\sigma F_0 \qquad (6)$$

Solving for the number of companies yields

$$N = \frac{S}{\sigma F_0} \qquad (7)$$

For S, the number of companies increases. If the market becomes larger, there are more companies entering the industry. For a fixed cost, the number of companies decreases as expected.

We are interested in seeing how N changes with the adoption of private standards, especially in the export market. Particular private standards that we are interested are the private standard schemes with third-party certification[7] such as ISO and GLOBALG.A.P. In a typical third-party certification scheme, a company incurs the recurring fixed cost of the certification fees (in the case of GLOBALG.A.P., this is annual). Therefore, a company obtaining a certificate for a particular private standard scheme will have higher fixed costs than companies without it.[8] Thus, the effect of private standard schemes

---

[7] There are many types of private standards with different assessment methods. For instance, many companies create a supplier code of conduct, which is also a private standard. The assessment is typically done by the buyer company to see whether the supplier meets the code of conduct. Thus, the audit cost is borne by the buyer, not by the supplier. There is also a private standard with certification. In this kind of scheme, the audit cost of compliance to a standard is borne by the suppliers.

[8] It is also conceivable that a company may need to incur a fixed cost associated with changes in production process (e.g., additional investment necessary to ensure safety) to comply with a private standard. However, that would be a one-off cost to obtain the certificate. What we are interested in is the cost of *maintaining* the certificate, so we do not consider this one-time adjustment cost in this model.

on the fixed cost is clear and $F_1 > F_0$ where F_1 is a fixed cost associated with maintaining certification.[9]

In contrast, the effects of a private standard scheme on variable costs are mixed. On the one hand, the certification may increase variable costs if a company is required to use inputs that are of higher quality. On the other hand, private standards, especially those focused on processes and management practices, may lower variable costs. It is also conceivable that obtaining and maintaining certification may not change variable costs. In this study, we assume that obtaining and maintaining certification has no effect on the variable costs (and hence marginal costs), and that only the fixed costs change. Below, we explore various cases for how private standard schemes can affect the number of companies in the industry, especially in the domestic and export market.

To make the analysis tractable and simple, we assume that consumer preferences in the domestic and export market are the same, with the exception of the size of the industry sales, S, in the domestic and export market. In addition, to export, a company is required to obtain and maintain certification based on the private standard scheme, whereas sales in the domestic market do not require certification, although a company can voluntarily obtain a certificate. This means that the exporting companies face higher fixed costs compared with those producing exclusively for the domestic market.

6.2.2 Case 1: Effect of Private Standard Schemes for Only the Domestic Market

In this case, there is no incentive for a company to obtain certification if there are enough potential companies with a fixed cost, F_0. This essentially means that $N \leq N_0$, where N_0 is a number of potential companies with a fixed cost, F_0. Because of the zero profit conditions, there would be entry of companies until the profit is driven down to

---

[9] For instance, Thai farms consider that the initial cost and recurring costs of GLOBALG.A.P. certification is a significant hurdle (Kersting and Wollni 2012).

zero. In this situation, a company with higher fixed costs (a company with a certification) does not enter. Therefore, the domestic market is populated purely by non-certified companies with the number of companies specified in equation (7). This is the baseline result. There might be a case where $N \geq N_0$, that permits the entry of companies with higher fixed cost, $F_1 > F_0$. In this situation, the total number of companies in the market will be lower than the baseline because of the inclusion of companies with higher fixed costs. There are two situations where this applies. One is the autarky situation. The other is where the industry is regarded as a traditionally non-tradable sector, such as services, where the domestic industry operates mainly under the standards and regulations prevailing in the domestic market.

6.2.3 Case 2: Effect of Private Standard Schemes for a Segregated Export Market

As mentioned above, we assume that the export market requires exporting companies to obtain and maintain a certificate. This requirement may be required from the importers. This situation reflects the mode 1. We model the fixed cost as

$$F_1 = (1 + \theta)F_0 \tag{8}$$

where $\theta \geq 0$

We also assume that industry spending in the export market is S^*. This can be treated as the consumers' demand for imported goods in the importing country. For now, we assume that the domestic market and the export market are completely segregated. This means that the export market does not affect the domestic market.[10] Furthermore, we assume that companies producing for the domestic

---

[10] Because we are only looking at the industry sector level, we assume that companies do not face resource constraints.

and foreign markets are different entities.[11] Thus, to produce for export, a company needs to pay the full fixed cost. Therefore, the solutions for the domestic market are unchanged, and the number of companies in the domestic market is still defined as $N = \frac{S}{\sigma F_0}$. Because the consumer preference is the same and the marginal cost is the same, and the only differences from the baseline case are the market size and the fixed cost, the number of companies exporting, M, is

$$M = \frac{S^*}{\sigma F_1} \tag{9}$$

We assume for now that companies selling to the domestic and the export market are different. The number of companies operating is

$$N + M = \frac{S}{\sigma F_0} + \frac{S^*}{\sigma F_1} \tag{10}$$

Substituting equation (8), we obtain

$$N + M = \frac{(1 + \theta)S + S^*}{\sigma(1 + \theta)F_0} \tag{11}$$

Equation (11) shows that if θ is large, then the number of exporting companies will approach zero. Thus, even if trade is liberalized, the difference in requirements can be large enough to discourage trade altogether. Because of the assumption of the segregated market, the number of companies producing for the domestic market is unchanged.

---

[11] This can be regarded as two different companies, or a company with two different production lines, one for the domestic market and the other for the foreign market.

6.2.4 Case 3: A Private Standard Scheme Is Required to Sell in the Domestic Market in Addition to the Export Market

Next, we consider the case where obtaining and maintaining certification is necessary for the domestic market. This may arise from the actions of the private sector or the government corresponding to modes 2, 3, and 4, depending on who sets the standard. We can treat the domestic and export markets as the same with a larger market size, as $S + S^*$. In addition, all companies have to incur fixed cost F_1. In this situation, the number of companies is

$$L = \frac{S + S^*}{\sigma F_1} \tag{12}$$

An interesting question is whether $L > N + M$, namely whether the domestic market should also adopt the private standard that prevails in the export market or whether a country is better off keeping the domestic and export market segregated.[12]

Using the results from equations (11) and (12), we see that the number of companies in an integrated domestic and export market is smaller than when the market was segregated.

$$N + M - L = \frac{(1 + \theta)S + S^*}{\sigma(1 + \theta)F_0} - \frac{S + S^*}{\sigma(1 + \theta)F_0} = \frac{\theta}{1 + \theta} \frac{S}{\sigma F_0} > 0 \tag{13}$$

As $\theta \to 0$, namely the cost of the certificate decreases, the number of companies in the segregated and the integrated case approaches equality. As θ increases, the difference in the number of companies approaches the number of companies selling to the domestic market. This happens because the fixed cost for the domestic market is raised from F_0 to F_1,

---

[12] Another interesting question is whether foreign companies will enter the domestic market. If the foreign company's fixed cost is F_1, they cannot penetrate the domestic market, although if we assume that the domestic market is also segregated, then foreign companies may be able to enter. However, if the fixed cost in the domestic market is increased to F_1, then the foreign companies would be better positioned to enter because the playing field is leveled.

while no other variables and constants change. In this model, a higher fixed cost leads to a lower number of companies.

6.3   Discussion

Our model is simple; however, it yields interesting results. Although not explicitly considered, if an export market exists with no additional fixed cost, then the number of companies (L′) is higher compared with the autarky situation (N), as expected. However, if the integration of the market increases the fixed cost for the domestic market, then the number of companies will depend on parameter θ.

$$L' - L = \frac{\theta}{1+\theta} \frac{S+S*}{\sigma F_0} \tag{14}$$

θ is a parameter that measures the differences in institutional settings that would affect fixed costs. The more different they are, the more adjustment is needed. This leads to a smaller number of companies when the fixed costs are forced to increase in the domestic market. Equation (14) is positive, meaning that trade integration that involves an increase in fixed costs (e.g., to comply with regulations) could mean a smaller number of companies because some companies are forced to exit, even when foreign companies do not enter the domestic market. After the equalization of the fixed cost, it is expected that foreign companies would be able to access the domestic market, decreasing the number of domestic companies further.[13] This may be a reason why developing countries may resist higher quality free trade agreements which may include regulatory issues.

For example, take the discussion on intellectual property rights (IPRs) under the Trans-Pacific Partnership (TPP) that were negotiated. This is a contentious issue dividing the negotiating countries

---

[13] In this model, we treat the foreign demand as exogenous to make the analysis simpler. In this kind of model with identical companies, the composition of domestic and foreign companies is unknown, and only the trade volume is known (Krugman 1979).

into two camps: those favoring stronger protection of IPRs (mainly developed countries) and those against (mainly developing countries). From the developing countries' point of view, stronger IPR, including lengthening the protection periods, may lead to higher recurring fixed costs, especially if enforcement is strengthened.[14] Stricter labor and environmental regulations can have similar effects.

6.3.1 Extension to Case 2

The fixed cost is a driving force in this kind of model. In case 2, we assumed that the domestic market and the export market are segregated, and that serving the export market incurred the full fixed cost, F_1. However, it may be reasonable to consider the case where the company that is already operating in the domestic market has a lower fixed cost than F_1 if there are some overlaps in the requirements. For instance, a country may have something that is similar to the certificate required by the buyers in the foreign countries and such costs are already included in the fixed cost for the domestic market. In that case, an exporting company that is already operational in the domestic market may incur only θF_0. This implies that if the exporting companies are a subset of the domestic companies, the number of exporting companies can be expressed as,

$$M' = \frac{S^*}{\sigma \theta F_0} = \frac{1}{\theta} \frac{S^*}{S} N \qquad (15)$$

The fraction of the exporting companies will depend positively on the relative market size, $\frac{S^*}{S}$, and inversely on θ. If the relative market size is large enough to outweigh θ, then, $M' > N$, implying that there are new companies entering the market to serve the export market exclusively. If the relative market size difference is small, or differences in fixed costs are large,

---

[14] Most countries have adequate IPR laws, especially WTO members, because they need to sign the Agreement on Trade-Related Intellectual Property Rights, which specifies the minimum level of IPR protection. However, enforcement varies widely among countries (Park 2008).

or both, then the exporting companies will be those already operating domestically. However, at a certain point, the advantage of operating in the domestic market vanishes if the differences in fixed cost are very large.

θ is large when the requirements specified by the buyers abroad are sufficiently different from the typical requirements in the domestic market. This could cover situations where there may be no requirements similar to those requested by the foreign buyers, which may apply to developing countries where the quality of institutions may be sufficiently different. This may also cover situations where regulations and standards in the domestic market are sufficiently different from foreign standards, which would apply more to developed countries. Equation (15) suggests that a large foreign market relative to the domestic market can continue to attract a certain number of exporters even if the difference measured by θ is large. For instance, the integrated European Union (EU) market is large enough that companies or the EU Commission can require stringent rules or requirements, and the large market size is attractive enough for many small countries to follow these rules and requirements, despite the need to incur higher fixed costs. Therefore, there are many companies in many countries who would follow the rules and requirements from the EU, making these rules and requirements effectively global or international. Thus, for smaller countries, standards set in major importing countries have large impacts on the number of domestic companies, and hence, the development of this industry. For small countries, standards (and difference of such standards prevailing in importing countries and domestically) have much larger impacts on the development of industry compared to countries with large internal markets.

6.4 Relationship with the Diffusion of Private Standards

Considering these results, we examine the ways in which private standards can diffuse across countries and how this relates to the theoretical model.

Mode 1 (foreign private standards adopted by domestic companies) is represented by case 2 and the extension to the case 2 in this section. Mode

2 (adoption of foreign private standards by the government) is closely related to case 3, especially when the government adopts the standards in mandatory public regulations. Modes 3 and 4 are closely related to the extension to case 2. In both modes, modifications to foreign standards are made to fit local conditions. This could have a direct effect on θ, which is the difference or distance between the domestic and the foreign market requirements. Modifications can be made to increase or decrease θ.

From the simple theoretical model developed in this chapter, mode 1 seems to be desirable, assuming that the domestic and export markets are completely segregated. Imposing additional requirements domestically when there is no domestic demand for certification is not helpful. To the extent that the compliance cost is modeled as fixed cost, even though not explicitly considered in this model, imposition of additional fixed cost will inevitably favor larger firms. In addition, policymakers must be cautious in implementing modes 3 and 4, although in mode 3, it is mainly left to the private sector. Creating similar standards (private or public) may not be effective, unless these private or public voluntary standards closely mirror the requirements for the export market. Caution is needed for mode 3; if it is implemented, even by the private sector, it may create a domestic standard that is significantly different from the rest of the world, and make it harder for companies to export by raising the apparent fixed costs, again creating burden to small- and medium-sized enterprises (SMEs). Governments do have some influence on the development of domestic private standards by encouraging them to be closer to foreign private standards. Adopting international standards may be a good option, as long as these international standards are meaningful in international transactions.

Mode 4 may be a viable option for countries that are aspiring to export to a more regulated market,[15] through gradually aligning their institutional differences, and moving towards harmonization in the long run,[16] although our

---

[15] A regulated market here refers to markets governed by stricter public mandatory regulation and markets governed by a private standards. As argued earlier, for a private company, a requirement is a requirement regardless of the origin.

[16] Although monopolistic competition is a long-run model, we may need to incorporate longer time horizons where the fixed cost can change.

analysis does not consider the dynamics of this process. Harmonization would make it easier for domestic companies to export to a regulated market, especially for SMEs. However, such a move needs to be gradual, otherwise a large number of companies would exit the market. Moreover, there is the problem of identifying the most useful regulations and standards to adopt. There is a wide variety of standards that are available in the marketplace,[17] some of which have better market potential than others. The future relevance of these private standards is also uncertain, because there are multiple competing standards for similar areas. In addition, the relevance and importance of standards depend on the preferences and intentions of companies. Thus, picking a standard to support publicly is a difficult and challenging task that governments must approach with caution.

The model developed here is a simple one assuming homogeneity in preferences and companies, except for some key parameters. Future extensions of the model can explore the effect of private standards on marginal costs in addition to the fixed costs that are considered in this chapter. Furthermore, differences in consumer preference between certified and uncertified goods could be incorporated.

Acknowledgment Part of this work was supported by JSP KAKENHI Grant Number 15K00675 and 15H03350.

References

Chen, S. S., Mohd, H. bin M. H., Michida, E., & Nabeshima, K. (2014). *Role of laboratories for adapting product-related environmental regulations (PRERs)*. (IDE Discussion Paper No. 452). Institute of Developing Economies. Chiba, Japan.

Henson, S., Masakure, O., & Cranfield, J. (2011). Do fresh produce exporters in Sub-Saharan Africa benefit from GlobalGAP certification? *World*

---

[17] For instance, in a sample of companies studied by Schuster and Maertens (2015), GLOBALG.A.P. certification was the main private standard adopted by the Peruvian asparagus industry, accounting for 34% of certification, and Hazard Analysis and Critical Control Point (HACCP) and British Retail Consortium (BRC). Global Standards are the next two most popular processing standards.

Development, 39(3), 375–386. http://dx.doi.org/10.1016/j.worlddev.2010.06.012.

Honda, K. (2012). *The effect of EU environmental regulation on international trade: Restriction of hazardous substances as a trade barrier.* (IDE Discussion Paper No.431). Institute of Developing Economies, Japan External Trade Organization (IDE-JETRO). Chiba, Japan.

Jaffee, S., & Masakure, O. (2005). Strategic use of private standards to enhance international competitiveness: Vegetable exports from Kenya and elsewhere. *Food Policy, 30*(3), 316–333. http://dx.doi.org/10.1016/j.foodpol.2005.05.009.

Kersting, S., & Wollni, M. (2012). New institutional arrangements and standard adoption: Evidence from small-scale fruit and vegetable farmers in Thailand. *Food Policy, 37*(4), 452–462. http://dx.doi.org/10.1016/j.foodpol.2012.04.005.

Kleemann, L., Abdulai, A., & Buss, M. (2014). Certification and access to export markets: Adoption and return on investment of organic-certified pineapple farming in Ghana. *World Development, 64*(0), 79–92. http://dx.doi.org/10.1016/j.worlddev.2014.05.005.

Krugman, P. R. (1979). Increasing returns, monopolistic competition, and international trade. *Journal of International Economics, 9*(4), 469–479. http://dx.doi.org/10.1016/0022-1996(79)90017-5.

Michida, E., Nabeshima, K., & Ueki, Y. (2014). *Impact of product-related environmental regulations in Asia: Descriptive statistics from a survey of firms in Vietnam.* (IDE Discussion Paper No. 466). Institute of Developing Economies. Chiba, Japan.

Michida, E., Ueki, Y., & Nabeshima, K. (2014a). *Impact of product-related environmental regulations in Asia: Descriptive statistics from a survey of firms in Penang, Malaysia.* (IDE Discussion Paper No. 457). Institute of Developing Economies. Chiba, Japan.

Michida, E., Ueki, Y., & Nabeshima, K. (2014b). *Impact on Asian firms of product-related environmental regulations through global supply chains: a study of firms in Malaysia.* (IDE Discussion Paper No. 453). Chiba, Japan: Institute of Developing Economies.

Nabeshima, K., Michida, E., Suzuki, A., & Nam, V. H. (2015). *Emergence of Asian GAPs and its relationship to Global G.A.P.* (IDE Discussion Paper No. 507). Chiba, Japan: Institute of Developing Economies, Japan External Trade Organization.

Otsuki, T., Michida, E., Nabeshima, K., & Ueki, Y. (2014). *Estimating the effect of chemical safety standards on firm performance in Malaysia and*

Vietnam. (IDE Discussion Paper No. 455). Institute of Developing Economies. Chiba, Japan.

Park, W. G. (2008). International patent protection: 1960–2005. *Research Policy, 37*(4), 761–766. http://dx.doi.org/10.1016/j.respol.2008.01.006.

Ramungul, N., Michida, E., & Nabeshima, K. (2013). *Impact of product-related environmental regulations/voluntary requirements on Thai firms*. (IDE Discussion Paper No. 383). Institute of Developing Economies. Chiba, Japan.

Schuster, M., & Maertens, M. (2015). The impact of private food standards on developing countries' export performance: An analysis of asparagus firms in Peru. *World Development, 66*(0), 208–221. http://dx.doi.org/10.1016/j.respol.2008.01.006.

Subervie, J., & Vagneron, I. (2013). A drop of water in the Indian Ocean? The impact of GlobalGap certification on lychee farmers in Madagascar. *World Development, 50*(0), 57–73. http://dx.doi.org/10.1016/j.worlddev.2013.05.002.

Kaoru Nabeshima is an Associate Professor at the Graduate School of Asia-Pacific Studies, Waseda University. He holds a PhD in Economics from University of California-Davis, and a BA in Economics from Ohio Wesleyan University. Prior to joining Graduate School of Asia-Pacific Studies, Waseda University in 2015, he worked for the Institute of Developing Economies, Japan External Trade Organization and the World Bank. Some of his publications include *Meeting Standards, Winning Markets: Regional Trade Standards Compliance Report East Asia 2013* (IDE-JETRO/UNIDO 2013), *Tiger Economies under Threat* (co-authored with Shahid Yusuf, 2009), and *Some Small Countries Do It Better: Rapid Growth and Its Causes in Singapore, Finland, and Ireland* (co-authored with Shahid Yusuf, 2012). His research interests lie in examining the relationship between regulations and international trade, the issue of middle income trap, and the innovation capabilities of firms in East Asia.

Part II

Regulatory Impacts on Firms and Supply Chains

7

A Snapshot of the Effects of Product-Related Environmental Regulations on Firms in Vietnam, Malaysia, and Japan

Etsuyo Michida, Yasushi Ueki,
and Kaoru Nabeshima

7.1   Introduction

As discussed in Part I, product-related environmental regulations (PRERs) imposed in major markets have raised concerns among exporting countries. In particular, the European Union (EU) Restriction of Hazardous Substances (RoHS) directive and the

E. Michida (✉)
Institute of Developing Economies, Japan External Trade Organization
(IDE-JETRO), Chiba, Japan
e-mail: etsuyo_michida@ide.go.jp

Y. Ueki
Economist, Economic Research Institute for ASEAN and East Asia, Jakarta,
Indonesia
e-mail: yasushi.ueki@eria.org

K. Nabeshima
Waseda University, Tokyo, Japan
e-mail: kknabeshima@waseda.jp

© The Author(s) 2017   **151**
E. Michida et al. (eds.), *Regulations and International Trade*,
IDE-JETRO Series, DOI 10.1007/978-3-319-55041-1_7

Registration, Evaluation, Authorization and Restriction of Chemicals (REACH) regulations are particularly important for the developing countries. To comply with these regulations, firms must confirm that their products do not contain hazardous materials exceeding the thresholds stipulated in regulations and they must inform EU legislators and customers of which chemicals are used in their product through layers of supply chains. If exported products do not satisfy the regulatory requirements, non-compliant products cannot be sold in regulated markets and firms may face technical barriers to trade. Asia has been the center of world manufacturing for decades. Many parts and component suppliers for global assemblers are located in these countries and these firms are required to meet PRERs in their manufacturing activities (Hiratsuka and Uchida 2010).[1] As PRERs become more demanding and increase in variety, especially in important markets, concerns about these regulations have been most prevalent in developing Asian countries.

We have conducted firm surveys to assess the effect of PRERs in Vietnam, Malaysia, and Japan. This chapter presents the background to these surveys, including research issues and survey questions. The results are discussed to show a snapshot of the problems affecting firms arising from increasing regulation and standards under globalization. The objective is not to identify a causal relationship or to compare different countries. Analysis that is more rigorous is provided in later chapters of this book.

Although the developing Asian countries have improved their manufacturing capabilities throughout their phases of industrial development, many firms appear to lack the capacity to comply with technical regulations imposed in major importing countries. How have firms changed their operations to meet product regulations? What are the main obstacles that firms have faced? Moreover, what kind of policies could support firms faced with product and process regulations under globalization? To examine these questions, we conducted a series of interviews and surveys with manufacturing firms in Vietnam in 2011, in Penang, Malaysia in 2012, and in Japan in 2013. Our research focuses on regulations and

---

[1] See Chen et al. (2014) for Malaysia.

requirements related to chemicals contained in products. Two primary EU regulations are the main examples of PRERs examined in this chapter. These regulations, enacted by the EU Parliament and the Council, are the RoHS directive and the REACH regulations. The RoHS directive, which restricts the use of certain hazardous substances in electrical and electronic equipment, was implemented in 2006.[2] The REACH regulations were implemented in 2007, and they regulate chemicals that can severely affect consumer health and the environment that are contained in products. Under REACH, if a product contains chemicals classified as substances of very high concern in excess of 0.1% by weight, firms are required to notify the European Chemicals Agency, which is the relevant regulatory body, and obtain authorization for use. In addition to the EU regulations, businesses must also comply with domestic regulations and regulations imposed by other markets, and these also affect the final products.

When chemicals contained in the final products are regulated, the materials, parts, and components used in the products must be redesigned, monitored, tested, and proven to meet the mandated chemical thresholds. The factories that make the parts and component suppliers are located in different countries; therefore, production networks must be managed across firms, industries, and countries. Chemical regulations often affect multiple industries, making adaptation even more complicated. Firms affected by the EU REACH and RoHS regulations are not only those in the chemical industry, but also the textile, wood products, plastic, rubber, machinery, electric, and electronic industries, among many others.[3] Many of these potentially affected industries are located in developing as well as in developed countries. Any firms that are part of a production network that exports final products to EU markets will be affected. This includes both direct exporters to the EU markets and indirect exporters whose parts and components are incorporated into the

---

[2] Prohibited substances include lead, mercury, cadmium, polybrominated biphenyl, and polybrominated diphenyl ether.

[3] The target products of RoHS are electrical and electronic products. However, RoHS affects sectors other than the target sector because, for example, the final products use plastics that may be distributed with textile bags, or the products, such as electrical outlets, are assembled into wooden desks.

final products that are shipped to the EU. Thus, the problem is not limited to exporting firms, but extends to some domestic firms. Our research interest lies in examining the effect of PRERs on Asian firms that directly or indirectly export to regulated markets. Differences in capacity and strategies in adapting to PRERs in different industries are also highlighted.

Beyond anecdotal evidence drawn from firms' experiences or case studies, no statistics about adaption to PRERs have been collected on a larger scale. This means that no in-depth examination on the effect of PRERs on firms and their adaptation behavior has been undertaken. To our knowledge, no research has been conducted that allows for extensive examination of how firms adapt to PRERs in Asia. The chapters in this book fill this gap. We conducted a series of surveys of firms in three Asian countries at different stages of economic development: Vietnam in 2011, representative of low-income countries; Malaysia in 2012, in the middle-income category; and Japan in 2013, a high-income country. Using surveys of firms in these countries, we have constructed a unique data set. The data set is used extensively in later chapters. This chapter shows the basic descriptive statistics from the three country surveys.

7.2   Research Questions

The surveys were constructed based on the following research issues. The first is examining the magnitude of the effect of chemical regulation on firms.

Issue 1: Effects of chemical PRERs on firms: How are firms affected by regulations/requirements for chemicals in products?

As chemical regulations in manufactured products are imposed by the EU and a small number of other countries, the number of affected firms may be limited. Nevertheless, if the effect of chemical regulations is extensive, more attention should be paid to PRERs such as RoHS and REACH. Also when a firm fails to meet regulations or customer requirements on chemicals, it may result in product rejection by customers.

The rate of product rejections can indicate the hurdles that a firm faces in implementing measures on chemicals.

Issues 2-4 address how firms adapt to PRERs and the effect of these regulations on global supply chain structures.

Issue 2: Material procurement: How do firms optimize their behavior with regard to purchasing materials to meet PRERs?

Issue 2 refers to our hypothesis that changing input materials to meet regulations may require firms to change their suppliers to businesses that can produce compliant inputs. Consequently, compliance with regulations could change supply chain structures by prompting firms to switch from non-compliant to compliant suppliers. Changing inputs may involve changes of suppliers, and thus it affects supply chain structures.

Issue 3: Market diversification: Do firms change their destination markets due to PRERs?

Issue 3 addresses whether PRERs prompt firms to change their destination markets. If firms cannot comply with regulations in the EU market, they may switch selling markets from the EU to other countries with looser regulations. This hypothesis leads to the next question, "If PRER is implemented only in developed countries, does it lead to the creation of pollution havens in developing countries?"[4]

Issue 4: Implications for supply chains: How do PRERs and private product requirements affect the structural management of supply chains?

Issue 4 assesses whether PRERs lead to changes in the structural management of supply chains. With PRERs, managing the supply chain and coordination among firms within the chain may be increasingly complex and burdensome. Because the strictness of regulations is uneven among

---

[4] The problem of pollution havens is typically discussed in the literature as the decision to locate production process of "dirty" industries. However, with the spread of PRERs, this could lead to segregation of markets into "clean" (regulated) and "dirty" (unregulated) consumption markets.

markets, structural management of supply chains and their quality may differ across firms.

Issues 5 and 6 ask about measures taken by firms to adapt to PRERs and their implications for businesses.

Issue5: Actions taken by firms: What were the motivations for firms to take these measures? What specific actions did firms take to adopt PRERs?

Issue 5 relates to the motivations of firms to take adaptation measures and measures for compliance. Depending on the types of firms and products, the motivations and the measures that were taken were different. By examining the motivations, firms are categorized as either proactive or reactive to regulatory changes. The attitude of firms to risk management also affects the types of measures that firms take.[5]

Issue 6: Business implications: What are the implications for business of adapting to PRERs?

Compliance with regulations may have business implications. Because measures are required, the questionnaire asked about changes in production costs and prices arising from compliance with regulations.[6] Lastly, issue 7 relates to the implications of government policy. What can policy do to improve the situation for domestic firms, especially for SMEs?

Issue 7: Policy implications: What can policy do to help firms adapt to PRERs?

Throughout the interviews in Vietnam, Malaysia, and Japan, it was found that many firms have not received complaints about chemicals in products from customers; therefore, these firms recognize no problems with chemicals in their products. Firms' compliance with PRERs has been achieved in a variety of ways, including testing products, changing production processes, changing inputs, and responding to customer specifications for

---

[5] See Chapter 11 for further argument of this point.
[6] Chapter 8 also examines the cost of compliance.

input materials in other ways. These measures are taken mainly to meet customers' demands without much knowledge of which regulations these demands are coming from. When firms decide to export to regulated markets, individual firms must collect regulatory information and decide how best to meet the regulatory requirements. To understand how firms are prepared to meet these requirements, the surveys asked firms whether they know why or for what regulations customers request that certain chemical requirements be met.

7.3   Survey and Data Description

The issues were explored by questionnaires conducted in three countries. The questionnaires consisted of four sections: (1) basic information, (2) input procurement and certification, (3) chemical management, and (4) export activities. The surveys in the countries share common core questions, although other questions differ to reflect differences in countries. Therefore, some data are not available for all three countries.

7.3.1   Vietnam Survey

Firm survey in Vietnam was conducted from December 2011 to January 2012. After the main content of the questionnaire was developed, the questionnaire was translated into Vietnamese and administered by the Vietnam Chamber of Commerce and Industry. For sampling, the manufacturing and commercial sectors, which are likely to be required to manage chemicals in products, were targeted. The geographical scope of the survey covered 63 provinces in Vietnam. The sample was taken from a list of firms from the General Department of Taxation containing 1954 foreign-owned firms and 10,024 private domestic firms, totaling 11,978 firms. For our purposes, foreign-owned firms are defined as all firms receiving foreign direct investment (FDI) and include both entirely foreign-owned firms and joint ventures between local and multinational firms. We refer to these firms as FDI firms hereafter. The survey was sent to all FDI firms and 70% of domestic firms that were randomly selected. The Vietnam survey was conducted from December 2011 to January 2012. The questionnaire was distributed via mail, with follow-up phone calls made when necessary. Over the month that the survey was conducted, we sent out a total of 11,978 questionnaires and received 1,055 responses, giving a response rate of 8.8%. Comparing the distribution of the firms to which the questionnaire was sent and the distribution of firms from which a response was received, FDI firms accounted for 16.3% of questionnaire recipients and 31.9% of the responses.

7.3.2 Malaysia Survey

We collected firm-level data in Penang, Malaysia, from November 2012 to February 2013. Penang has developed as an industrial zone over decades and hosts many manufacturing industries that make a major contribution to the state economy. The geographical coverage was limited to Penang because of the availability of the nationwide Industrial Census that we could take our sample from; Penang has a new Industrial Census. Surveyed firms were sampled from firms recorded in the 2011 Penang Industrial Census, which holds data on 2,116 firms, including 1,898 manufacturing and manufacturing-related firms, and 218 firms in other service sectors. The questionnaire was adjusted to reflect the specific characteristics of Malaysia, such as firm categories and asset levels, and it was also translated into Chinese. Depending on the firm, either English or Chinese versions of questionnaires were used. Beginning in November 2012, we contacted 732 firms by distributing questionnaires by mail, followed up by phone calls. The number of replies was 374, giving a response rate of approximately 51%.

7.3.3 Japanese Survey

This survey drew the sample from the Tokyo Shoko Research company database, a commercial database of firms operating in Japan. The database contains 84,324 firms that are involved in the manufacturing sectors, excluding food, cosmetics, and others that are not relevant industries for the current topic. For sampling, a stratified sampling method was used, requiring that the share of each sector is the same as that of our population. This resulted in a sample of 2,000 firms. From

January 17, 2014 to February 14, 2014, the questionnaire was distributed to 2,000 firms by post. Out of 2000 firms, 493 firms responded, giving a response rate of 24.7%.

7.4 Results from Descriptive Statistics

Three datasets are intended to reflect differences in the stage of development of each country. However, the samples show significant differences in firm size. As Table 7.1 shows, the firm size in the three surveys varies. The firms in the Vietnam sample have the largest number of employees, and the Japanese firms have the smallest number of employees. This survey took lists with the largest possible coverage of firms for each survey for sampling: the taxation list for Vietnam, the industrial census list for Malaysia, and one of the largest private company databases in Japan. In Vietnam, small firms are not captured by the tax office list. In Malaysia, Penang is a region containing many FDI firms, which tend to be larger. Moreover, larger firms are more likely to respond to surveys because they are more experienced in product quality control and smaller firms do not have the capacity to do so, especially in less developed countries.

This section presents the responses to the questions about chemical management for the three data sets.

Issue 1: Effects of chemical PRERs on firms: How are firms affected by regulations/requirements for chemicals in products?

For this research issue, firms were asked "Have you ever taken measures related to chemicals in products after 2000?" and "Have your products

Table 7.1 Firm size indicators

Number of employees					
	Obs	Mean	Std. Dev.	Min	Max
Vietnam	978	630	1,407	1	16,175
Malaysia	370	158	310	1	3,000
Japan	493	84	466	1	6,362

been rejected by your customers because of chemicals the products contained?" In translating the research issue into questions in our questionnaire, we encountered various problems. First, although our interest lies in whether firms take action in relation to specific regulations, our pre-survey interviews with firms revealed that many small and medium enterprises were not aware that customers' requests, such as limiting use of hazardous substances, were to comply with specific regulations. This is because there are different methods of regulatory compliance. Many firms have received requests relating to regulatory compliance through their customers' private requirements, for example, requirements described in green procurement manuals. Therefore, the question intends to capture both regulations and private requirements that were developed for compliance.

Tables 7.2–7.4 summarize the results for the two questions. The results for the first and second questions are in the left and right columns, respectively. The data are categorized by firm characteristics. The firm categories differ among the three data sets, reflecting the industrial differences. For Vietnam, the firm categories are domestic, state-owned, and FDI. For Malaysia the categories are domestic, joint-venture, and FDI. The Japanese data do not offer firm ownership categories; thus, the data are categorized by the firm size by the number of employees. The data show that 43.1% of Vietnamese firms, 60.9% of Malaysian firms, and 30.2% of Japanese firms needed to take specific actions related to chemicals used in their products after 2000. In addition, FDI firms tend to implement measures more often than domestic firms, and larger firms take measures more often than smaller firms in Malaysia and Japan. In Vietnam, state-owned firms show the highest rate in taking measures for chemical management of products.

The right column of Tables 7.2, 7.3 and 7.4 show the number of rejections. For Vietnam, of the 552 firms that responded, 54 firms (9.8%) reported having products rejected by customers because of improper use of chemicals in products. The figures for domestic and FDI firms show that 14.2% of FDI firms experienced rejection compared with 3.7% of domestic firms. For Malaysia and Japan, the results are similar, with a rejection rate of 9.2% for both countries. In Vietnam, state-owned enterprises show the highest rate of product rejection. The categories of firms that were more likely to take measures to respond to

Table 7.2 Vietnam: Measures for chemicals and product rejection by firm type

| | Took measures for chemicals in products | | | | | | Experience of product rejection | | | | | |
| | Yes | | No | | Total | | Yes | | No | | Total | |
	No.	%	No.	%	No.	%	No.	%	No.	%	No.	%
Domestic firm	248	40.5	365	59.5	613	66.8	26	7.2	336	92.8	362	65.5
State-owned firm	5	55.6	4	44.4	9	1.0	2	28.6	5	71.4	7	1.3
FDI firm	142	48.1	153	51.9	295	32.2	26	14.2	157	85.8	183	33.2
All firms	395	43.1	522	56.9	917	100	54	9.8	498	90.2	552	100

Note: The percentages for Yes and No are the number of firms answering yes or no divided by the total number of firms for each firm type. The percentages for total are the share of each type of firms in all firms. Total number of firms differ across tables depending on the number of firms that answered each question

Table 7.3 Malaysia: Measures for chemicals and product rejection by firm type

| | Took measures for chemicals in products | | | | | | Experience of product rejection | | | | | |
| | Yes | | No | | Total | | Yes | | No | | Total | |
	No.	%	No.	%	No.	%	No.	%	No.	%	No.	%
Domestic firm	149	55.8	118	44.2	267	72.6	10	6.6	141	93.4	151	66.2
Joint venture	21	65.6	11	34.4	32	8.7	1	4.5	21	95.5	22	9.6
FDI firm	54	78.3	15	21.7	69	18.7	10	18.2	45	36.8	55	24.1
All firms	224	60.9	144	39.1	368	100	21	9.2	207	90.8	228	100

Note: The same as the table above

Table 7.4 Japan: Measures for chemicals and product rejection by firm size

| No. of employees | Took measures for managing chemicals in products | | | | | | Experience of product rejection | | | | | |
| | Yes | | No | | Total | | Yes | | No | | Total | |
	No.	%	No.	%	No.	%	No.	%	No.	%	No.	%
1–9	44	24.2	138	75.8	182	39.3	1	2.0	49	98.0	50	32.9
10–99	69	28.0	177	72.0	246	53.1	1	1.3	74	98.7	75	49.3
100–299	13	65.0	7	35.0	20	4.3	1	7.7	12	92.3	13	8.6
300max	14	93.3	1	6.7	15	3.2	3	21.4	11	78.5	14	9.2
All firms	140	30.2	323	69.8	463	100	6	9.2	146	90.8	152	100

Note: The same as the table above

regulations or customer requirements were also the ones that experienced greater levels of product rejection because of chemicals in products. Although this might seem contradictory, it reflects the fact that firms that have greater obligations to manage the content of their products are also subject to more careful checking of their products.

Question 2: Material procurement: How do firms optimize their behavior with regard to purchasing materials to meet PRERs?

To examine how firms optimize material procurement, the questionnaire asked, "If your products are exported to multiple markets, do you change inputs depending on the destination markets?" Choosing appropriate raw materials, including chemicals, is key to meeting regulations without compromising price competitiveness. Table 7.5 shows that some firms use different chemicals depending on the target markets. It may reflect that some firms use safer but more expensive chemicals for regulated countries and cheaper chemicals for unregulated markets. This has prompted concern in some developing countries that they may become pollution havens by consuming substandard products that cannot be exported to regulated

Table 7.5 Firms changing chemicals in products for different markets by firm type

Vietnam	Domestic firms		State-owned firms		FDI firms		All firms	
	No.	%	No.	%	No.	%	No.	%
Yes	90	52.6	4	100.0	33	45.8	127	51.4
No	81	47.4	0	0.0	39	54.2	120	48.6
Total	171	100.0	4	100.0	72	100.0	247	100.0
Malaysia	**Domestic firms**		**Joint venture**		**FDI firms**		**All firms**	
Yes	35	26.3	6	28.6	16	29.6	57	27.4
No	98	73.7	15	71.4	38	70.4	151	72.6
Total	133	100	21	100	54	100	208	100
Japan								
Yes							8	6.6
No							113	93.4
							221	100

markets. Other firms use the same chemicals across different markets. In this case, it is assumed that firms use inputs that meet the most stringent regulations for products sold in regulated or unregulated markets. Firms that answered that they changed chemicals depending on markets were 51.4% of Vietnamese respondents, 27.4% of Malaysian respondents, but only 6.6% of 221 Japanese respondents. Thus, how firms optimize the choice of chemicals is different across countries and firms.

Question 3: Market diversification: Do firms change their destination markets due to PRERs?

One concern raised about PRERs has been that such regulations could act as a trade barrier for exporters. During research in Vietnam, which involved a tea-processing firm, when the product contained an excessive amount of agricultural chemical residues, rather than correcting the problem, the firm abandoned sales to a large-brand tea processor that sold to regulated developed country markets, including the EU and the United States of America (USA).[7] Instead, the firm opted to export its tea to countries that did not require the same level of examination of chemical residues and accepted a much lower price for the product. If countries do not have regulations that are strict enough owing to a lack of scientific or government capacity, do they become pollution havens for lower quality consumer products? That is, these unregulated markets could be flooded with lower quality products, including those that are rejected in regulated markets, which could pose serious risks to health and the environment. To examine these concerns, the questionnaire posed the question, "Have you changed export markets because of chemical regulations or requirements?" Very few firms said that they had done so. As can be seen in Table 7.6, only 4.0% of Vietnamese firms and 1.8% of Malaysian firms answered that they had changed their target market. A small fraction of firms needed to exit supply chains connected to regulated markets.

Question 4: Implications for supply chains: How do PRERs and private product requirements affect the structural management of supply chains?

---

[7] We visited this tea firm in 2011. See Michida and Nabeshima (2012) for details.

Table 7.6 Firms changing export market because of PRERs

	Vietnam	Malaysia
Changed market	25 (4.0%)	4 (1.8%)
Did not change market	603 (96.0%)	222 (98.2%)

For firms that are eager to comply with their customer's requirements for supplier codes of conduct, specifying or making recommendations about input materials to their own suppliers is a way to control chemicals in the products used by suppliers. Customer requests and recommendations, where a supplier chooses certain input materials, are an indicator of the level of control of chemicals in products. The survey asked firms about the type of requests and specifications from customers in different countries in terms of the selection of input materials. As shown in Table 7.7, depending on the customers' country of origin, the degree of specification of raw materials differs. For each firm category, the left column is the number of firms with customers that specify materials. The middle column is the total number of firms that have customers from each country or region. The right column is the percentage of firms with customers who specify materials. For Vietnamese firms with customers in the EU, 39.2% reported that customers from the EU requested the use of specified materials, followed by 34.4% of firms with Japanese customers, and 32.6% of firms with American customers. A similar trend was also observed in the Malaysian survey. This result indicates that customers from the EU, Japan, and the USA are more likely to specify input materials than any Asian countries. Comparing Vietnam and Malaysia, the percentage shares of firms with customers who specify materials in Malaysia are higher than in Vietnam across the board.[8]

An overall supply chain map (Fig. 7.1) was constructed from the survey results for the three research questions. This finding raises concerns that products containing cheaper, less safe chemicals may end up in unregulated

---

[8] The surveys asked firms to identify themselves if they supply their main products to global supply chains. The question was "Do you supply your main product for global supply chains?" Then global supply chains were defined here as referring to the network of companies that procure inputs from various countries and sell the products globally, such as automotive assemblers, electronics and electric producers, garment producers, etc. There are both direct exporting firms and non-direct exporting firms that can be part of global supply chains for the current definition.

Table 7.7 Specification of input materials by customer country of origin and firm type

	Domestic firms			State-owned firms			FDI firms			All firms		
Vietnam	No.	Total No.	%	No.	Total No.	%	No.	Total No.	%	No.	Total No.	%
EU	53	142	37.3	0	0	0.0	29	66	43.9	82	209	39.2
Japan	32	105	30.5	1	2	50.5	20	47	42.6	53	143	34.4
USA	36	119	30.3	0	0	0.0	21	56	37.5	57	175	32.6
China	23	106	21.7	1	2	50.0	20	59	33.9	44	167	26.3
South Korea	23	101	22.8	0	0	0.0	15	57	26.3	38	158	24.1
Vietnam	53	241	22.0	0	0	0	13	63	20.6	66	304	21.7
Taiwan	12	84	14.3	1	1	100.0	13	46	28.3	26	131	19.8
ASEAN	17	87	19.5	0	1	0.0	7	39	17.9	24	127	18.9
India	7	72	9.7	2	2	100.0	1	22	4.5	10	96	10.4

	Domestic firms			Joint venture			FDI firms			All firms		
Malaysia	No.	Total No.	%	No.	Total No.	%	No.	Total No.	%	No.	Total No.	%
EU	34	51	66.7	9	12	75.0	21	26	80.8	64	89	71.9
USA	38	58	65.5	6	10	60.0	17	25	68.0	61	93	65.6
Japan	22	34	64.7	4	7	57.1	14	20	70.0	40	61	65.6
Taiwan	11	19	57.9	3	6	50.0	7	10	70.0	21	35	60.0
ASEAN	62	119	52.1	6	10	60.0	18	30	60.0	86	159	54.1
China	25	44	56.8	2	4	40.0	12	24	50.0	39	73	53.4
Malaysia	84	199	42.2	14	22	63.6	25	44	56.8	128	265	48.3
South Korea	2	7	28.6	1	5	20.0	4	5	80.0	7	17	41.2
India	6	15	40.0	0	2	0.0	3	6	50.0	9	23	39.1

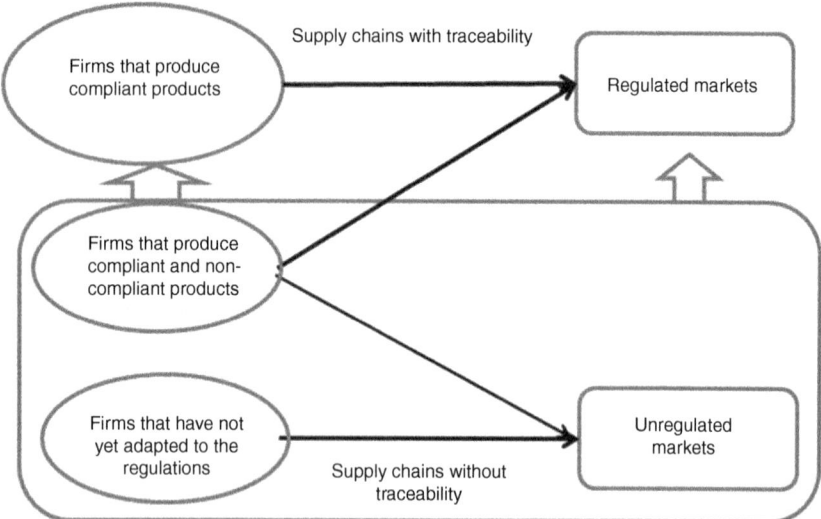

Fig. 7.1 Potential for the creation of pollution havens in unregulated countries

markets, leading to market segmentation. Stringency in regulations differs between countries because environmental and health-related regulations are usually set at the country level to achieve an optimal balance between multiple factors, such as geography, climate, culture, and people's behavior. Therefore, it must be stressed that looser regulations compared with other countries do not necessarily create pollution havens. Such problems occur when a country lacks the capacity to set or enforce appropriate regulations.

Question 5: Measures taken by firms: What were the motivations for firms to take these measures? What did firms do to adapt to PRERs?

Table 7.8 shows the key determinants for firms to adapt to PRERs on chemicals. Most firms answered that they adapted to PRERs to avoid rejection of products by their customers. The next most common response was seeking full compliance with domestic regulations and

Table 7.8 Reasons for compliance with regulation

	Vietnam		Malaysia	
	No	%	No.	%
Avoid customer rejection	139	41.2	101	44.7
Comply fully with domestic regula-tion/requirements	84	24.9	53	23.5
Increase export	40	11.9	6	2.7
Improve brand image	20	5.9	9	4.0
Maintain current business Relationships	18	5.3	14	6.2
Increase domestic sales	18	5.3	1	0.4
Develop new business relationship	10	3	4	1.8
Attain higher sales price	4	1.2	2	0.9
Other	4	1.2	36	15.9
Total	337	100	226	100.0

requirements. "Other" referred to instructions from headquarters in many cases. Compliance with PRERs or chemical requirements is often seen more as a need to react to regulations or requirements in a passive manner rather than as proactive measure to increase competitiveness or brand image, especially in Malaysia. The results for the next research question confirm that this perception reflects what firms experienced. In Malaysia and Vietnam, 41.2% and 44.7% of respondents answered that avoiding product rejections by customers is the reason for complying with regulations.

The most common measures taken by firms to comply with PRERs are sending products for testing, followed by changing production processes (Table 7.9). The results are similar for Vietnam and Malaysia. To meet product quality expectations, testing is inevitable. However, testing costs can take up a large portion of profits, especially for smaller businesses. The Japanese survey asked specifically about testing costs and price relationship. The survey shows that out of 46 firms, 78% of firms bear the testing costs, customers bear costs for 9% of firms, and suppliers bear costs for 13% of firms. Moreover, 75% of 45 firms answered that it is very hard or relatively hard to increase prices to cover testing costs.

Table 7.9 Measures taken to adapt to regulations

	Vietnam		Malaysia	
	No.	%	No.	%
Send products for testing	65	27.9	99	45.0
Change production process	49	21.0	66	30.0
Invest in testing facility	32	13.7	25	11.4
Invest in new production facility	31	13.3	30	13.6
Change inputs	28	12.0	64	29.1
Change product design	2	0.9	25	11.4
Obtain certification	N/A	N/A	30	13.6
Obs. (multiple answered allowed)	233	100.0	220	100.0

Although many firms need to test their products before distributing to their customers, there are some firms that need to invest more extensively in production processes or testing facility to meet PRERs.

Question 6: Business implications: What were the implications for business of adapting to PRERs?

Does adaptation to chemical regulations and requirements improve firms' competitiveness? Firms were asked, "Did your export level change after meeting PRER or other chemicals requirement?" Overall, 65.7% of Vietnamese firms and 55.8% of Malaysian firms responded that compliance did not change their exports (Table 7.10). This shows that compliance with regulations offers an opportunity to keep exporting to regulated markets for a majority of firms. Chapters 7 and 9 offer further analysis of export performance.

Table 7.10 Change in export levels after regulatory compliance

	Vietnam		Malaysia	
	No.	%	No.	%
Do not export	61	13.4	40	17.7
Exports increased	42	9.2	58	25.7
Exports decreased	53	11.6	2	0.9
No impact	299	65.7	126	55.8
Total	455	100.0	226	100

Table 7.11 Cost and price changes after regulatory compliance in Vietnam and Malaysia

Vietnam

Price change→ ↓Cost change	Increase		Decrease		Unchanged		Total	
	No.	%	No.	%	No.	%	No.	%
Increase	194	79.2	2	0.8	49	20.0	245	59.8
Decrease	14	60.9	6	26.1	3	13.0	23	5.6
Unchanged	12	8.5	0	0.0	130	91.5	142	34.6
Total	220	53.7	8	2.0	182	44.4	410	100.0
Malaysia								
Increase	55	43.3	4	3.1	68	53.5	127	55.5
Decrease	0	0.0	1	50.0	1	50.0	2	0.9
Unchanged	3	3.0	2	2.0	95	95.0	100	43.6
Total	58	25.3	7	3.1	164	71.6	229	100.0

However, some firms experienced a decrease in exports after regulatory compliance. Compliance with regulations can increase costs from investing in production processes or testing laboratories, and compliance costs may reduce the price competitiveness of firms in some situations. Table 7.11 shows the cross tabulations for compliance cost and price changes owing to regulatory compliance. In both Malaysia and Vietnam, more than 50% of firms answered that costs increased because of compliance (see Chapter 8 for further analysis on production costs). Of the firms whose production costs increased, about 80% of firms increased sale prices in Vietnam. However, in Malaysia, the share of firms that could pass on the cost increases in higher prices was 43.4%, which is lower than in Vietnam. Compliance to regulation or requirements does not guarantee an increase in export competitiveness or prices. Compliance is often considered as a ticket to enter the regulated market without additional benefits.

Question 7: Policy implications: What can policy do to help firms adapt to PRERs?

The questionnaire asked firms involved with chemical management "Do you know which regulations of chemicals in products you need to

Table 7.12 Firm with knowledge of regulations

Vietnam	Domestic firms		State-owned firms		FDI firms		All firms	
	No.	%	No.	%	No.	%	No.	%
Yes	173	52.7	4	80.0	104	69.3	281	58.2
No	155	47.3	1	20.0	46	30.7	202	41.8
Total	328	100.0	5	100.0	150	100.0	483	100.0
Malaysia	**Local firm**		**Joint venture**		**FDI firms**		**All firms**	
	No.	%	No.	%	No.	%	No.	%
Yes	109	72.2	20	90.9	43	78.2	172	75.4
No	42	27.8	2	9.1	12	21.8	56	24.6
Total	151	100	22	100	55	100	228	100

comply with?" Table 7.12 shows the firms' knowledge of chemical regulations. Overall, 58% of Vietnamese firms and 75% of Malaysian firms stated that they knew the regulations with which they need to comply, whereas the remaining firms comply without specific knowledge of the regulations. Firms that do not know the regulations are taking measures as required by their customers. This could lead to firms relying solely on their customers for information and make it difficult for firms to take proactive measures. Moreover, if the firm stops doing business with its current customers, the firm could lose its standing in the market because of its lack of regulatory knowledge. This risk is real because regulations tend to be revised periodically.

In the Japanese questionnaires, firms were asked "Do you know EU RoHS and REACH?" to examine firms' knowledge of EU RoHS and REACH regulations. Table 7.13 shows that as the firm size decreases, fewer firms are aware of either set of regulations, even though all the firms in our sample could be affected. Even for the products that are exported to non-EU countries, various countries have introduced RoHS-like regulations (see Chapter 2). As similar regulations have been implemented in more markets, being prepared for newer regulatory environments is important to stay in a variety of markets.

In addition to the policy implications drawn from the survey, firms provided comments and suggestions for improving their adoption of PRERs. These responses were categorized as (1) more information and

Table 7.13 Knowledge on EU RoHS and REACH in Japan

No. of employees	RoHS				REACH			
	Yes	No	Total	Share of Yes (%)	Yes	No	Total	Share of yes
0–4	11	13	24	45.8	8	16	24	33.33
5–9	17	12	29	58.6	11	21	32	34.38
10–19	23	13	36	63.9	16	21	37	43.24
20–99	31	6	37	83.8	24	11	35	68.57
100–299	13	0	13	100.0	11	2	13	84.62
More than 300	13	0	13	100.0	13	0	13	100.00
Total	108	44	152	71.1	83	71	154	53.90

training is needed, (2) subsidy or financial support is needed, (3) lack of laboratories and high testing costs are the major hurdles, (4) stricter domestic regulations should be introduced to avoid unsafe chemicals/products being imported, and (5) more awareness about chemical safety is needed. Of the 319 comments received, the majority of firms expressed an urgent need for information and training (1) and they expected governments, chambers of commerce, and industrial associations to provide them with training courses or information and guidelines. Specifically, firms would like to have information on RoHS, REACH, and similar regulations in each export market. In addition, some firms would like to obtain information about pending regulations so that they have enough time to comply.

The second largest responses (17 responses) were concerned with awareness about chemical safety (5). Some of the responses were as follows. "We understand that it is absolutely necessary to control chemicals. On the other hand, if control of chemicals is too strict, it may discourage business activities. Enhancing the understanding and responsibility is necessary. To do so, we need guidelines for using chemicals. Or we need secured inputs that meet all requirements and standards to produce our products." "Our firm is ready to bear the cost to comply with any requirements or regulations."

There were 16 comments related to laboratories or testing (3) which makes this the third largest category. Some firms mentioned that it would be good to have a national laboratory that can meet the requirements and satisfy their customers at a lower cost. Other firms complained that testing takes a long time.

Some firms commented that chemicals are not related to their businesses. The answers included, "We are a small business so chemical controls have not been required so far" or "The parent firm controls all the chemicals so that we don't know about chemicals." There are 12 comments that request stricter than domestic regulations (4) because some firms are concerned that less safe or lower quality products are imported into the Vietnamese market. Finally 10 comments are related to requests for subsidy for testing or other financial support from the government.

7.5 Conclusion

This chapter presented the firm survey results to assess the effect of PRERs in Vietnam, Malaysia, and Japan. The descriptive statistics give a snapshot of the problems relating to firms adapting to increasing regulation and standards arising from globalization. Across the three surveys, requirements about chemicals in products are imposed on larger firms or FDI firms and more rejections are observed for those firms than for smaller or domestic firms. Knowledge about PRERs, such as EU RoHS and REACH, is better in larger firms and FDI firms and worse in smaller firms. Compared with other manufacturing sectors in developing Asian countries, the results show that the competitiveness of Japanese manufacturing industries, especially smaller firms, is weak in terms of management of chemicals in products. They have not been well equipped with foreign regulatory knowledge because their customers have not yet required this of them. Smaller firms face the challenge of acquiring the necessary skills and capacity to keep up with the changing regulatory environment and customer requirements as PRERs are increasingly strengthened.

The results show that PRERs, as well as customer requirements for chemicals, have affected various industries in Vietnam. Firms in both Malaysia and Vietnam have also needed to take measures to comply with regulations and requirements about chemicals in products and have experienced product rejections because of non-compliant chemicals. The results also confirmed that FDI firms have experienced more rejections and are facing tougher compliance requirements compared with domestic firms. This clearly shows that it is more difficult to enter global supply chains that target highly regulated markets if firms have not yet entered such markets.

More firms in Vietnam than in Malaysia could increase their product prices after cost increases arising from compliance with chemical regulations and requirements. However, compliance with PRERs is a minimum standard for competing in regulated markets and an increase in sales price following compliance becomes more difficult.

Although Malaysian firms consider cooperation with customers and suppliers along supply chains as important in adapting to chemical PRERs, Vietnamese firms consider assistance from government and industrial organizations as being particularly important.

The survey revealed the situation of firms in Penang in adapting to PRERs, specifically chemical regulations such as RoHS and REACH. The results confirm that firms involved in production networks have adapted to chemical PRERs through various measures. The product rejection rate statistics reflect that firms supplying products to regulated markets face tougher compliance requirements from customers and the data reveal that firms often struggle to comply with the required processes. Entry to global supply chains is becoming more difficult for firms targeting highly regulated markets that do not yet serve such markets.

In addition, lower rejection rates for local firms do not necessarily mean that there are fewer problems. It simply means that the requirements imposed on firms are lower in the destination markets they serve, where the level of regulation is lower. As incomes rise in developing countries and consumer demand for safer and healthier products increases, more firms are expected to face tougher requirements for their products.

Acknowledgement Authors thank Toshi H. Arimura, Tsunehiro Otsuki, Shunsuke Managi, and Hakaru Iguchi for their valuable advice and comments for the Vietnam survey. We would also like to thank the Vietnam Chamber of Commerce and Industry for assisting in administering the survey in Vietnam and all the firms who kindly filled out the questionnaire. We would like to thank the Ministry of International Trade and Industry, the governments of Malaysia and the Penang government, especially YB Phee Boon Poh, Penang Executive Councilor for Health, Welfare and Caring Society, for endorsing our survey, as well as Invest Penang, the Federation of Malaysian Manufacturers in the Northern Region, and the Free Industrial Zone Firms' Association in Penang for distributing the survey to their member firms, and all the firms who kindly filled out the questionnaire. The survey was conducted by PE Research. For the Japanese survey, we are grateful to the Ministry of Economy, Trade and Industry, the Japan Environmental Management Association for Industry, to Tetsuya Matsuura for comments on survey sheets, and to Tokyo Shoko Research, Ltd., for conducting the Japanese survey. All errors and limitations in this paper are the responsibility of the authors. The views in this paper are those of the author and do not reflect the views of the organizations and individuals mentioned above. The research was partly supported by JSPS KAKENHI Grant No. 15K00675 (Michida, Nabeshima).

References

Chen, S. S., Helme, b. M. H. M., Michida,E., & Nabeshima,K. (2014). *Role of laboratories for adapting product-related environmental regulations (PRERs)*. (IDE Discussion Paper No. 452). Chiba: Institute of Developing Economies.

Hiratsuka, D., & Uchida Y. (Eds.). (2010). *Input trade and production networks in East Asia*. New York: Edward Elgar.

Michida, E., & Nabeshima, K. (2012). *Role of supply chains in adopting product related environmental regulations: Case studies of vietnam*. (IDE Discussion Papers No.343). Chiba: Institute of Developing Economies.

Etsuyo Michida is an Associate Senior Research Fellow at Institute of Developing Economies, Japan External Trade Organization (IDE-JETRO) and was a Visiting Scholar at Haas School of Business, University of

California, Berkeley from 2015 to 2017. Her research interest lies in trade and the environment with a special focus on developing countries.She has recently researched on the relationship between environmental regulation, firm behavior, and global supply chains. She holds a PhD in Economics from Graduate School of International Cooperation Studies, Kobe University.

Yasushi Ueki is an Economist at Economic Research Institute for ASEAN and East Asia (ERIA), Jakarta, Indonesia. He is specialized in technology transfer, innovation, and industrial development. Prior to joining ERIA in January 2014, he was a research fellow at Institute of Developing Economies (IDE), Japan from 1999. From 2002 to 2005, he worked as an expert at United Nations Economic Commission for Latin America and the Caribbean, Santiago, Chile. From 2007 to 2012, he was stationed at IDE Bangkok Research Center, Thailand. He holds a PhD in international public policy from Osaka University, Japan.

Kaoru Nabeshima is an Associate Professor at the Graduate School of Asia-Pacific Studies, Waseda University. He holds a PhD in Economics from University of California-Davis, and a BA in Economics from Ohio Wesleyan University. Prior to joining Graduate School of Asia-Pacific Studies, Waseda University in 2015, he worked for the Institute of Developing Economies, Japan External Trade Organization and the World Bank. Some of his publications include *Meeting Standards, Winning Markets: Regional Trade Standards Compliance Report East Asia 2013* (IDE-JETRO/UNIDO 2013), *Tiger Economies under Threat* (co-authored with Shahid Yusuf, 2009), and *Some Small Countries Do It Better: Rapid Growth and Its Causes in Singapore, Finland, and Ireland* (co-authored with Shahid Yusuf, 2012). His research interests lie in examining the relationship between regulations and international trade, the issue of middle income trap, and the innovation capabilities of firms in East Asia.

·

8

Transmission Channels of Requirements for Chemicals in Products to Firms in Vietnam

Yasushi Ueki, Etsuyo Michida, and Kaoru Nabeshima

8.1 Introduction

International trade has been liberalized to eliminate tariff barriers through the General Agreement on Tariffs and Trade/World Trade Organization (WTO) rounds of negotiations, and regional and bilateral

Y. Ueki (✉)
Economist, Economic Research Institute for ASEAN and East Asia, Jakarta, Indonesia
e-mail: yasushi.ueki@eria.org

E. Michida
Institute of Developing Economies, Japan External Trade Organization (IDE-JETRO), Chiba, Japan
e-mail: etsuyo_michida@ide.go.jp

K. Nabeshima
Waseda University, Tokyo, Japan
e-mail: kknabeshima@waseda.jp

© The Author(s) 2017   **179**
E. Michida et al. (eds.), *Regulations and International Trade*,
IDE-JETRO Series, DOI 10.1007/978-3-319-55041-1_8

trade agreements. However, various groups of non-tariff measures (NTMs) classified by the United Nations Conference on Trade and Development (UNCTAD)(2013) remain untouched, or even proliferate in importing developed and developing countries. Consequently, sanitary and phytosanitary measures, technical barriers to trade, and other NTMs have been highlighted in recent trade negotiations and disputes.

UNCTAD defines NTMs as policy measures other than ordinary customs tariffs that can potentially have an economic effect on international trade in goods, changing quantities traded, or prices, or both (UNCTAD, 2010: xvi). NTMs contain product-related regulations, standards, or requirements for the environmental, health, safety, and other social reasons, rather than economic reasons such as protecting domestic and infant industries.

Among the various NTMs, this study focuses on product-related environmental regulations (PRERs) including standards, specifications, and requirements that restrict or control the use of chemical substances contained in products. PRERs are imposed on suppliers by countries where there are concerns mainly about the safety and environmental impact of products. The European Union (EU) is a pioneer in introducing PRERs such as the Restriction of Hazardous Substances (RoHS) directive for electrical and electronic products and equipment, and the Registration, Evaluation, Authorization and Restriction of Chemicals (REACH) regulation, which came into force in 2006 and 2007, respectively.

In addition to mandatory public regulations, voluntary private standards limit the use of chemicals in products or require firms to manage and monitor chemicals strictly (UNIDO, 2010). Private standards contain firm-specific codes of conduct and sector-specific standards. An example of a firm-specific standard is IKEA's IWAY. IKEA is a multinational furniture retailer that requires its suppliers to comply with IKEA's code of conduct on purchasing products, materials, and services, IWAY, including requirements related to the environment, chemicals, and hazardous and non-hazardous waste. An example of a sector-specific consortium standard is OEKO-TEX standard 100. OEKO-TEX is an association organized by institutes for textile research and testing in Europe and Japan. OEKO-TEX standard 100 provides testing methods for harmful substances and its label proves that certified textiles will not harm health.

A common aspect of these mandatory and voluntary standards is the increasing demand for suppliers to record data about chemical substances contained in raw materials, intermediate goods, and their products, or to report such data to their buyers. Even firms in developing Asian countries like Vietnam must shoulder management responsibility for complying with PRERs introduced in developed country markets. In Vietnam, several firms require their suppliers to change inputs, provide training, and conduct supplier audits to comply with their own private standards regarding chemical management, many of which have been developed according to mandatory regulations (Michida & Nabeshima, 2012). Because production networks have become more globalized, it is more complicated and expensive for private firms, particularly those in developing countries, to comply with PRERs. Consequently, local firms in developing countries are likely to be excluded from international production networks and developed markets.

PRERs also bring a new policy challenge to developing countries. PRERs take a different approach from traditional environmental regulations. Environmental regulations used to be originated and institutionalized in producer countries and imposed on production sites. The governments implement these policies by monitoring only potential sources of pollutants such as production sites. However, PRERs are introduced by consumer countries and they affect producer countries through production networks.

To meet PRERs, including private standards, and gain an advantage in competing for consumers and corporate buyers, it is essential for suppliers and policy makers to obtain information about PRERs and take necessary measures as accurately and quickly as possible. Therefore, it is important for suppliers and policy makers to get a better understanding of the mechanism of transmitting information about PRERs, including private standards, from consumer countries and downstream buyers to upstream suppliers.

Considering the discussion above, this study attempts to identify the transmission channels of requirements for chemicals in products to developing countries. The effects of PRERs are significant in developing countries, especially those in East Asia that form the world production base in global production networks. However, latecomer countries to East Asian production networks like Vietnam lack strong supporting industries. Suppliers in these countries struggle in establishing collaborative relationships with domestic and international buyers. Therefore, this empirical study focuses on transmission channels for information about PRERs that firms in Vietnam can access.

This chapter has the following structure. Sections 8.2 and 8.3 discusses the hypotheses and model. Section 8.4 explains the data and summary statistics. Section 8.5 presents the results. Section 8.6 presents the summary and conclusions.

8.2   Hypotheses and Model

A firm in production networks can obtain information on PRERs imposed in its target market through indirect and direct information access channels to the information sources. Indirect access channels connect the firm to the information sources in the market through its business partners, which are typically corporate buyers and trading firms that are positioned near the final consumers. Direct access channels connect the firm directly with the market through its own market research activities, sales personnel, foreign affiliates, and other own activities and networks.

Firms can also be categorized according to their attitude toward acquisition of information about PRERs: proactive and reactive in response to the introduction of PRERs. Proactive firms may obtain information about PRERs by using their own information channels or by making necessary investments in information acquisition to satisfy PRERs. Reactive firms may obtain information in response to pressure from their corporate buyers, or through technical assistance from the buyers.

Most local firms in developing countries are less capable and lack resources for establishing their own information channels directly linked with foreign markets. Therefore, local firms are expected to depend on indirect channels to obtain information on PRERs through their corporate buyers, although their dependency will be affected by the corporate buyers' characteristics and local suppliers' capability and attitudes toward PRERs.

8.2.1 Global Value Chains as PRER Transmission Channels

Corporate buyer channels can be categorized according to the types of governance in the global value chain (GVC). Gereffi et al. (2005) constructed the theory of value chain governance based on the following factors: complexity of information and knowledge, codification of information and knowledge, and capability of suppliers. Gereffi et al. (2005) consider that the value chain tends to be the captive type when the codification and complexity of product specifications are both high but supplier capabilities are low. Local suppliers in developing countries like Vietnam tend to less capable and belong to chains where their buyers have a strong influence on the information that the suppliers receive.

This study assumes that the lead firm in the GVC is a multinational corporation (MNC), probably from a developed country. Suppliers in Vietnam ship their products to the lead firm directly or indirectly through a downstream firm linked directly to the lead firm. The lead firm requires strict quality control of its suppliers. For suppliers in developing countries, the transaction with the lead firm is equivalent to exporting markets in developed countries, even if the lead firm is located in the home country of the suppliers. However, the lead firm is more knowledgeable about PRERs than local suppliers are. The lead firm can provide its upstream suppliers with information about PRERs through the chain. This study categorizes this type of information transmission channel as an indirect channel for upstream suppliers.

Indirect channels can be important for transmitting information about PRERs to suppliers in developing countries because lead firms in GVCs have more information about and solutions for PRERs and they play a leading role in collaboration on PRERs with their suppliers from developing countries. Jeppesen and Hansen (2004) observe that MNCs issue directives and standards for their suppliers and even provide environmental technical assistance and training to their partners in developing countries.

Asymmetry of information about PRERs and the capability to meet the regulations are particularly important in the relationship between local suppliers and their lead firms in the EU, which often issues complicated and abstruse PRERs. The EU's PRERs are so complex and underspecified that even the affiliates of MNCs in the EU have difficulty complying with them. Hence, we propose the following hypotheses.

H1. Firms that engage with GVCs are more likely to manage chemical substances in products than firms that are disengaged from GVCs.

H1a. Firms that engage with GVCs led by EU firms are more likely to manage chemical substances in products than firms that are disengaged from GVCs.

8.2.2 Direct Export Chains as PRER Transmission Channels

Capable suppliers are more independent of their upstream buyers than suppliers in captive chains are. Firms that can acquire information on foreign markets have an advantage in international competition (Morgan et al., 2004). Such suppliers can export their products directly to their overseas buyers and use their own direct trading channels as direct access channels to information about PRERs. In other words, information inefficiencies hinder the internationalization of less capable firms such as small firms (Leonidou, 2004). Similarly, many local firms may have difficulty in finding and accessing international markets.

Exporting firms are more likely to acquire information on foreign government regulations and other market information, including environmental policies, than domestic firms. Exporting enables firms to obtain market and technological knowledge (Salomon & Jin, 2010). As Aguilera-Caracuel et al. (2012) discuss, firms that have complex international environmental experiences are likely to generate organizational capabilities useful for environmental development and taking a proactive environmental strategy. Hence, we propose the following hypothesis.

H2. Exporting firms are more likely to manage chemical substances in products than non-exporting firms are.

The difference between firms that engage in GVCs (GVC firms) and exporters should be noted. We define GVC firms as firms supplying their product for GVCs that refer to the networks of firms that procure inputs from various countries and sell the products globally. We define exporters are firms exporting their main product to one or more countries by themselves. A precise definition of exporters includes indirect exporters whose products are not exported by the producers but are used for producing export products by a downstream firm. In this study, GVC firms include both direct and indirect exporters, whereas exporters are firms that export directly and exclusive of indirect exporters. Even if firms are exporters, they do not necessarily engage in GVCs that result in firms playing a leading role in chain governance.

8.2.3 Firm Capacity and Access to PRER Information

Firm capacities affect the probability of direct exportation and of participation in GVCs. Firms with the minimum capacity necessary for entering international production networks are eligible for learning and complying with PRERs. Even if firms can join a network and access new knowledge, they need to have the capacity to apply it commercially. Therefore, acquiring this capacity used to be a serious concern for practitioners and policy makers.

Cohen and Levinthal (1990) call the ability of a firm to recognize the value of new external information, assimilate it, and apply it to commercial ends as absorptive capacity. Many previous studies have investigated the association of absorptive capacity with firm innovation and performance. However, absorptive capacity also influences environmental management (Hervani et al., 2005). Because the variable related to research and development (R&D) is a standard measure for absorptive capacity (Cohen & Levinthal, 1990), we propose the following hypothesis.

H3. Firms that conduct R&D activities are more likely to manage chemical substances in products than firms that do not conduct R&D activities.

The discussion above emphasizes the importance of participation in GVCs or the connection with the international market, and the absorptive capacity in learning and adopting management practices for chemical substances in products, without considering the characteristics of the firms. However, the foreign affiliates of MNCs, including joint ventures, have already been involved in GVCs if their parent firm is a lead firm in a GVC. MNC affiliates are more likely to be linked to foreign markets directly or through their parent firms. Even these affiliates need a certain level of absorptive capacity to receive technology transfer from their parent firms (Lanen et al., 2001; Minbaeva et al., 2003), and the affiliates are more likely to receive information about PRERs from their parent firms and to comply with the regulations. Therefore, we propose the following hypothesis.

H4. Foreign-owned firms are more likely to manage chemical substances in products than locally owned firms are.

8.3 Model

This study uses the following simple regression model to examine these hypotheses.

$$Pr(CMR_i = 1) = \alpha + \beta 1 * GVC_i + \beta 2 * EXPORTER_i + \beta 3 * R\&D_i$$
$$+ \beta 4 * FDI_i + \beta 5 * X_i + \varepsilon_i$$

The dependent variable, CMR_i, is a binary variable for chemical management requirements (CMRs), which is equal to 1 if firm i has to manage chemicals in products, and is otherwise 0. CMRs in this study include measures for preventing products from being contaminated by hazardous chemical substances, for example, testing products, changing inputs to reduce or eliminate certain chemicals, and providing information on chemicals in products. Because the dependent variable is dichotomous, we apply the probit estimation.

The regression model includes four independent variables, of which GVC_i is an important dummy variable capturing firm i's engagement in GVCs. If firm i provides its main product to networks of firms that procure inputs from various countries and sell products globally, GVC_i is equal to 1, and is otherwise 0. The first probit estimation includes this variable as a baseline result. Then, GVC_i are categorized into two types according to the nationalities of the GVCs' lead firms: EU GVC (EU_GVC_i) and non-EU GVC ($NON\text{-}EU\_GVC_i$). If firm i's lead firms are from the EU, the independent variable for firm i that engages in GVCs led by EU firms (EU_GVC_i) is equal to 1, and is otherwise 0. Similarly, if the lead firms of GVCs that firm i belongs to are non-EU, variable $NON\text{-}EU\_GVC_i$ is equal to 1, and is otherwise 0. The nationalities of the lead firms are self-reported by firm i.

The independent variable $EXPORTER_i$ takes a value of 1 if firm i exports its main product, and is otherwise 0. The variable, $R\&D_i$, is equal to 1 if firm i conducts R&D activities, and is otherwise 0. The variable, FDI_i, identifies whether firm i accepts foreign direct investments (FDI) and is equal to 1 if firm i is foreign-owned, and is otherwise 0.

The regression model also includes a set of control variables, X_i, that consists of the number of employees ($EMPLOYEES_i$) and seven industry dummies including the reference category. The number of employees is an indicator of firm size and can be disregarded if the probability of receiving CMRs is dependent on fixed costs other than investments associated with R&D activities and entries into GVCs and foreign markets. Among the variables in the regression model, the variable $EMPLOYEES_i$ is the unique variable that is continuous instead of binary.

Industrial dummy variables, which control for industry specific effects, categorize firm i's main product or process into (1) food, beverages, or tobacco products; (2) textiles, apparel, or leather and related products; (3) wood and wood products, paper and paper products, or printing; (4) chemicals and chemicals products, pharmaceuticals, or rubber and plastic products; (5) metals, metal products, or machinery; (6) other manufacturing; and (7) wholesale trade, retail trade, or repair and installation of machinery and equipment.

The transmission channels that this study focuses on are not necessarily accessible to all firms (Leonidou, 2004). Firms that enter into foreign consumer markets or conduct R&D are capable of establishing direct accesses to information about chemical substances in products that consumer countries regulate or GVCs' lead firms manage. However, it is necessary for firms to bear a substantial amount of the fixed costs and take risks when they attempt to develop foreign markets or to innovate. Small- and medium-sized enterprises (SMEs) and local firms in developing countries may have difficulty affording large investment costs. GVCs may bring resource-limited firms indirect access to information about public product-related chemical requirements. Firms that participate in GVCs can gain preferential access to information about product-related public and private requirements that are transmitted into their value chains. Lead firms and their direct/indirect suppliers may also provide firms in their value chains with technical support or specifications to enable all firms in their chains to comply with public and private requirements. However, GVCs are not necessarily open to all firms that would like to participate. In developing countries, local firms, especially SMEs, have difficulty satisfying lead firms' high-level requirements for quality, cost, and delivery management. The regression analysis also attempts to detect transmission channels that are available for SMEs and local firms.

8.4   Data

The data set for this study comes from a questionnaire survey in Vietnam (Michida & Nabeshima, 2012; Michida et al., 2014). The main objective of the survey is to assess the impact on local industry development in developing countries of public chemical regulations, such as RoHS and REACH, and of private standards and requirements for managing chemical substances in products that consumer countries and corporate buyers impose on producers in developing countries.

For the questionnaire survey, we collaborated closely with the Vietnam Chamber of Commerce and Industry (VCCI). We developed a questionnaire, and the VCCI translated it into Vietnamese and administered the survey. The survey covered target firms operating in 63 provinces in Vietnam in the manufacturing and commercial sectors that are likely to receive requests for complying with chemical-related product requirements. VCCI took the sample from the list of firms that the General Department of Taxation maintains. The list contains 13,404 local firms and 1,954 FDI firms that include both 100% foreign-owned firms and joint ventures between local firms and MNCs. The VCCI sent the questionnaire to 11,978 firms, including 10,024 local firms that the VCCI selected randomly and all FDI firms, and they collected 1,055 responses between December 2011 and January 2012. The resulting response rate was 8.8%. We used only responses in which all of the questions necessary for the study were completed and the nationalities of lead firms were given. Consequently, a total of 436 respondents, including 262 local firms (60.1%) and 174 FDI firms (39.9%), were used for the regression analysis.

Table 8.1 summarizes the mean values of the dependent and independent variables. About 45% of the respondents need to or receive requests to take measures to comply with requirements for chemical substances in their products and 31% recognize their participation in GVCs. About 11% of the respondents engage in GVCs where firms in the EU take a leadership role in value chain governance. The respondent firms were larger and more capable than average Vietnamese firms were. The average number of employees is 742.2, about 85% are exporters, and 17% conduct R&D activities. The respondents focus mainly on producing or processing textiles, apparel, or leather and related products (40%); wood and wood products, paper and paper products, or printing (15%); and food, beverages, or tobacco products (13%).

The percentage of local firms that need to take appropriate measures to comply with CMRs (44%) is similar to that of the FDI firms (47%), even though local firms have different characteristics from FDI firms. Local firms are less likely to participate in GVCs that non-EU firms govern and are less likely to be exporters than FDI firms are. There is a considerable gap in firm size between local and FDI firms. More local firms engage in manufacturing of food, beverages, or tobacco products (18%) and wood or paper products (19%) than FDI firms, whereas 59% of the FDI firms manufacture textiles, apparel, or leather and related products. All these characteristics of local firms may cause the differences in determining the probability of encountering CMRs compared with

Table 8.1 Mean values of the dependent and independent variables

	Entire sample	Local firms	FDI firms
CMR (0/1)	0.45	0.44	0.47
GVC (0/1)	0.31	0.29	0.36
EU_GVC (0/1)	0.11	0.13	0.08
NON-EU_GVC (0/1)	0.20	0.16	0.28
EXPORTER (0/1)	0.85	0.79	0.93
R&D (0/1)	0.17	0.18	0.14
FDI (0/1)	0.40		
EMPLOYEES	742.19	496.94	1,111.48
(S.D.)	(1,404.91)	(1,252.93)	(1,538.29)
Min	2	2	3
0.25	40	20	200
Median	200	100	600
0.75	800	450	1,300
Max	10,954	10,954	10,000
Industry dummy (0/1)			
Food, beverages, tobacco	0.13	0.18	0.06
Textiles, apparel, leather	0.40	0.27	0.59
Wood, paper, printing	0.15	0.19	0.09
Chemicals, pharmaceuticals, rubber	0.06	0.06	0.07
Metal, machinery	0.08	0.08	0.08
Other manufacturing	0.15	0.18	0.10
Wholesale, retail, repair, and installation	0.03	0.03	0.01
Observations	436	262	174

Note: Table contains standard deviation, range, and percentiles of EMPLOYEES

FDI firms. This study investigates local firms' characteristics by restricting the sample to local firms and estimating the model.

8.5   Regression Results

8.5.1   Entire Sample

Columns 1 and 2 of Table 8.2 show the baseline results of the binary probit estimations that use the entire sample. Column 1 of Table 8.2 shows that the coefficient for GVC is 0.164 and is significant at the 1% level. This estimated marginal effect indicates that firms that engage in

Table 8.2 Transmission channels of chemical management requirements (entire sample, marginal effect)

	(1)	(2)	(3)	(4)	(5)	(6)
	Entire Sample		Employees < 200		Employees ≥ 200	
GVC	0.164***		0.040		0.171**	
	(0.057)		(0.093)		(0.070)	
EU_GVC		0.214***		0.180		0.168*
		(0.080)		(0.141)		(0.091)
NON-EU_GVC		0.136**		-0.041		0.168**
		(0.066)		(0.109)		(0.077)
EXPORTER	0.098	0.096	0.037	0.035	0.078	0.077
	(0.073)	(0.074)	(0.084)	(0.084)	(0.199)	(0.199)
R&D	0.185***	0.187***	0.102	0.117	0.186**	0.186**
	(0.068)	(0.067)	(0.115)	(0.117)	(0.085)	(0.085)
FDI	-0.001	0.004	-0.051	-0.048	0.005	0.005
	(0.056)	(0.057)	(0.084)	(0.086)	(0.074)	(0.076)
EMPLOYEES (100 persons)	0.006**	0.006**	0.136*	0.137*	0.005**	0.005**
	(0.003)	(0.003)	(0.071)	(0.072)	(0.002)	(0.002)
Industry dummy	Yes	Yes	Yes	Yes	Yes	Yes
Observations	436	436	208	208	228	228
LR Chi2	45.23	46.06	18.36	20.95	25.14	25.14
Prob < Chi2	0.000	0.000	0.074	0.051	0.005	0.009
Pseudo R-squared	0.082	0.083	0.078	0.084	0.103	0.103

Notes: Robust standard errors in parentheses, *** $p < 0.01$, ** $p < 0.05$, * $p < 0.1$

GVCs are 16.4% more likely to need to or receive requests to take necessary measures for complying with requirements for chemical substances in their products than those that do not engage in GVCs.

The regression model in column 2 of Table 8.2 replaces the independent variable GVC with EU_GVC (firms that engage in GVCs with EU lead firms) and NON-EU_GVC (firms that engage in GVCs with non-EU lead firms). The estimated coefficient for EU_GVC is 0.214, significant at the 1% level. The coefficient for NON-EU_GVC is 0.136, significant at the 5% level. These results suggest that firms that engage in GVCs with EU lead firms are 21.4% more likely to adopt chemical substances management than those that do not engage in GVCs. Firms that engage in GVCs with non-EU lead firms are 13.6% more likely to adopt chemical substance management than those that do not engage in GVCs. Although the estimated coefficient for EU_GVC is larger than that for NON-EU_GVC, the Wald test does not reject the hypothesis that these two coefficients are equal.

The coefficients for R&D are 0.185 and 0.187, significant at the 1% level in columns 1 and 2, indicating that firms that conduct R&D activities are 18.5–18.7% more likely to face pressure to manage chemical substances in products. The coefficients for EXPORTER and FDI in columns 1 and 2 are not statistically significant, contrary to our expectations.

We performed the same estimations as in columns 1 and 2 of Table 8.2, dividing the entire sample into two subsamples according to the median number of employees. The estimation results of the regression model in columns 3 and 4 of Table 8.2 use the observations for firms with fewer than 200 employees. The estimated coefficients for the main independent variables are not significant, contrary to the estimation results using the entire sample in columns 1 and 2.

Columns 5 and 6 of Table 8.2 present the results of the probit estimations using the observations for firms that hire 200 or more employees. The estimation results are similar to those in columns 1 and 2. The estimated coefficient for GVC in column 5 is significant at the 5% level. The coefficients for EU_GVC and NON-EU_GVC in column 6 are significant at the 10% and 5% level, respectively. The estimated marginal effect of the engagement in GVCs is about 17%, irrespective of the lead firms' home countries. The estimated coefficients for R&D in columns 5 and 6 are 0.186, significant at the 5% level.

Of the estimated coefficients for the control variables, this study reports only the coefficients for EMPLOYEES. Table 8.2 shows that the estimated coefficients are positively significant at the 5% or 10% level for all estimations in columns 1–6.

8.5.2 Local Firms

The regression analyses in Table 8.3 restrict the sample to local firms. In contrast to the estimation results that use the entire sample in columns 1–2 of Table 8.2, the coefficients for GVC, NON-EU_GVC, and EMPLOYEES are not significant. The coefficients for EU_GVC and R&D are significant at the 5% level.

The entire sample of local firms is divided into two subsamples according to the median number of employees. The probit estimations in columns 3 and 4 of Table 8.3 use the observations for local firms that hire fewer than 100 employees. Although the median values that divide the sample are different, the estimation results in columns 3 and 4 of Table 8.3 are similar to those in columns 3 and 4 of Table 8.2. The estimated coefficients for the main independent variables are not significant, whereas the coefficient for EMPLOYEES is significant at the 5% level.

The probit estimations in columns 5 and 6 of Table 8.3 use the observations for local firms that hire 100 or more employees. The estimation results are similar to those in columns 1 and 2 of Table 8.3. The estimated coefficient for EU_GVC in column 6 is significant only at the 10% level and the coefficients for R&D in columns 5 and 6 are significant at the 1% level. In contrast to columns 5 and 6 of Table 8.2, the coefficients for GVC and EMPLOYEES in columns 5 and 6 of Table 8.3 are not significant.

8.6 Conclusion

Regression analyses that use the entire sample support the first hypothesis and do not support the second hypothesis. GVCs transmit information to firms in Vietnam about chemical management that consumer countries or

Table 8.3 Transmission channels of chemical management requirements (local firms, marginal effect)

	(1)	(2)	(3)	(4)	(5)	(6)
	Local firms		Employee < 100		Employee ≥ 100	
GVC	0.113		0.022		0.096	
	(0.080)		(0.135)		(0.094)	
EU_GVC		0.238**		0.195		0.202*
		(0.097)		(0.180)		(0.107)
NON-EU_GVC		0.015		-0.092		0.006
		(0.098)		(0.152)		(0.113)
EXPORTER	0.134	0.134	0.067	0.074	-0.287	-0.288
	(0.084)	(0.085)	(0.102)	(0.102)	(0.187)	(0.182)
R&D	0.208**	0.213**	-0.007	0.005	0.267***	0.271***
	(0.085)	(0.084)	(0.138)	(0.140)	(0.095)	(0.092)
EMPLOYEES (100 persons)	0.004	0.004	0.516**	0.492**	0.002	0.002
	(0.004)	(0.004)	(0.206)	(0.207)	(0.004)	(0.004)
Industry dummy	Yes	Yes	Yes	Yes	Yes	Yes
Observations	262	262	129	129	133	133
LR Chi2	27.85	33.09	19.00	21.37	20.80	24.66
Prob < Chi2	0.002	0.001	0.040	0.030	0.014	0.006
Pseudo-R-squared	0.082	0.091	0.119	0.126	0.099	0.111

Notes: Robust standard errors in parentheses, *** $p < 0.01$, ** $p < 0.05$, * $p < 0.1$.

lead firms in GVCs require, regardless of whether the GVCs' lead firms are EU or non-EU. However, although exporting firms may have direct links with foreign markets, exporting firms are not necessarily more likely to take necessary measures to comply with requirements for chemical substances in their product than non-exporting firms as export markets include those with and without stricter regulations.

These findings indicate that GVCs are conduits for transmitting information about requirements regarding chemical substances in products. Firms in GVCs capture a global market and the lead firms in GVCs require all suppliers in their chains to assure product safety that meets various strict standards, even if they do not ship their products directly to consumer markets like the EU that restrict various chemical substances in many products. Michida and Nabeshima (2012) present several cases of firms that provide their suppliers in Vietnam with information and training necessary for complying with mandatory regulations or private standards regarding chemical substances in products. However, exporters include firms in GVCs and firms that target customers and countries without strict chemical-related requirements. Exporters include firms facing different chemical-related requirements according to final destinations of their products and corporate customers. Vietnamese exporters are not necessarily capable of entering markets with strict chemical regulations because customers in Vietnam and its neighboring countries have less stringent product safety requirements than those in developed countries. Consequently, the probability of receiving CMRs is not statistically different between exporters and non-exporters in Vietnam.

Regression analyses support the third hypothesis that firms conducting R&D activities are more likely to have to meet chemical substance requirements than firms that do not conduct R&D activities. However, the effect of R&D activities is not significant for smaller firms. These findings imply a substantial gap between larger and smaller firms in the ability to recognize CMRs, as previous work on absorptive capacity suggests (Cohen & Levinthal, 1990).

The estimated coefficients for the variable for FDI were not statistically significant, even though hypothesis 4 expects a positive relationship with the requirement to conduct chemical management. This result implies that the variable for GVC may capture information exchange between foreign affiliates and their parent firm because transactions with GVCs' lead firms can include transactions among group firms in the case of foreign-owned firms.

We recognize that there is plenty room for improvement in this study. One of the limitations is a lack of detailed analysis of indirect exporters in GVCs. Firms in GVCs include both direct and indirect exporters. Indirect exporters in GVCs are important for developing countries because local firms are more likely to participate in international markets as suppliers to GVCs than as direct exporters. However, the entire sample (436 observations) includes only 6 observations of indirect exporters in GVCs. The small number of indirect exporters in GVCs makes it difficult to examine whether GVCs transmit information on CMRs to indirect exporters.

The other limitation is a lack of international comparison between Vietnam and other countries in Southeast Asia that have undergone more advanced industrial development than Vietnam. Vietnamese firms are less capable of controlling production than those in advanced countries in Southeast Asia. Lead firms in GVCs may not ask Vietnamese firms in their chains to handle production processes that require complex chemical management. It is necessary to perform a comparative analysis with more advanced countries to determine whether GVCs transmit information about CMRs to locally owned firms.

Acknowledgement: The authors thank the Vietnam Chamber of Commerce and Industry (VCCI) for their cooperation in the survey conducted in Vietnam. All errors and limitations in this study are the responsibility of the authors. The views in this study are those of the author and do not necessarily reflect the views of the organizations. Please send correspondence to: Yasushi Ueki, Economic Research Institute for ASEAN and East Asia, Sentral Senayan II 6th Floor, Jalan Asia Afrika No.8. Gelora Bung Karno, Senayan, Jakarta Pusat 10270, Indonesia, Tel: +62-21-5797-4460 (e-mail: yasushi.ueki@eria.org).

References

Aguilera-Caracuel, J., Hurtado-Torres, N. E., & Aragón-Correa, J. A. (2012). Does international experience help firms to be green? A knowledge-based view of how international experience and organisational learning influence proactive environmental strategies. *International Business Review, 21*(5), 847–861. doi:http://dx.doi.org/10.1016/j.ibusrev.2011.09.009.

Cohen, W. M., & Levinthal, D. A. (1990). Absorptive capacity: A new perspective on learning and innovation. *Administrative Science Quarterly, 35*(1), 128–152. doi:http://dx.doi.org/10.2307/2393553.

Gereffi, G., Humphrey, J., & Sturgeon, T. (2005). The governance of global value chains. *Review of International Political Economy, 12*(1), 78–104. doi: http://dx.doi.org/10.1080/09692290500049805.

Hervani, A. A., Helms, M. M., & Sarkis, J. (2005). Performance measurement for green supply chain management. *Benchmarking: An International Journal. 12*(4), 330–353. doi:http://dx.doi.org/10.1108/14635770510609015.

Jeppesen, S., & Hansen, M. W. (2004). Environmental upgrading of Third World enterprises through linkages to transnational corporations. Theoretical perspectives and preliminary evidence. *Business Strategy and the Environment. 13*(4), 261–274. doi:http://dx.doi.org/10.1002/bse.410.

Lane, P. J., Salk, J. E., & Lyles, M. A. (2001). Absorptive capacity, learning, and performance in international joint ventures. *Strategic Management Journal, 22*(12), 1139–1161. doi: http://dx.doi.org/10.1002/smj.206.

Leonidou, L. C. (2004). An analysis of the barriers hindering small business export development. *Journal of Small Business Management, 42*(3), 279–302. doi: http://dx.doi.org/10.1111/j.1540-627X.2004.00112.x.

Michida, E., & Nabeshima, K. (2012). *Role of supply chains in adopting product related environmental regulations: Case studies of Vietnam.* (IDE Discussion Paper No. 343). Chiba: Institute of Developing Economies.

Michida, E., Nabeshima, K., & Ueki, Y. (2014). *Impact of product-related environmental regulations in Asia: descriptive statistics from a survey of firms in Vietnam.* (IDE Discussion Papers No. 466). Chiba: Institute of Developing Economies.

Minbaeva, D., Pedersen, T., Björkman, I., Fey, C. F., & Park, H. J. (2003). MNC knowledge transfer, subsidiary absorptive capacity, and HRM. *Journal of International Business Studies, 34*(6), 586–599. doi:http://dx.doi.org/10.1057/palgrave.jibs.8400056.

Morgan, N. A., Kaleka, A., & Katsikeas, C. S. (2004). Antecedents of export venture performance: A theoretical model and empirical assessment. *Journal of Marketing, 68*(1), 90–108. doi:http://dx.doi.org/10.1509/jmkg.68.1.90.24028.

Salomon, R., & Jin, B. (2010). Do leading or lagging firms learn more from exporting? *Strategic Management Journal, 31*(10), 1088–1113. doi:http://dx.doi.org/10.1002/smj.850.

United Nations Conference on Trade and Development (UNCTAD). (2010). *Non-tariff measures: Evidence from selected developing countries and future research agenda*. New York and Geneva: United Nations.

UNCTAD. (2013). *Non-tariff measures to trade: Economic and policy issues for developing countries*. Geneva: United Nations.

United Nations Industrial Development Organization (UNIDO). (2010). *Making private standards work for you: A guide to private standards in the garments, footwear and furniture sectors*. Vienna: UNIDO.

Yasushi Ueki is an Economist at Economic Research Institute for ASEAN and East Asia (ERIA), Jakarta, Indonesia. He is specialized in technology transfer, innovation, and industrial development. Prior to joining ERIA in January 2014, he was a Research Fellow at Institute of Developing Economies (IDE), Japan from 1999. From 2002 to 2005, he worked as an expert at United Nations Economic Commission for Latin America and the Caribbean, Santiago, Chile. From 2007 to 2012, he was stationed at IDE Bangkok Research Center, Thailand. He holds a PhD in international public policy from Osaka University, Japan.

Etsuyo Michida is an Associate Senior Research Fellow at Institute of Developing Economies, Japan External Trade Organization (IDE-JETRO) and was a Visiting Scholar at Haas School of Business, University of California, Berkeley from 2015 to 2017. Her research interest lies in trade and the environment with a special focus on developing countries. She has recently researched on the relationship between environmental regulation, firm behavior, and global supply chains. She holds a PhD in Economics from Graduate School of International Cooperation Studies, Kobe University.

Kaoru Nabeshima is an Associate Professor at the Graduate School of Asia-Pacific Studies, Waseda University. He holds a PhD in Economics from University of California-Davis, and a BA in Economics from Ohio Wesleyan University. Prior to joining Graduate School of Asia-Pacific Studies, Waseda University in 2015, he worked for the Institute of Developing Economies, Japan External Trade Organization and the World Bank. Some of his publications include *Meeting Standards, Winning Markets: Regional Trade Standards Compliance Report East Asia 2013* (IDE-JETRO/UNIDO 2013),

Tiger Economies under Threat (co-authored with Shahid Yusuf, 2009), and *Some Small Countries Do It Better: Rapid Growth and Its Causes in Singapore, Finland, and Ireland* (co-authored with Shahid Yusuf, 2012). His research interests lie in examining the relationship between regulations and international trade, the issue of middle income trap, and the innovation capabilities of firms in East Asia.

9

Effects of Chemical Safety Standards on Production Cost in Malaysia and Vietnam

Keiichiro Honda and Tsunehiro Otsuki

9.1 Introduction

Technical regulations for domestic or international sales, such as safety and quality requirements, are primarily designed to ensure acceptable levels of safety and quality in products. However, the regulations may

This chapter is a revised version of our article, "Effects of RoHS and REACH regulations on firm-level production and export, and the role of global value chains: The cases of Malaysia and Vietnam," published in IDE Discussion Papers No.526, IDE-JETRO. We gratefully acknowledge the financial supports given by JSPS KAKENHI Grant Number JP15H03350 and JP26780152.

K. Honda (✉)
Faculty of Administration, Prefectural University of Kumamoto, Kumamoto, Japan
e-mail: khonda@pu-kumamoto.ac.jp

T. Otsuki
Osaka School of International Public Policy, Osaka University, Osaka, Japan
e-mail: otsuki@osipp.osaka-u.ac.jp

also affect producers' production and marketing performance by requiring greater effort to meet the safety and quality requirements. Empirical studies of the effect of technical regulations on international trade have shown mixed results, partly because of the complexity of channels through which regulations affect producers and consumers (Honda et al. 2015). Xiong and Beghin (2014) suggested that the effects of technical regulations could be split into demand-side and supply-side effects, which they refer to as demand-enhancing effects and tradecost effects, respectively. The demand-side effect occurs when compliance with technical regulations increases consumer confidence in the safety and performance of the products, promoting trade. The supply-side effect occurs when compliance with technical regulations in the export market requires additional production costs from firms.

In this chapter and Chapter 10, we examine these two effects separately by using the firm-level data sets in Malaysia and Vietnam. The most important advantage of using firm-level data sets is that, unlike analysis using cross-country data sets, the effect of technical regulations on firms' production costs can be isolated from the total effects. The analyses in these chapters, particularly Chapter 10, also explicitly consider the channels of global value chains to promote the compliance of firms with Restriction of Hazardous Substances (RoHS) and Registration, Evaluation, Authorization and Restriction of Chemicals (REACH), which are examined in Chapter 8 in detail. We focus on RoHS and REACH, which are technical regulations targeting consumer and environmental safety in the EU. We analyze the effect of RoHS and REACH requirements on the performance of firms in Malaysia and Vietnam. The EU RoHS is a directive of the European Parliament and the Council restricting the use of certain hazardous substances in electrical and electronic (E&E) equipment that took effect in 2006.[1] This directive restricts the amount of hazardous substances allowed in E&E equipment. EU REACH came into force in 2007 and it regulates the use in products of chemical

---

[1] The regulated substances are lead, mercury, cadmium, polybrominated biphenyls, and polybrominated diphenyl ethers.

substances that have serious effects on consumer health and the environment. Under REACH, if a product contains chemicals classified as Substances of Very High Concern in excess of 0.1% by weight, firms are required to apply to the European Chemicals Agency for authorization.

This chapter focuses on the effect of RoHS and REACH requirements on firms' costs in Vietnam and Malaysia because the cost represents the supply-side effects of technical regulations. Chapter 10 addresses the demand-side effect, particularly the effect in export markets, because RoHS and REACH affect the demand in the export destination. We intend to provide a complete picture of the effects of these regulations on the export performance and cost-effectiveness of firms. Although production costs may increase, exports may do so as well. The empirical results will allow us to examine whether these requirements have a positive or negative net effect on firms by assessing which effect is dominant.

In this study, we use the survey data set for manufacturing firms in Malaysia and Vietnam collected by the Institute of Developing Economies during 2011–2012. The survey covered firms in a wide range of industries with respect to export and production in Malaysia and Vietnam. In the cost analysis, we evaluated the increase in variable costs arising from RoHS and REACH compliance by using an estimation from a translog cost function according to Maskus et al. (2013).

The reminder of this chapter is organized as follows. Section 9.2 gives an overview of the effects of technical regulations on firms' performance. Section 9.3 reviews related studies. Sections 9.4 and 9.5 presents the empirical methodology and describes the data. Section 9.6 shows the results and discusses implications. Section 9.7 provides the conclusion.

9.2   Background

When firms face technical regulations, such as RoHS and REACH, in the export market, their products must be redesigned, monitored, and tested, and must demonstrate compliance with the standards. Thus, technical regulations tend to impose additional costs on firms. Firms exporting to the EU will be directly affected by RoHS and REACH. In addition to the chemical industry, RoHS and REACH affect the textile, garment, wood product, plastic, rubber, machinery, and E&E industries, among others. Potentially affected industries are often located in developing countries, with those aiming to export to EU markets most affected.

Malaysia and Vietnam are rapidly industrializing countries in East Asia, and manufacturing exports have become an increasingly important engine of export-led growth for these countries. Exports of goods from Malaysia and Vietnam have grown rapidly during the past two decades (Figs. 9.1 and 9.2). Malaysia has been a World Trade Organization (WTO) member since 1995, and Vietnam joined the WTO in 2007. Although Malaysia is a larger exporter than Vietnam, exports from both countries have been increasing rapidly. This is especially true for manufactured goods, where growth has been higher than that of exports of agricultural products.

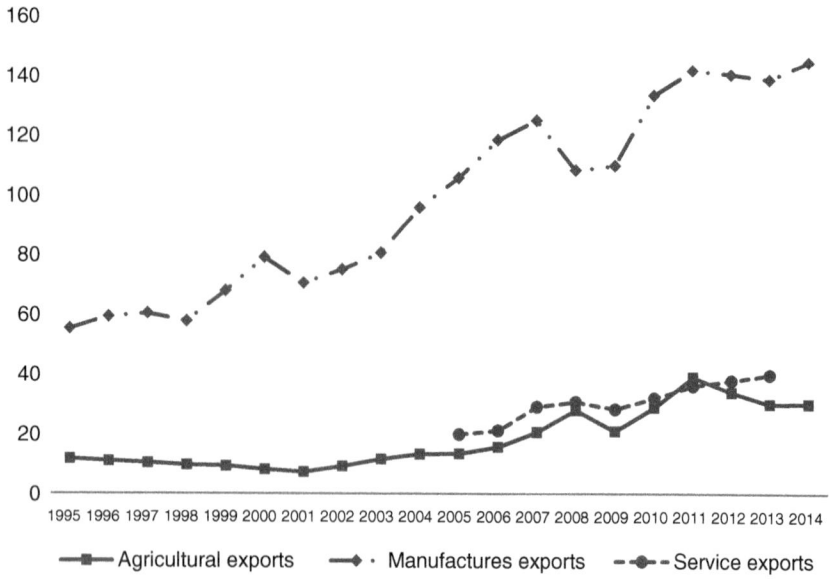

Fig. 9.1 Malaysia's exports (in billions of USD)

Source: Author's calculations from World Development Indicators data

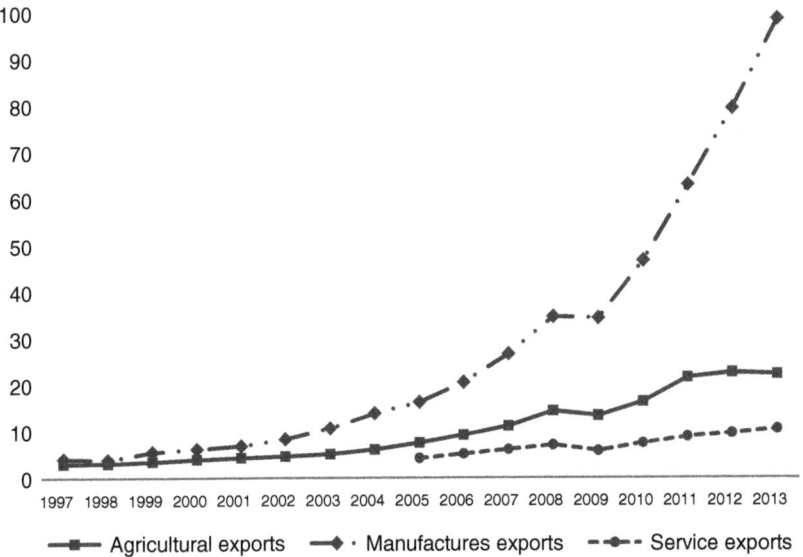

Fig. 9.2 Vietnam's exports (in billions of USD)

Source: Author's calculations from World Development Indicators data

Figure 9.2 shows the positive impact of WTO membership on Vietnam's exports. Figures 9.1 and 9.2 show the recovery from the financial crisis and a continued increase in exports. Our data show that 70% and 74% of sampled firms in Malaysia and Vietnam, respectively, exported their products.

As trade expands, these countries have faced increasing pressure from importing countries, particularly from developed countries and downstream buyers in the region, to meet safety and quality requirements. Despite the importance of building capacity to meet foreign safety and quality requirements, the rate of compliance with RoHS and REACH is not necessarily high in Malaysia and Vietnam. Based on our data, the share of firms in Malaysia complying with RoHS and REACH is 34.1% and 24.1%, respectively. Moreover, in Vietnam, the share is 8.4% for both RoHS and REACH. Thus, firms in Vietnam face much stronger pressure to upgrade their capacity in product safety and quality because the country's export trade is expected to grow.

9.3   Related Studies on the Supply-Side Effect of Technical Regulations

Producers in developing countries face capacity constraints when complying with food safety and quality standards, which are typically imposed by developed countries. The significance of this is still unclear because firm-level quantitative studies of technical regulations are limited, with research on developing countries being especially scarce.

However, country-level empirical studies that examine the effects of technical regulations on trade are more abundant, particularly in the food and agricultural sectors. Otsuki et al. (2001) used a gravity model to show that the EU's aflatoxin standards discouraged African groundnut exports to the EU. A majority of studies of this kind have found negative effects of food safety standards (e.g., Otsuki et al. (2001), Wilson et al. (2003), Chen et al. (2008), Drogué and DeMaria (2012), and Winchester et al. (2012)). Honda (2012) published one of the few studies focusing on the manufacturing sector. A gravity model was used to examine the effects of the EU's RoHS on exports to the EU market from EU and non-EU countries, and the results showed that RoHS promoted intra-EU trade, but discouraged exports from non-EU countries. Unlike the other country-level studies, Xiong and Beghin (2014) attempted to isolate the positive demand-enhancing effect of food safety standards from the negative tradecost effect by using a more sophisticated gravity model. They called these the demand-enhancing effect and tradecost effect, respectively, through structural parameters in the gravity model.

In contrast, there have been few firm-level studies. Wilson and Otsuki (2004) used the World Bank's Technical Barriers to Trade Survey Database to describe the benefits and difficulties that technical regulations pose to firms in developing countries. They showed that in 17 developing countries, approximately 70% of the surveyed firms across various industries claimed that the costs of testing and certification were likely to prevent them from exporting to major developed country markets. Approximately 80% of the surveyed firms also responded that the assurance of product quality and safety was important for expanding their exports. The firms tried to comply with the technical regulations by expanding their plants or equipment, by redesigning products, and by hiring labor for production and testing.

By using the Technical Barriers to Trade Survey Database, Maskus et al. (2013) and Chen, Otsuki and Wilson (2008) developed methods for using firm-level data to analyze the effect of technical requisitions. Maskus et al. (2013) used a translog cost function to estimate whether the presence of technical regulations would increase a firm's recurring variable production costs in addition to the initial setup costs. The initial setup costs to meet safety and quality requirements were non-trivial. From Table 4 in the study by Maskus et al. (2013), the per-firm cost of additional plant or equipment needed to meet these requirements was calculated to be 20% of investment on average, based on the firm-level survey data set of 16 selected developing countries worldwide. The cost of product redesign was 24% of investment.

Chen, Otsuki, and Wilson (2008) estimated firm-level export functions of intensive and extensive margins. They identified the factors that increase the amount of exports in a firm's total sales (intensive margin), and the number of export markets and products that are exported (extensive margin). Compliance with quality standards increased both the amount of exports and the number of export markets and products exported. In contrast, standard certification procedures reduced the number of export markets and products exported.

9.4 Empirical Strategy and Data

9.4.1 Model for Cost Estimation

Compliance with technical regulations imposes various costs on firms. Maskus et al. (2013) distinguished the initial setup costs and the running or variable costs of complying with technical regulations. Although firms can be asked directly about their initial setup costs, they often cannot give an exact amount, especially if many years have passed since they first complied with the regulations. The additional running costs associated with regulations affect the consistency and amount of exports because these costs reduce profit margins. Therefore, we follow the approach of Maskus et al. (2013) for cost function estimation and use a translog cost function, which is flexible and can incorporate non-price variables, such as factors for technical regulations.

Assuming a short-run cost function

$$C = C(w, y; s, z) \qquad (1)$$

where w is a vector of factor prices, y is output, s indicates the stringency of the technical regulations (e.g., RoHS or REACH), and z is a vector for other variables affecting firm-level costs. The firm minimizes variable costs, wx, where x is a vector of variable inputs. The cost function is assumed to have some standard properties: it does not decrease with w and y, it is concave with w, and it is homogeneous of degree one with respect to w. This general cost function has a variable for technical regulations, s, as an argument because different technical regulations should affect the choice of inputs for producing a given output level. Maskus et al. (2013) used the initial setup costs for technical regulations as a measure of the stringency of technical regulations, although we use a dummy variable indicating compliance with RoHS or REACH because of a lack of data about the setup costs associated with these regulations.

We assume that the cost function is weakly separable from the aggregator for material inputs and other inputs (separability). The separability assumption is necessary because we do not have data on the prices of materials and other inputs. Therefore, equation (1) is specified as the cost of producing net output or added value, introducing only labor and capital as variable inputs, and obtaining weak separability in this instance. This implies that the choice of the relative labor and capital inputs is independent of the material and intermediate input prices.[2] As a result, the cost function that reflects this technology is rewritten as

$$C(w, y; s, z) = (C^1(y, w^1; s, z), C^2(y, w^2; s, z)) \qquad (2)$$

---

[2] In our specific case, the separability condition is expressed as

$$\frac{\partial}{\partial w_j}\left(\frac{\partial C(w,y;s,z)/\partial w_L}{\partial C(w,y;s,z)/\partial w_K}\right) = 0,\ j \neq L, K \text{ or } \frac{\partial}{\partial w_j}\left(\frac{\partial L(w,y;s,z)}{\partial K(w,y;s,z)}\right) = 0,\ j \neq L, K.$$

where $w^1 = \{w_L, w_K)$ and w^2 is the vector of prices for variable inputs other than labor and capital. For consistency with the linear homogeneity of C with respect to w, these subcomponents of the overall cost function are assumed to be homogeneous of degree one with respect to $w1$ and $w2$, as appropriate. Separating the cost function allows us to ensure that the elasticity of cost (value added) with respect to our technical regulation variables derived from the first component ($C1$) is unaffected by the presence of the second component ($C2$). This cost elasticity can be written as[3]

$$\sigma_s \equiv \frac{\partial C^1}{\partial s}\frac{s}{C^1} = \partial \ln C^1 / \partial \ln s. \tag{3}$$

Our specification of a short-run variable cost is a translog function. This translog function allows a flexible second-order approximation to a cost structure depending on output, input prices, and other factors, including technical regulations. The specification of costs for firm i is

$$
\begin{aligned}
\ln \tilde{C}_i = {} & \beta_0 + \beta_y \ln y_i + \beta_L \ln w_{Li} + \beta_K \ln w_{Ki} + \frac{1}{2}\beta_{LL}(\ln w_{Li})^2 \\
& + \frac{1}{2}\beta_{KK}(\ln w_{Ki})^2 + \frac{1}{2}\beta_{yy}(\ln y_i)^2 + \beta_{LK} \ln w_{Li} \ln w_{Ki} + \beta_{Ly} \ln w_{Li} \ln y_i \\
& + \beta_{Ky} \ln w_{Ki} \ln y_i + \beta_s s_i + \beta_{Ls}s_i \ln w_{Li} + \beta_{Ks}s_i \ln w_{Ki} + \beta_{ys}s_i \ln y_i \\
& + \frac{1}{2}\beta_{ss}s_i^2 + \sum_{n=1}^{N}\beta_{zn}z_n + \sum_{c=1}^{C}\beta_{zc}z_c + \varepsilon_i.
\end{aligned}
$$

$$\tag{4}$$

Here, $\tilde{C}$ is value-added cost (cost of labor and capital, referred to as production costs hereafter), w_L is the wage rate, w_K is the unit price of capital, y is sales as a measure of output, and s is the firm-specific measure of technical regulations. The variables z_n and z_c are industry-specific and country-specific factors, respectively, that affect firm costs. We use industry and country dummies to control for these effects.

This translog cost function is estimated jointly with an equation for the share of labor cost in production costs as

---

[3] When the technical regulation variables are binary, we have $\sigma_s \equiv C^1(y, w^1; 1, z) - C^1(y, w^1; 0, z)$.

$$S_{Li} = \beta_L + \beta_{LL} \ln w_{Li} + \beta_{LK} \ln w_{Ki} + \beta_{Ly} \ln y_i + \beta_{Ls}s_i + \mu_i. \qquad (5)$$

We eliminate the capital share equation from the estimation because it is fully determined by the constraints below. Note that in writing these equations, we have imposed the required symmetry in cross-variable coefficients. Furthermore, the linear homogeneity condition imposes the constraints

$$\beta_L + \beta_K = 1 \qquad (6)$$

$$\beta_{KK} + \beta_{LK} = 0$$

$$\beta_{LL} + \beta_{LK} = 0$$

$$\beta_{Ly} + \beta_{Ky} = 0$$

$$\beta_{Ls} + \beta_{Ks} = 0$$

Equations (4) and (5) are estimated jointly in an iterative three-stage least squares procedure (I3SLS), subject to the constraints in equations (6). In addition to consistency and asymptotic efficiency, the I3SLS procedure guarantees identical translog cost parameters irrespective of which shared equation is dropped (Berndt and Wood 1975). The parameters for the dropped equation can be recovered by using the symmetry condition and the conditions in equations (6).

From equations (4), we can calculate the direct elasticity of production costs with respect to foreign standards as $\sigma_s^d = \beta_s + \beta_{ss} \ln s_i$, which varies with the level of technical regulations. We are also interested in the impact of the standards on factor demands. The coefficient β_{Ls} in equations (6) measures the bias toward labor use (effect on labor share) from an increase in foreign technical regulations ($\varphi_{Ls} \equiv \partial S_L / \partial \ln s = \beta_{Ls}$), and the bias toward capital use, ($\varphi_{Ks} \equiv \partial S_K / \partial \ln s = \beta_{Ks}$). The need to satisfy these technical regulations could result in an overall increase in costs, along with a bias in factor use toward either labor or capital.

In addition to the direct elasticity of cost, we can calculate the total elasticity of cost with respect to a change in the stringency of technical regulations while accounting for effects on factor use as

$$\sigma_S \equiv \frac{\partial \ln \tilde{C}}{\partial \ln s} = \beta_s + \beta_{ss} \ln s_i + \beta_{Ls} \ln w_{Li} + \beta_{Ks} \ln w_{Ki} + \beta_{ys} \ln y_i. \quad (7)$$

We are constrained to use the binary variable regarding firm's compliance with technical regulations to represent s instead of a continuous variable to measure the stringency of technical regulations. However, the use of the instrumental variables for s conveniently allows us to redefine the variable as a continuous variable. The use of instrumental variables is desirable due to possible endogeneity of firm's compliance; a firm with greater productivity or cost-efficiency is more willing to or capable of complying with technical regulations. Furthermore, applying a probit model for the RoHS/REACH adoption equation allows us to impose a range between 0 and 1 on the predicted value of s. The use of probit model for the first stage of instrumental variable estimation is acceptable under certain conditions (Wooldridge 2010). The instrumental variables include dummy variables for a request to implement measures regarding chemical substances in the firm's products, the status of acquisition of either ISO 9001 or 14001 certification, and the difficulty in procuring inputs. The question for the first instrumental variable is "Have you ever needed or been asked to implement measures regarding chemical substances in your products? Examples include the testing of products, changing inputs to reduce or eliminate certain chemicals, and providing information about chemicals contained in your products since 2000." The question for the second variable is "Do you have any internationally recognized certificates, such as ISO, and, if so, which ones?" The question for the last variable is "Have you ever experienced difficulty in procuring inputs in order to meet chemical regulations/private requirements?"

9.5   Data

9.5.1 Survey in Malaysia

The data for Malaysia were collected in the Malaysian state of Penang from 2012 to 2013.[4] Penang was chosen because of its large agglomeration of industries, with many of the target firms located in the area. The project was also endorsed by the government of Penang, as the state government recognizes the importance of the effect of regulations. The survey was conducted by PE Research of Malaysia.

Our questionnaire comprised four sections: 1) basic information, 2) input procurement and certificates, 3) chemical management, and 4) export status. The surveyed firms were sampled from the firms recorded in the Penang Industrial Census of 2011, which collected data on 2116 firms, of which 1898 were manufacturers and 218 were service firms. Beginning in November 2012, questionnaires were sent to 732 of these firms, and the questionnaires were followed up with phone calls. We received replies from 374 firms, giving us a response rate of approximately 51%.[5] From the manufacturing industries, 346 firms were chosen, and 23 firms were taken from the service sectors. We targeted sectors for which the management of chemicals contained in products was likely to be necessary. The share of small and medium enterprises, here defined as having fewer than 200 employees, was 83.4%, or 308 of the chosen firms. Among the chosen firms, 72.6% (268) were 100% locally owned, and 18.7% (69) firms were 100% foreign-owned firms; the remaining 32 firms were joint ventures between local and foreign owners.

---

[4] The data were collected under the IDE-JETRO research project "Impact of product-related environmental regulations on international trade and technological spillovers through supply chain in Asia."

[5] The authors wish to thank the local governments, Invest Penang and Penang industrial associations, Federation of Malaysian Manufacturers in the Northern Region and the Free Industrial Zone, Penang, Firms' Associationfor endorsing our research project and also those firms who kindly filled out our form.

9.5.2 Survey in Vietnam

The data for Vietnam were collected from throughout the entire country in 2011 and 2012. In Vietnam the survey was conducted by the Vietnamese Chamber of Commerce and Industry. The population consisted of firms operating according to the General Department of Taxation. Target firms included those in manufacturing and those in commerce, where the management of chemicals in products is an issue. Of the 15,358 firms, survey forms were sent to 11,978 firms across all provinces. A response rate of 8.8% (1055 firms) was obtained. Domestic firms account for 67.4% of respondents (710 firms), foreign direct investment (FDI) firms for 31.8% (335 firms), and state-owned enterprises for 0.9% (9 firms). Among respondents, 57.6% were small and medium enterprises, defined here as those with fewer than 300 employees.

9.5.3 Descriptive Statistics

The survey focused on a variety of industries in Malaysia and Vietnam. The industries studied and the number of firms are shown in Table 9.1. Hereafter, the number of samples is limited to those that are used in the subsequent empirical analysis. Table 9.2 shows descriptive statistics for the variables used in the cost analysis. The average value-added cost and sales are greater in Malaysia than in Vietnam. In Malaysia, we find that the wage rate and unit price of capital are higher. We define global value chains as networks of firms that procure inputs from various countries and sell the resulting products, such as automotive products, electronics, and garments, globally. Firms were asked whether they supplied their main products to global value chains. In Malaysia, more firms are integrated into global value chains. The number of firms complying with RoHS and REACH is also far greater in Malaysia. The survey also asked firms whether they were able to meet EU RoHS and REACH standards along with other regulations and requirements.[6]

---

[6] We assume that non-response implies non-compliance so as to prevent the loss of samples due to missing data.

Table 9.1 Industries and number of firms included in the analysis

	Number of firms	RoHS	REACH
Food products	51	3	3
Beverages	7	0	0
Textiles	25	3	5
Wearing apparel	113	11	10
Leather and related products	9	2	2
Wood and products of wood and cork, except furniture,	48	4	3
Paper and paper products	9	3	3
Printing and reproduction of recorded media	10	5	3
Coke and refined petroleum products	2	0	0
Chemicals and chemical products	17	6	6
Basic pharmaceutical products and pharmaceutical preparation	2	1	1
Rubber and plastics products	51	16	13
Other non-metallic mineral products	10	1	1
Basic metals	26	8	4
Fabricated metal products, except machinery, and equipment	43	12	8
Computer, electronic and optical products	23	13	10
Electrical equipment	17	7	3
Machinery equipment	19	2	0
Motor vehicles, trailers, and semi-trailers	5	2	1
Other transport equipment	6	0	0
Furniture	21	2	3
Other manufacturing	60	7	8
Wholesale and retail trade, and repair and installation of machinery and equipment including motor vehicles and motor-cycles	11	0	0
Others	50	3	3
Total (cumulative)	635	111	90

Source: Malaysia and Vietnam firm surveys. These counts are for the responses used in the empirical analyses

9.6   Results and Discussion

The cost function was run jointly with the labor share equation under alternative specifications. Instrumental variables were used for RoHS and REACH to mitigate the effects of endogeneity. The predicted value of RoHS or REACH from the ordinary least squares (linear probability

Table 9.2 Descriptive statistics of the variables used in the empirical analysis

	Obs.	Mean	Std. Dev.	Min	Max
Full sample					
Value added cost (million USD)	600	7.780	23.300	0.001	302.000
Sales (million USD)	600	11.900	32.100	0.049	324.000
Wage rate (USD)	600	4615.421	10249.190	0.996	194792.700
Unit capital price (USD)	600	2.166	4.038	0.000	38.333
Participation in global value chain	600	0.318	0.466	0.000	1.000
RoHS compliance	600	0.178	0.383	0.000	1.000
REACH compliance	600	0.142	0.349	0.000	1.000
Malaysia					
Value added cost (million USD)	220	15.900	36.500	0.019	302.000
Sales (million USD)	220	23.700	50.000	0.049	324.000
Wage rate (USD)	220	7129.422	8180.298	215.750	70466.650
Unit capital price (USD)	220	3.389	5.466	0.000	38.333
Participation in global value chain	220	0.518	0.501	0.000	1.000
RoHS compliance	220	0.341	0.475	0.000	1.000
REACH compliance	220	0.241	0.429	0.000	1.000
Vietnam					
Value added cost (million USD)	380	3.104	5.054	0.001	28.300
Sales (million USD)	380	5.092	7.430	0.049	28.300
Wage rate (USD)	380	3159.946	11025.540	0.996	194792.700
Unit capital price (USD)	380	1.458	2.672	0.001	20.630
Participation in global value chain	380	0.203	0.402	0.000	1.000
RoHS compliance	380	0.084	0.278	0.000	1.000
REACH compliance	380	0.084	0.278	0.000	1.000

Source: The authors' calculations from Malaysia and Vietnam firm survey data

model) of the reduced-form regression, which is a model with instruments and exogenous variables as regressors, is used in place of the original RoHS/REACH dummy. The parameter estimates with respect to translog models are presented in Table 9.3. For comparison, we also show the parameters estimated by the Cobb–Douglas functional form. Robust standard errors are reported in parentheses. The translog I model

Table 9.3 Cost function estimation

	(1)	(2)	(3)	(4)	(5)	(6)
	RoHS			REACH		
Variables	CobbDouglas	Traslog I	Traslog II	CobbDouglas	Traslog I	Traslog II
$\log y$	0.939***	0.395	0.254	0.941***	0.541**	0.563**
	(0.0107)	(0.249)	(0.291)	(0.0110)	(0.246)	(0.284)
$(\log y)^2$		0.0290*	0.0383*		0.0175	0.0150
		(0.0170)	(0.0206)		(0.0168)	(0.0202)
$\log w_L$	-0.0384***	-0.0302	-0.0634	-0.0397***	-0.0418	-0.0537
	(0.0128)	(0.0594)	(0.0619)	(0.0129)	(0.0593)	(0.0622)
$\log w_K$	0.124***	1.030***	1.063***	0.123***	1.042***	1.054***
	(0.00910)	(0.0594)	(0.0619)	(0.00917)	(0.0593)	(0.0622)
$(\log w_L)^2$		0.0674***	0.0674***		0.0684***	0.0684***
		(0.00257)	(0.00257)		(0.00255)	(0.00255)
$(\log w_K)^2$		0.0674***	0.0674***		0.0684***	0.0684***
		(0.00257)	(0.00257)		(0.00255)	(0.00255)
$\log w_L \log w_K$		-0.0674***	-0.0674***		-0.0684***	-0.0684***
		(0.00257)	(0.00257)		(0.00255)	(0.00255)
$\log w_L \log y$		-0.0153***	-0.0123***		-0.0150***	-0.0139***
		(0.00357)	(0.00393)		(0.00356)	(0.00394)
$\log w_K \log y$		0.0153***	0.0123***		0.0150***	0.0139***
		(0.00357)	(0.00393)		(0.00356)	(0.00394)
s (= RoHS or REACH)	-0.155	0.799***	2.154	-0.204	1.940***	1.736
	(0.122)	(0.279)	(1.683)	(0.158)	(0.346)	(2.123)
s^2			2.990*			-0.0358
			(1.591)			(2.468)
$s* \log w_L$			-0.0636*			-0.0271

$s^* \log w_K$					0.0636*	0.0271
					(0.0339)	(0.0423)
$s^* \log y$					-0.0999	0.0292
					(0.120)	(0.0423)
Global value chain	0.0290	-0.121	0.0373	-0.319***	-0.138	-0.322***
	(0.0458)	(0.107)	(0.0490)	(0.111)	(0.108)	(0.152)
Malaysia dummy	0.160***	-0.544***	0.154***	-0.570***	-0.561***	-0.569***
	(0.0506)	(0.116)	(0.0493)	(0.110)	(0.116)	(0.113)
Constant	0.655***	5.287***	0.647***	4.403**	6.264***	4.305**
	(0.150)	(1.822)	(0.151)	(1.798)	(2.054)	(2.006)
Observations	600	600	600	600	600	600
R-squared	0.962	0.788	0.962	0.796	0.789	0.796

Robust standard errors are in parentheses*** p<0.01, ** p<0.05, * p<0.1. The instrumental variables for 2SLS include dummy variables for the experience of a request to take chemical measures about chemical substances, the status of acquisition of either ISO 9001 or ISO 14001, and experience of a difficulty to procure inputs follows a specification without interaction terms with RoHS (or REACH); the translog II model follows the full translog specification. Robust standard errors are reported in parentheses. The equation includes industry and country fixed effects. The fit of each model is good based on adjusted R-squared coefficients. We examine local concavity in input prices and the positivity of input shares for the translog model according to procedures described by Berndt and Wood (1975). Our translog cost function satisfies these conditions.

The results of the Cobb–Douglas model estimation show that the coefficients for RoHS and REACH are both statistically insignificant. However, the Cobb-Douglas specification may be too simple to represent the underlying technology. In the translog models (translogs I and II), the coefficients for the linear RoHS and REACH variables are positive and significant in both specifications. This indicates that the direct effect of RoHS and REACH is significant and increases variable production cost. The coefficients for the quadratic RoHS and REACH are not significant. According to the translog I model, cost increases arising from tightening RoHS and REACH by a 1% equivalent increase, based on the RoHS or REACH values predicted by the first-stage regression, are 0.8% and 1.9% of total labor and capital costs, respectively.

When we take the indirect costs of technical regulations into account in the translog II model according to equation (5), the cost increases caused by RoHS and REACH under the same scenario as in translog I are 2.2% and 1.5%, respectively (Table 9.4).

Our estimate includes only labor and capital costs; thus, additional cost variables may be necessary. These could include the cost of raw materials,

Table 9.4 The effects of RoHS and REACH on the variable cost (in percentage)

RoHS			REACH		
CobbDouglas	Translog I	Traslog II	CobbDouglas	Translog I	Traslog II
−0.155	0.799***	2.184*	−0.204	1.940***	1.516**
(0.122)	(0.279)	(1.243)	(0.158)	(0.346)	(0.677)

These estimates are based on the full sample. Standard errors are in parentheses*** $p<0.01$,** $p<0.05$,* $p<0.1$.Those for translog II model are evaluated at the mean values of the variables

intermediate inputs, and other costs. Firms have also already incurred the initial setup costs for compliance with these regulations. Therefore, the costs associated with RoHS and REACH compliance appear to be non-trivial.

The effect of participating in a global value chain is only evident because the coefficients for the global value chains dummy are only significant for REACH. Thus, evidence is limited to REACH concerning a cost-saving effect from participation in global value chains.

9.7   Conclusions

This study used firm-level data to examine the impact of foreign chemical safety regulations, such as RoHS and REACH, on the production costs of firms in Malaysia and Vietnam. We found that in addition to the initial setup costs for compliance, EU RoHS and REACH implementation causes firms to incur additional variable production costs by requiring additional labor and capital expenditures of around 2.2% and 1.5% of the variable costs, respectively. Thus, this finding highlights a negative aspect of these technical regulations to obligate firms to make non-trivial effort to comply with them. A question that follows would be what are the benefits of compliance and how large they are. This question will be addressed in Chapter 10. Further work that focuses on differences in RoHS- and REACH-type chemical safety regulations across countries, in particular, between EU and non-EU countries, is necessary to make useful recommendations for exporting firms and regulating countries to avoid technical regulations that create unnecessary barriers to trade. Harmonizing regulations globally may increase economic benefits if they aim to achieve the same public goals and if cross-country differences in regulations are small.

References

Berndt, E. R., & Wood, D. O. (1975). Technology, prices, and the derived demand for energy. *The review of Economics and Statistics, 59*(3), 259–268.

Chen, C., Yang, J., & Findlay, C. (2008). Measuring the effect of food safety standards on China's agricultural exports. *Review of World Economics, 144*(1), 83–106. doi:10.1007/s10290-008-0138-z.

Chen, M. X., Otsuki, T., & Wilson, J. S. (2008). Standards and export decisions: Firm-level evidence from developing countries. *The Journal of International Trade & Economic Development*, *17*(4), 501–523. doi:http://dx.doi.org/10.1080/09638190802250027.

Drogué, S., & DeMaria, F. (2012). Pesticide residues and trade, the apple of discord? *Food Policy*, *37*(6), 641–649. doi:http://dx.doi.org/10.1016/j.foodpol.2012.06.007.

Honda, K. (2012). The effect of EU environmental regulation on international trade: Restriction of hazardous substances as a trade barrier. *IDE Discussion Papers, No.341*. http://ir.ide.go.jp/dspace/bitstream/2344/1134/1/ARRIDE_Discussion_No.341_honda.pdf.

Honda, K., Otsuki, T., & Wilson, J. S. (2015). Food safety standards and international trade: The impact on developing countries' export performance. In A. Hammoudi, C. Grazia, Y. Surry, & J. B. Traversac (Eds.), *Food safety, market organization, trade and development* (pp.151–166). London: Springer.

Maskus, K. E., Otsuki, T., & Wilson, J. S. (2013). Do foreign product standards matter? Impacts on costs for developing country exporters. *Asia-Pacific Journal of Accounting & Economics*, *20*(1), 37–57. doi:http://dx.doi.org/10.1080/16081625.2013.744685.

Otsuki, T., Wilson, J. S., & Sewadeh, M. (2001). What price precaution? European harmonisation of aflatoxin regulations and African groundnut exports. *European Review of Agricultural Economics*, *28*(3), 263–284. doi:10.1093/erae/28.3.263.

Wilson, J. S., & Otsuki, T. (2004). Standards and technical regulations and firms in developing countries: New evidence from a World Bank technical barriers to trade survey. Washington D.C.: The World Bank. http://siteresources.worldbank.org/INTRANETTRADE/Resources/Topics/Services/TBT_Data_Description.pdf.

Wilson, J. S., Otsuki, T., & Majumdsar, B. (2003). Balancing food safety and risk: do drug residue limits affect international trade in beef? *Journal of International Trade & Economic Development*, *12*(4), 377–402. doi:10.1080/0963819032000154810.

Winchester, N., Rau, M. L., Goetz, C., Larue, B., Otsuki, T., Shutes, K., & Nunes De Faria, R. (2012). The impact of regulatory heterogeneity on agri-food trade. *The World Economy*, *35*(8), 973–993. doi:10.1111/j.1467-9701.2012.01457.x.

Wooldridge, J. M., (2010). *Econometric Analysis of Cross Section and Panel Data*. Second Edition. Cambridge, MA: MIT Press.

Xiong, B., & Beghin, J. (2014). Disentangling demand-enhancing and trade-cost effects of maximum residue regulations. *Economic Inquiry*, *52*(3), 1190–1203. doi:10.1111/ecin.12082.

Keiichiro Honda is a Associate Professor at Faculty of Administration, Prefectural University of Kumamoto, Japan. He has a MA in Commercial Science from Meiji University and a PhD in Applied Economics from Osaka University. His research fields are International Economics, Industrial Organization and Applied Econometrics. His main research interests include non-tariff barriers, trade and environment, firm behavior, demand system and agricultural trade.

Tsunehiro Otsuki is a Professor of Economics at Osaka School of International Public Policy, Osaka University, Japan. Dr. Otsuki's fields of research include international trade, environmental economics and development economics. He has a wide range of publications in technical regulations such as food safety and chemical safety standards on international trade and firm performance with a particular focus on developing countries.

10

Effects of Chemical Safety Standards on Export Performance in Malaysia and Vietnam

Keiichiro Honda and Tsunehiro Otsuki

10.1 Introduction

Using a firm-level dataset in Malaysia and Vietnam, Chapter 9 presented estimates of the supply-side (trade cost) effects of selected technical regulations imposed by the EU on its imports of manufactured products: the Restriction of Hazardous Substances (RoHS) Directive, and Registration, Evaluation, Authorisation and Restriction of Chemicals (REACH). The demand-side effects of these technical regulations are also important; compliance with their requirements could enhance

K. Honda (✉)
Faculty of Administration, Prefectural University of Kumamoto, Kumamoto, Japan
e-mail: khonda@pu-kumamoto.ac.jp

T. Otsuki
Osaka School of International Public Policy, Osaka University, Osaka, Japan
e-mail: otsuki@osipp.osaka-u.ac.jp

© The Author(s) 2017   **223**
E. Michida et al. (eds.), *Regulations and International Trade*,
IDE-JETRO Series, DOI 10.1007/978-3-319-55041-1_10

demand in the export market by signaling better product safety and quality. Compliance with these requirements is therefore expected to help firms compete in the regulated market and possibly other markets as well.

Moreover, linkage between firms in upstream and downstream industries might hold important implications for compliance decisions concerning technical regulations because firms purchasing intermediate inputs could require the suppliers to comply with the regulations. This supply chain effect was investigated in Chapter 9 from the viewpoint that buyers transmit regulatory information to input suppliers, thus promoting compliance with the regulations through global value chains. Accordingly, non-exporting firms might also have an incentive to comply with technical regulations if firms exporting to the regulated market are in the same supply chains. Furthermore, pressure and assistance related to compliance with the regulations would exist for firms in upstream industries, so we can expect that compliance will be promoted if there is vertical linkage between firms.

This chapter examines the effects of compliance with the EU RoHS and REACH on the export performance of firms in Malaysia and Vietnam by using the same data sets as in Chapter 9—a survey of manufacturing firms in Malaysia and Vietnam collected by Institute of Developing Economies in 2011–2012. Also, we investigate here the indirect role of supply chains via RoHS and REACH compliance. We attempt to reveal the entire mechanism comprising regulations, supply chains, compliance, and the export performance of firms in Malaysia and Vietnam. Thus, this chapter provides an integrated view of exports, compliance with the regulations, and supply chains. Toward this end, an empirical strategy of estimating instrumental variables is adopted as it allows a two-stage model structure.

The reminder of this chapter is organized as follows. Section 10.2 reviews the literature on the effects and determinants of technical regulations. Section 10.3 presents our empirical methodology and describes the data used. Section 10.4 shows the results and discusses their implications. Section 10.5 concludes the chapter.

10.2 Effects of Technical Regulations on Export Performance

10.2.1 Demand-Side Effects of Technical Regulations

As explained in Chapter 9, most gravity model analyses have not separated the demand- and supply-side effects of technical regulations and thus end up with mixed signs of their trade impacts. Honda (2012) is the only study to use a gravity model to examine the effects of RoHS on manufacturing trade. The study's prominent finding is the contrasting effects between intra-EU trade and trade with non-EU partners (positive for the former and negative for the latter). The positive effect on intra-EU trade seems to reflect the dominance of demand-side effects over trade-cost effects. Several gravity model analyses, however, use a two-step sample selection framework, combining the export entry equation and export amount equations to investigate the supply-side (trade cost) effect of the former, and the demand-side effect of the latter, as the fixed cost of compliance affects only export entry (see, e.g., Xiong and Beghin (2014) and Ferro et al. (2015)). Xiong and Beghin (2014) developed a theory-oriented gravity model to identify the demand- and supply-side effects separately.

Demand-side effects are more likely to be seen in firm-level studies because the effect can be identified by focusing on variables for firm's export performance. Several studies support the demand-enhancing effect of compliance with technical regulations. Maertens and Swinnen (2008) point out that developed countries' stringent food safety standards do not always discourage firms in developing country. Maertens and Swinnen (2009), and Maertens et al. (2011) demonstrate through a case study of Senegal's fresh and processed fruits and vegetables industry that compliance with the food safety standards of developed countries can increase a developing country's exports to developed countries that appreciate high-quality products. Maertens et al. (2011) also point out the important role played by multinational enterprises as leaders in the food product supply chain in improving product quality and safety.

Expanding our scope to include international standards, Acharyya (2005) shows that firms certified as meeting international standards create favorable perceptions of their company or brand and attract buyers. Otsuki (2011) uses a firm-level data set from Eastern and Central Europe to show a positive impact of compliance with ISO 9001 or ISO 14001.

10.2.2 Supply Chains

East Asia is a region where international production networks are among the world's most sophisticated, as many studies have demonstrated (see, e.g., Ando and Kimura (2005)). Compliance with technical regulations is likely to be encouraged when a downstream buyer orders upstream supplies, and this supply chain management tends to work effectively for firms along the entire chain. For example, Koh et al. (2012) demonstrate the mechanism by which supply chain management encourages upstream suppliers to comply with safety requirements such as the EU's Waste Electrical and Electronic Equipment Directive and RoHS.

If the chemicals contained in a final product are regulated, then the materials, parts, and components that make up the final product must be redesigned, monitored, tested, and shown to meet the stipulated chemical thresholds. Because parts and components suppliers are often located across borders, management of supply chains, value chains, and production networks takes place across firms, industries, and countries. To add to this complexity, product-related environmental regulations on chemicals affect various industries.

10.3 Empirical Strategies and Data

10.3.1 Econometric Model

We use an estimation approach for the effects of technical regulations on various measures of the export performance of firms, namely, the firm's entry into export markets, the number of export markets entered, and the export amount.

We begin by considering a firm's entry into export markets. A binary variable is given a value of one when the firm exports to at least one foreign country and zero otherwise. A probit model is used to estimate the effects of technical regulations along with other regressors. We then focus on the number of export markets entered as a measure of export diversification. This model allows us to examine whether compliance with RoHS or REACH will afford opportunities for the firm to export to a greater variety of markets. Since we are dealing with an ordered dependent variable, an ordered probit model is used for this estimation. We focus on a firm's amount of exports as a measure of the magnitude of exports instead of entry or number of markets in order to capture the intensity of exports. Since the ordered probit estimation addresses market diversification, a complementary measure of export intensity would be (the logarithm of) the average export amount per market instead of the total export amount. It is also common in the literature to estimate the export amount model using the Heckman sample selection model while taking the sample selection into account. This sample selection is represented by the above probit model, as is typical.

We also admit the possibility of endogeneity of the RoHS and REACH variables in the export analysis because exporting firms are expected to face these regulations and are thus more inclined to comply with them. Thus, these probit models for the export regime are estimated using an instrumental variable probit (IV probit) model. The same instrumental variables as in the production analysis are used. They are selected based on the major tests to qualify instrumental variables, namely, the Cragg-Donald statistic for weak instruments, the Sargan J statistic for over-identifying restrictions, the Anderson canonical correlations Lagrange multiplier statistic for under-identification, and the Wu-Hausman statistic for exogeneity of instruments. These tests are conducted based on two-stage least squares as some of the tests are not available for the IV probit model. It is not guaranteed that the instrumental variables selected based on the export regime regression will apply to the regressions for the number of export markets, for the export amount, or for the cost function, but we use the same set of instrumental variables throughout the production and export analysis in order to maintain the integrity of the analyses. Fortunately, these instruments satisfy these tests for most of the regression models.

The role of global value chains in promoting compliance with RoHS and REACH regulations is analyzed by probit regression. We are particularly interested in whether the positive effect of global value chains remains even when a firm is a non-exporter or upstream supplier that is unlikely to be subject to a direct request from buyers in importing countries to comply with the regulations. In this way, we can examine the indirect effect of quality and safety management through the supply chain.

A firm's decision to export is appropriately modeled by a probit model. Including explanatory variables for RoHS and REACH possibly gives rise to endogeneity bias, so we use the IV probit model.

$$\Pr(Exporter_{ij}) = \beta_0 + \beta_1 s_{ij} + \beta_2 GVC_{ij} + \gamma \mathbf{Z}_{ij} + \varepsilon_{ij} \tag{1}$$

$Exporter_{ij}$ is a binary variable of export status for firm i in j industry, which takes a value of one when the firm exports to at least one foreign country and zero otherwise. A binary variable s_{ij} represents firm i's compliance with technical regulations, either RoHS or REACH. It is considered to be endogenous and, thus, is instrumented. The instrumental variables are specified as in Chapter 8: A request to implement measures regarding chemical substances in the firm's products, acquisition status of either ISO 9001 or ISO 14001 certification, and difficulty in procuring inputs. GVC_{ij} denotes the firm's participation in the global value chain. $\mathbf{Z}_{ij}$ represents the other control variables, firm age, wage, number of employees, multinational enterprise dummy, and Malaysia dummy.

To investigate the scope and nature of the effect, we extend the analysis to examine the effects of RoHS and REACH on destination-specific export behavior, diversification of export markets, and intensity or amount of exports. The previous export regression limiting the export destination to only the EU market is

$$\Pr\left(Exporter_{ij}^{EU}\right) = \beta_0 + \beta_1 s_{ij} + \beta_2 GVC_{ij} + \gamma \mathbf{Z}_{ij} + \varepsilon_{ij}. \tag{2}$$

Here, $Exporter_{ij}^{EU}$ takes a value of one when the firm exports to the EU markets and zero otherwise.

Furthermore, we examine how RoHS and REACH affect the number of export markets (destination countries of exports) by using an ordered probit model:

$$y^* = \alpha_0 + \alpha_1 s_{ij} + \alpha_2 GVC_{ij} + \lambda \mathbf{Z}_{ij} + v_{ij} \tag{3}$$

y^* is an unobservable latent regressand. The observed number of markets, y, is then given by

$$y = \begin{cases} 0 & \text{if } y^* \le 0 \\ 1 & \text{if } 0 < y^* \le \mu_1 \\ 2 & \text{if } \mu_1 < y^* \le \mu_2 \\ \vdots & \\ J & \text{if } y^* \mu_{J-1} \end{cases} \tag{4}$$

µ indicates unknown threshold parameters to be estimated with α_1, α_2, and λ.[1]

The effect of RoHS and REACH on the export amount should be estimated using the sample selection method because export decision works as the selection equation. For the selection equation, we modify the previous export regression by adding a variable for exclusion restriction. For the additional variable, we use the number of years since the main product was first produced,[2] Age_{ij}^{prod}. Thus, we estimate model

$$Exp_{ij} = \delta_0 + \delta_1 s_{ij} + \delta_2 GVC_{ij} + \varphi \mathbf{Z}_{ij} + u_{ij} \tag{5}$$

with the export entry equation (1) with Age_{ij}^{prod} being an additional regressor. Here, Exp_{ij} is the average export value per export market.

---

[1] We control for the endogeneity of the technical regulation variable in the ordered probit model by running a linear probability model in the first stage and replacing Std_{ij} by the predicted value from the first-stage estimation.

[2] We also use the predicted value of the linear probability model of the technical regulation variable for Std_{ij} in this model.

10.3.2 Indirect Effects of Global Value Chains

We also examine the effects of global supply chains by using alternatives to the global value chain variable, GVC_{ij}, which captures a firm's direct participation to global value chains and thus should capture whether a firm is likely under pressure to comply with RoHS or REACH when the firm belongs to a supply chain subject to these technical regulations. However, firms may have incentive to comply with these technical regulations to meet potential demand from buyers in downstream industries in their country for compliant intermediate inputs. This might happen even when the firm is not a part of a global supply chain. Thus, we construct linkage indices to capture the intensity of domestic vertical linkage and the influence of the export market according to the method proposed by Chenery and Watanabe (1958). We particularly focus on forward vertical linkage because RoHS and REACH compliance is expected to attract potential buyers in downstream industries. It is necessary to have the inputoutput table of a country to calculate its linkage indices, but this is available for only Vietnam not Malaysia. Thus, we limit the analysis using linkage indices to Vietnam.

We use the Chenery and Watanabe (1958)'s forward linkage index, which is defined as the sum of the output coefficients excluding the intermediate output of the firm's own.

$$FL_j = \sum_{k \neq j} \varphi_{kj}$$

Here, the output coefficient φ_{kj} is defined as x_{hj}/X_h. x_{hj} indicates elements of an $h \times j$ intermediate inputs matrix in the Vietnamese inputoutput table and X_j is the total output of sector j.

Additionally, we use the modified indices for considering linkage with other sectors. Export forward linkage is defined as

$$FL_j^{EXP} = \sum_{k \neq j} \left(\varphi_{kj} \times \frac{Export_k}{X_k} \right)$$

where $Export_k/X_k$ is the proportion of total export to total output in sector k.

Exports to the EU forward linkage is defined as

$$FL_j^{EU} = \sum_{k \neq j} \left(\varphi_{kj} \times \frac{Export_k}{X_k} \times \frac{Export_k^{EU}}{Export_k} \right)$$

where $Export_k^{EU}/Export_k$ is the proportion of exports to the EU relative to total exports in sector k.

Standard forward linkage is defined as follows:

$$FL_j^{EU} = \sum_{k \neq j} \left(\varphi_{kj} \times Share_k^s \right)$$

Here, $Share_k^s$ is the rate of compliance with each technical regulation in sector k.

10.3.3 Data

Here, we use the same firm-level survey data set of Malaysia and Vietnam as was used in the cost function analysis of Chapter 8. Therefore, the details of the survey are omitted here. The empirical analysis in this chapter uses the data on firms' export performance and export determinants including RoHS and REACH compliance. Table 10.1 shows the count of firms belonging to each industry. Table 10.2 shows descriptive statistics for the variables used in the cost analysis. The number of firms that enter the export market and the number of export markets entered are greater in Malaysia than in Vietnam. In contrast, the number of firms that export to the EU is greater in Vietnam.

Our analysis using the indices of indirect transmission of regulations is conducted for only the Vietnam samples because our linkage indices rely on the inputoutput table of Vietnam for the year 2007, obtained from the General Statistics Office of Vietnam. We match industries in our data set to the 138 categories of the Vietnam Standard Industrial Classification in the inputoutput table. A higher linkage index indicates that a firm is more closely linked with

Table 10.1 Industries included in the analysis

	Number of firms	RoHS	REACH
Food products	44	3	3
Beverages	4	0	0
Textiles	20	2	4
Wearing apparel	95	10	9
Wood and products of wood and cork, except furniture,	40	3	2
Paper and paper products	8	3	3
Printing and reproduction of recorded media	8	5	3
Coke and refined petroleum products	2	0	0
Chemicals and chemical products	16	5	5
Basic pharmaceutical products and pharmaceutical preparation	0	0	0
Rubber and plastics products	47	15	11
Other non-metallic mineral products	0	0	0
Basic metals	24	8	4
Fabricated metal products, except machinery and equipment	42	12	8
Computer, electronic and optical products	22	13	10
Electrical equipment	15	7	3
Machinery equipment	16	2	0
Motor vehicles, trailers, and semi-trailers	4	1	0
Other transport equipment	5	0	0
Furniture	16	2	3
Other manufacturing	56	7	7
Others	42	2	2
Total	526	100	77

Source: Malaysia and Vietnam firm surveys. These counts are for the responses used in the empirical analyses

downstream industries. The share of firms in downstream industries complying with REACH is greater than that complying with RoHS.

10.4 Results and Implications

In the empirical analysis, we investigated the effect of RoHS and REACH compliance on the export performance of firms. Our primary focus is whether the regulations affect the entry of firms into export markets in

Table 10.2 Descriptive statistics of the variables used in the empirical analysis

	Obs	Mean	Std. Dev.	Min	Max
Full sample					
Entry to export market	526	0.637	0.481	0.000	1.000
Entry to EU market	526	0.289	0.454	0.000	1.000
Number of export markets	526	2.036	2.348	0.000	15.000
Average export per export market (million USD)	526	2.328	9.745	0.000	162.000
Number of years since the firm was established	526	13.994	11.947	1.000	67.000
Wage rate (USD)	526	4730.319	10790.070	0.996	194792.700
Number of employees	526	359.072	907.244	2.000	10000.000
Multinational enterprise	526	0.270	0.444	0.000	1.000
Participation in global value chain	526	0.321	0.467	0.000	1.000
Number of years since the main product was first produced	526	11.966	10.203	0.000	62.000
RoHS compliance	526	0.190	0.393	0.000	1.000
REACH compliance	526	0.146	0.354	0.000	1.000
Malaysia					
Entry to export market	212	0.684	0.466	0.000	1.000
Entry to EU market	212	0.245	0.431	0.000	1.000
Number of export markets	212	2.665	2.603	0.000	12.000
Average export per export market (million USD)	212	3.728	14.600	0.000	162.000
Number of years since the firm was established	212	19.344	12.717	1.000	67.000
Wage rate (USD)	212	7041.300	8255.681	215.750	70466.650
Number of employees	212	152.363	291.153	2.000	2500.000
Multinational enterprise	212	0.212	0.410	0.000	1.000
Participation in global value chain	212	0.514	0.501	0.000	1.000
	212	15.972	11.466	0.000	62.000

(continued)

Table 10.2 (continued)

	Obs	Mean	Std. Dev.	Min	Max
Number of years since the main product was first produced					
RoHS compliance	212	0.344	0.476	0.000	1.000
REACH compliance	212	0.241	0.428	0.000	1.000
Vietnam					
Entry to export market	314	0.605	0.490	0.000	1.000
Entry to EU market	314	0.318	0.467	0.000	1.000
Number of export markets	314	1.611	2.057	0.000	15.000
Average export per export market (million USD)	314	1.383	3.641	0.000	28.300
Number of years since the firm was established	314	10.382	9.894	1.000	55.000
Wage rate (USD)	314	3170.038	11969.850	0.996	194792.700
Number of employees	314	498.634	1129.141	2.000	10000.000
Multinational enterprise	314	0.309	0.463	0.000	1.000
Participation in global value chain	314	0.191	0.394	0.000	1.000
Number of years since the main product was first produced	314	9.261	8.234	1.000	55.000
RoHS compliance	314	0.086	0.281	0.000	1.000
REACH compliance	314	0.083	0.276	0.000	1.000
Export forward linkage	314	0.117	0.156	0.005	0.795
Export to EU forward linkage	314	0.027	0.044	0.000	0.178
RoHS forward linkage	314	0.043	0.060	0.001	0.332
REACH forward linkage	314	0.040	0.052	0.001	0.267

Source: The authors' calculations from Malaysia and Vietnam firm survey data

general, but we also examine the regulations' effects on entry to the EU export market, the number of export markets, and the amount of exports. The results for RoHS and REACH are presented in Tables 10.3 and 10.4, respectively. Models (1) and (2) in Table 10.3 (models (5) and (6) in Table 10.4), respectively, show the results from the IV probit regressions examining whether compliance with RoHS (REACH) increases the likelihood of entering export markets in general and the EU export markets in particular. Instrumental variables are used to deal with possible endogeneity of RoHS (REACH). The results from the second-stage regressions indicate that compliance with RoHS and compliance with REACH increase the probability of entering both foreign markets in general and EU markets in particular, as seen from the positive and significant coefficients for RoHS and REACH in the models. Multinational enterprises are found to export more actively than local firms, but not necessarily when the EU is the destination. The variable for global value chains representing direct participation in known supply chains is found to have no significant impact for either general and EU-bound exports. The first-stage results also hold important implications regarding the determinants of RoHS and REACH compliance such as the role of supply chains in promoting the compliance. These are discussed after the discussion of the second-stage results, as they are the major concern of this chapter.

Despite the above findings, it is still unclear whether improved access to foreign export markets is predominantly due to the improved access to the EU market. Thus, we use an ordered probit model to investigate whether compliance with RoHS and REACH actually helped firms to expand into export markets outside the EU. The endogeneity of RoHS or REACH compliance is controlled by using instrumental variables as in the IV probit model for the previous estimation. We now focus on the number of export markets as the dependent variable. Model (3) in Table 10.3 (model (7) in Table 10.4) shows the results of the ordered probit estimation for the effect of RoHS (REACH) on the number of export markets. We find that compliance with RoHS and REACH significantly decreases the number of export markets.

We therefore cannot conclude that compliance with RoHS and REACH helps firms access a greater variety of countries. This is contrary to the expectation that compliance with these regulations would signal

Table 10.3 Result of export regressions (RoHS)

Variables	(1) Export		(2) Export to EU		(3) Number of export markets	(4) Export amount	
	First stage	Second stage	First stage	Second stage	Ordered probit	Outcome equation	Selection equation
RoHS		1.669***		1.790***	-0.503***	-199,462	2.147***
		(0.302)		(0.287)	(0.0986)	(4.444e+06)	(0.447)
Firm age	-0.00104	0.0117*	-0.00121	0.0137**	-0.00195	19,733	0.0559***
	(0.00148)	(0.00628)	(0.00157)	(0.00551)	(0.00136)	(54,808)	(0.0160)
Wage	9.68e-07	4.24e-06	1.26e-06	2.09e-06	-5.52e-07	75.81	6.20e-06
	(7.92e-07)	(8.17e-06)	(8.14e-07)	(4.38e-06)	(1.06e-06)	(51.79)	(8.99e-06)
Size of employment	2.80e-06	0.000272	3.96e-06	0.000146	-5.97e-05***	581.4	0.000353**
	(1.68e-05)	(0.000195)	(1.68e-05)	(9.67e-05)	(1.94e-05)	(641.1)	(0.000152)
Multinational enterprise	0.0188	0.500***	0.0238	0.0651	-0.0815**	5.636e+06***	0.603***
	(0.0351)	(0.169)	(0.0355)	(0.145)	(0.0355)	(1.487e+06)	(0.168)
Global value chains	0.125***	0.217	0.126***	-0.00137	-0.0742*	753,943	0.181
	(0.0367)	(0.181)	(0.0374)	(0.162)	(0.0394)	(1.622e+06)	(0.181)
Malaysia	0.0494	-0.268	0.0463	-0.744***	-0.0863**	5.760e+06***	-0.306
	(0.0421)	(0.175)	(0.0430)	(0.162)	(0.0430)	(1.890e+06)	(0.209)
Chemical safety requested by buyer	0.246***		0.243***				
	(0.0330)		(0.0325)				

	(1)	(2)	(3)	(4)
ISO	0.149***	0.155***		
	(0.0329)	(0.0349)		
Difficulty to procure inputs	0.133**	0.109*		
	(0.0622)	(0.0654)		
Years of production				-0.0534***
				(0.0166)
Constant	-0.0477	-0.0478	1.206e+06	-0.891***
	(0.0358)	(0.0360)	(4.064e+06)	(0.227)
Anderson canon. Corr. LM test	103.212***	103.212***	103.212***	
Cragg-Donald F test	39.368***	39.368***	39.368***	
Sargan test	2.486	3.801	4.649*	
Wu-Hausman test	18.231***	13.430***	16.748***	
Observations	526	508	526	526

Notes: Robust standard errors are in parentheses *** p < 0.01, ** p < 0.05, * p < 0.1
The first-stage result of (3) has been omitted as it is the same as that in (1)
The second-stage coefficients are the marginal effect in (1) and (2)

Table 10.4 Result of export regressions (REACH)

Variables	(5) Export		(6) Export to EU		(7) Number of export markets	(8) Export amount	
	First stage	Second stage	First stage	Second stage	Ordered probit	Outcome equation	Selection equation
REACH		2.233***		2.179***	-0.649***	-1.145e+06	2.822***
		(0.349)		(0.335)	(0.130)	(5.777e+06)	(0.593)
Firm age	0.00164	0.00655	0.00142	0.00780	-0.000380	23,323	0.0485***
	(0.00147)	(0.00679)	(0.00157)	(0.00603)	(0.00144)	(57,045)	(0.0158)
Wage	-2.27e-07	6.21e-06	-1.54e-07	4.42e-06	-1.17e-06	75.03	8.94e-06
	(8.66e-07)	(8.35e-06)	(8.62e-07)	(3.55e-06)	(1.08e-06)	(51.90)	(9.05e-06)
Size of employment	-1.22e-05	0.000291	-1.20e-05	0.000171**	-6.93e-05***	576.3	0.000388***
	(1.13e-05)	(0.000189)	(1.14e-05)	(7.38e-05)	(1.93e-05)	(640.1)	(0.000151)
Multinational enterprise	-0.00406	0.535***	-0.00110	0.101	-0.0936***	5.625e+06***	0.657***
	(0.0341)	(0.173)	(0.0346)	(0.142)	(0.0352)	(1.491e+06)	(0.168)
Global value chains	0.139***	0.115	0.137***	-0.0846	-0.0488	918,325	0.0619
	(0.0361)	(0.190)	(0.0366)	(0.167)	(0.0425)		(0.195)
Malaysia	-0.0129	-0.167	-0.00801	-0.609***	-0.120***	5.796e+06***	-0.162
	(0.0378)	(0.171)	(0.0391)	(0.163)	(0.0411)	(1.812e+06)	(0.202)
Chemical safety requested by buyer	0.177***		0.181***				
	(0.0304)		(0.0294)				

ISO	0.115***	0.122***			
	(0.0312)	(0.0320)			
Difficulty to procure inputs	0.131**	0.102			
	(0.0643)	(0.0658)			
Years of production					−0.0526***
					(0.0165)
Constant	−0.0368	−0.0373		1.288e+06	−0.885***
	(0.0342)	(0.0344)		(4.025e+06)	(0.227)
Anderson canon. Corr. LM test	67.918***	67.918***	67.918***		
CraggDonald F test	24.082***	24.082***	24.082***		
Sargan test	3.258	4.987*	5.953*		
WuHausman test	13.175***	12.186***	10.458***		
Observations	526	508	526	526	

Notes: Robust standard errors are in parentheses *** $p < 0.01$, ** $p < 0.05$, * $p < 0.1$
The first-stage result of (7) has been omitted as it is the same as that in (3)
The second-stage coefficients are the marginal effect in (5) and (6)

the safety and quality of a firm's products and helps the products gain acceptance in other markets. The negative and significant coefficients for RoHS and REACH might be because firms in Malaysia and Vietnam end up concentrating their efforts in fewer markets, most probably EU markets. In this analysis, the EU market is counted as one market even though the number of export markets increases within the EU. Thus, the decrease in the number of markets is considered to have occurred outside the EU, implying concentration of the countries' exports to the EU market. This result also implies that compliance with RoHS and REACH is effective for attracting only EU buyers and seems to suggest that caused a diversion from non-EU markets. The diversion effect seems to have outweighed the signaling effect of EU RoHS and REACH compliance for better consumer and environmental safety.

In the regression analyses up to this point, the specification of the instrumental variables is mostly appropriate regarding the under-identification test, the CraggDonald test for weak instruments, the over-identification test, and WuHausman test. The only exception is that there are some cases where the over-identification test fails at the 10% level although it is valid at the 5% level. These tests are generally supportive of the specification of instrumental variables.

Model (4) in Table 10.3 (model (8) in Table 10.4) shows the effect of RoHS (REACH) on the amount of exports by a firm instead of the effect on the export regime. The Heckman sample selection estimation is used to examine the effect of compliance with RoHS and REACH on the average amount exported per market as a measure of the intensity of export.[3] Probit regression for export market entry in the first stage works as the selection equation. The results indicate that the (log) average export amount per export market does not significantly increase with compliance with RoHS or REACH. Thus, the major benefit of RoHS and REACH compliance is entry to foreign export markets, specifically the EU markets, rather than an increase in export amount. This result is consistent with the

---

[3] It should be noted that the inverse mills ratios are insignificant in both tables, implying that sample selection is not severe enough to cause the biased coefficient estimators.

findings of Ferro et al. (2015), who note that once firms enter a market, technical regulations do not affect the export amount.

The signs of the major coefficients are largely robust even when we split the sample into Malaysia and Vietnam. Table 10.5 shows the results of the market entry regression for the individual countries.

Overall, compliance with RoHS and REACH provides firms with better access to export markets but the advantage of compliance with REACH is likely to be found in accessing the export market. This may indicate that REACH is more universal than RoHS. RoHS-type regulations are more widely adopted worldwide, but its certification requires assurance of safety in only six hazardous substances. On the other hand, compliance with REACH may be more challenging due to its coverage of all chemicals. Therefore, compliance with REACH demonstrates a greater capability of a firm to assure product safety, resulting in greater coefficients with respect to REACH in those tables.

Now, we turn to interpreting the results of the first-stage regression—the adoption equation. The first-stage results for models (1) and (2) in Table 10.3 (models (5) and (6) in Table 10.4) estimated by ordinary least squares correspond to the adoption equation for RoHS (REACH). We find that firm's participation in supply chains significantly increases the likelihood of compliance with RoHS (REACH) (see columns (1), (2), (5), and (6)). This implies that participation in supply chains tends to increase pressure from buyers in the downstream industries to comply with RoHS and REACH.

We also examine the effects of indirect transmission of RoHS and REACH regulation by using our "linkage indices," which captures the linkage of industries in Vietnam. Sometimes, even firms that do not participate in global supply chains may encounter pressure to comply with RoHS and REACH indirectly through the vertical linkage channels. This occurs when buyers in the downstream industries who purchase the firms' products as intermediate inputs are subject to RoHS and REACH, or when industries subject to RoHS and REACH are present at any downstream level in the vertical linkage. When such pressure exists, firms may tend to comply with RoHS and REACH even though they are not a part of known global supply chains. This indirect transmission of regulations is also of interest whereas the direct transmission has been addressed in Chapter 7.

Table 10.5 Results for sub-sample analysis

Variables	(9) RoHS Malaysia First stage	(9) RoHS Malaysia Second stage	(10) Vietnam First stage	(10) Vietnam Second stage	(11) REACH Malaysia First stage	(11) REACH Malaysia Second stage	(12) Vietnam First stage	(12) Vietnam Second stage
RoHS or REACH		1.110***		2.285***		1.889***		2.615***
		(0.354)		(0.712)		(0.467)		(0.743)
Firm age	-0.00241	-0.00389	0.00152	0.0206	-0.00135	-0.00357	0.00551**	0.0138
	(0.00227)	(0.00829)	(0.00256)	(0.0142)	(0.00216)	(0.00809)	(0.00257)	(0.0162)
Wage	6.74e-07	9.52e-06	6.42e-07	-3.31e-06	-1.17e-06	1.13e-05	-4.42e-07	-8.74e-07
	(2.60e-06)	(1.32e-05)	(8.67e-07)	(7.01e-06)	(2.79e-06)	(1.33e-05)	(6.89e-07)	(7.60e-06)
Size of employment	-0.000100	0.00437***	9.04e-06	0.000156	2.41e-05	0.00400**	-1.79e-05	0.000229
	(9.81e-05)	(0.00166)	(1.75e-05)	(0.000143)	(0.000106)	(0.00170)	(1.02e-05)	(0.000146)
Multinational enterprise	0.0127	0.524	0.0346	0.398*	-0.0254	0.558	0.0349	0.418*
	(0.0700)	(0.339)	(0.0368)	(0.220)	(0.0746)	(0.340)	(0.0348)	(0.218)
Global value chains	0.150***	0.226	0.0970*	0.218	0.200***	-0.0117	0.0706	0.287
	(0.0562)	(0.256)	(0.0529)	(0.293)	(0.0561)	(0.282)	(0.0481)	(0.280)
Chemical safety requested by buyers	0.428***		0.134***		0.239***		0.140***	
	(0.0550)		(0.0412)		(0.0477)		(0.0414)	
ISO	0.160***		0.115**		0.0885*		0.0875*	
	(0.0578)		(0.0504)		(0.0517)		(0.0492)	
Difficulty to procure inputs	0.0982		0.107		0.0824		0.152	
	(0.0736)		(0.108)		(0.0833)		(0.110)	
Constant	0.0137		-0.0322		-0.0254		-0.0523	
	(0.124)		(0.0350)		(0.122)		(0.0348)	
Anderson canon. Corr. LM test	65.235***		32.707***		25.215***		33.054***	
CraggDonald F test	26.415***		10.823*		8.112		10.950*	
Sargan test	3.294		0.342		3.458		0.905	
WuHausman test	13.328***		3.787*		9.736***		2.287	
Observations	202		298		202		298	

Robust standard errors are in parentheses *** p < 0.01, ** p < 0.05, * p < 0.1.

A linkage index is constructed to capture the degree of indirect transmission of regulations, and replaces the *GVC* index in the first-stage regression as one of the instrumental variables. Because the linkage index is an industry-level variable, the industry dummies need to be suppressed to avoid perfect collinearity. The results in Tables 10.6 and 10.7 indicate no evidence of the effect of indirect transmission while the RoHS and REACH variables remain positive and significant in the second-stage regression using the IV probit model.[4] The lack of significant effect of indirect transmission of the RoHS and REACH regulations contrasts with the finding in Chapter 8 that participation in global value chain robustly had a significant and positive effect on RoHS and REACH compliance in Vietnam according to Chapter 8. This implies that direct participation in global value chains gives strong incentives for firms to comply with these regulations, and that firms should be aware of their participation in the global value chains. In the absence of explicit global value chain, however, firms are not aware of the demand for RoHS and REACH compliance from the downstream firms through indirect supply chain linkage.

10.5 Conclusions

This chapter examined the demand-side effects of the EU's RoHS and REACH regulations, investigating their effects on export market access using firm-level survey data in Malaysia and Vietnam. It was found that firms' compliance with both RoHS and REACH promoted access to the EU export market as expected. However, the negative effects of compliance on the number of export markets imply that RoHS and REACH may lead to concentration of exports to the EU market. Also, the regulations did not affect export

---

[4] We maintain our specification of instrumental variables from the previous tables (except that we replace the GVC variable with our linkage indices) despite the fact that the models in Tables 10.6 and 10.7 fail to satisfy some of the qualification tests for instrumental variables. This is done for the sake of comparison.

Table 10.6 Result of export regressions with linkage index (RoHS)

Variables	(13) First stage	(14) First stage	(15) First stage	(13) Second stage	(14) Second stage	(15) Second stage
	Export	Export to EU	RoHS	Export	Export to EU	RoHS
RoHS				2.564***	2.530***	2.596***
				(0.658)	(0.635)	(0.644)
Firm age	0.00196	0.00195	0.00195	0.0207	0.0211*	0.0202
	(0.00246)	(0.00245)	(0.00246)	(0.0128)	(0.0126)	(0.0126)
Wage	2.06e-07	2.15e-07	2.08e-07	1.74e-06	1.76e-06	1.76e-06
	(7.91e-07)	(7.85e-07)	(7.97e-07)	(6.21e-06)	(6.27e-06)	(6.21e-06)
Size of employment	8.38e-06	8.69e-06	8.00e-06	0.000214	0.000220	0.000209
	(1.69e-05)	(1.69e-05)	(1.69e-05)	(0.000184)	(0.000184)	(0.000181)
Multinational enterprise	0.0297	0.0300	0.0296	0.472**	0.478**	0.465**
	(0.0350)	(0.0349)	(0.0349)	(0.201)	(0.198)	(0.200)
Chemical safety requested by buyers	0.141***	0.142***	0.139***			
	(0.0394)	(0.0383)	(0.0397)			
ISO	0.0904*	0.0908*	0.0912*			
	(0.0470)	(0.0471)	(0.0467)			
R&D	0.0132	0.0133*	0.0129			
	(0.00802)	(0.00806)	(0.00797)			
Linkage index						

Export	-0.00473		
	(0.0103)		
Export to EU		-0.00304	
		(0.00851)	
RoHS			-0.00615
			(0.00957)
Constant	-0.0429	-0.0441	-0.0531
	(0.0325)	(0.0420)	(0.0384)
Anderson canon. Corr. LM test	37.531***	37.401***	36.858
CraggDonald F test	10.298*	10.258	10.09
Sargan test	7.498*	5.486	5.784
WuHausman test	7.743*	8.359***	8.910***
Observations	314	314	314	314

Robust standard errors are in parentheses *** $p < 0.01$, ** $p < 0.05$, * $p < 0.1$

Table 10.7 Result of export regressions with linkage index (REACH)

Variables	(16)	(17)	(18)	(16)	(17)	(18)
	First stage			Second stage		
	Export	Export to EU	RoHS	Export	Export to EU	RoHS
REACH	0.00545**	0.00545**	0.00542**	2.834***	2.802***	2.844***
	(0.00243)	(0.00243)	(0.00243)	(0.681)	(0.661)	(0.674)
Firm age	$-7.79e{-}07$	$-7.69e{-}07$	$-7.70e{-}07$	0.0136	0.0141	0.0134
	(6.35e-07)	(6.32e-07)	(6.38e-07)	(0.0138)	(0.0136)	(0.0137)
Wage	$-1.72e{-}05^*$	$-1.71e{-}05^*$	$-1.73e{-}05^*$	4.51e-06	4.50e-06	4.57e-06
	(9.61e-06)	(9.60e-06)	(9.74e-06)	(6.63e-06)	(6.70e-06)	(6.68e-06)
Size of employment	0.0269	0.0271	0.0270	0.000293	0.000297	0.000292
	(0.0331)	(0.0330)	(0.0330)	(0.000183)	(0.000183)	(0.000182)
Multinational enterprise	0.147***	0.149***	0.146***	0.502***	0.508***	0.500***
	(0.0381)	(0.0371)	(0.0382)	(0.194)	(0.192)	(0.193)
Chemical safety requested by buyers	0.0625	0.0620	0.0641			
	(0.0424)	(0.0426)	(0.0426)			
ISO	0.0185*	0.0186*	0.0182*			
	(0.00992)	(0.00988)	(0.00995)			
R&D						
Linkage index						

	(1)	(2)	(3)
Export	−0.00858		
	(0.00970)		
Export to EU		−0.00716	
		(0.00798)	
REACH			−0.00882
			(0.00927)
Constant	−0.0761**	−0.0853**	−0.0865**
	(0.0314)	(0.0401)	(0.0382)
Anderson canon. Corr. LM test	40.642***	40.532***	40.438***
CraggDonald F test	11.272*	11.237*	11.207*
Sargan test	5.099	3.210	3.858
WuHausman test	8.832***	9.320***	9.591***
Observations	314	314	314

Robust standard errors are in parentheses *** $p < 0.01$, ** $p < 0.05$, * $p < 0.1$

amounts, implying that RoHS and REACH compliance facilitates only entrance of previously non-exporting firms into export markets, but does not affect the activities of incumbent exporters. The results also confirm those suggested in Chapter 7—that participation in supply chains, particularly, the global supply chains, promotes compliance with RoHS and REACH perhaps by helping firms to comply or pressuring firms to do so. However, there is no evidence that firms' indirect connections with buyers in downstream industries promote compliance with these regulations, which are based on an extended definition of supply chains.

Despite Chapter 9's finding of cost-increasing effects of RoHS and REACH, this chapter's empirical findings of positive effects of RoHS and REACH on export performance provides an optimistic view that Malaysian and Vietnamese firms are likely to overcome compliance costs and gain access at least to EU markets. It can perhaps be recommended for these countries' governments use various channels to promote exports by their firms. Such channels include (1) technical or financial assistance to reduce firm's cost burden for compliance with these regulations or to give incentives for firms to comply, and (2) promotion of firms' participation in global or even domestic supply chains.

Acknowledgment We gratefully acknowledge the financial supports given by JSPS KAKENHI Grant Number JP15H03350 and JP26780152.

References

Acharyya, R. (2005). Consumer targeting under quality competition in a liberalized vertically differentiated market. *Journal of Economic Development, 30*(1), 129–150. https://core.ac.uk/download/pdf/6294588.pdf.

Ando, M., & Kimura, F. (2005). The formation of international production and distribution networks in East Asia. In T. Ito, & A. K. Rose (Eds.,) *nternational Trade in East Asia, NBER-East Asia Seminar on Economics 14*(pp. 177–216). University of Chicago Press.

Chenery, H. B., & Watanabe, T. (1958). International comparisons of the structure of production. *Econometrica: Journal of the Econometric Society, 26* (4), 487–521. doi:10.2307/1907514.

Ferro, E., Otsuki, T., & Wilson, J. S. (2015). The effect of product standards on agricultural exports. *Food Policy, 50*, 68–79. doi:http://dx.doi.org/10.1016/j.foodpol.2014.10.016.

Honda, K. (2012). The effect of eu environmental regulation on international trade: restriction of hazardous substances as a trade barrier. *IDE Discussion Papers, No. 341*. http://ir.ide.go.jp/dspace/bitstream/2344/1134/1/ARRIDE_Discussion_No.341_honda.pdf.

Koh, S. C. L., Gunasekaran, A., & Tseng, C. S. (2012). Cross-tier ripple and indirect effects of directives WEEE and RoHS on greening a supply chain. *International Journal of Production Economics, 140*(1), 305–317. doi:http://dx.doi.org/10.1016/j.ijpe.2011.05.008.

Maertens, M., & Swinnen, J. (2008). Standards as barriers and catalysts for trade and poverty reduction. *Journal of International Agricultural Trade and Development, 4*(1), 47–62.

Maertens, M., & Swinnen, J. F. (2009). Trade, standards, and poverty: Evidence from Senegal. *World development, 37*(1), 161–178. doi:http://dx.doi.org/10.1016/j.worlddev.2008.04.006.

Maertens, M., Colen, L., & Swinnen, J. F. (2011). Globalisation and poverty in Senegal: A worst case scenario? *European Review of Agricultural Economics, 38*(1), 31–54. doi:10.1093/erae/jbq053.

Otsuki, T. (2011). Effect of International Standards Certification on Firm-Level Exports: An Application of the Control Function Approach. *Empirical Economics Letters, 10(7)*, 623–630.

Xiong, B., & Beghin, J. (2014). Disentangling demand-enhancing and trade-cost effects of maximum residue regulations. *Economic Inquiry, 52*(3), 1190–1203. doi:10.1111/ecin.12082.

Keiichiro Honda is an Associate Professor at Faculty of Administration, Prefectural University of Kumamoto, Japan. He has a MA in Commercial Science from Meiji University and a PhD in Applied Economics from Osaka University. His research fields are International Economics, Industrial Organization and Applied Econometrics. His main research interests include non-tariff barriers, trade and environment, firm behavior, demand system and agricultural trade.

Tsunehiro Otsuki is a Professor of Economics at Osaka School of International Public Policy, Osaka University, Japan. Dr. Otsuki's fields of research include international trade, environmental economics, and development economics. He has a wide range of publications in technical regulations such as food safety and chemical safety standards on international trade and firm performance with a particular focus on developing countries.

11

Diffusion of Quality and Environmental Management Systems Through Global Value Chains: Cases of Malaysia and Vietnam

Hakaru Iguchi and Toshi H. Arimura

11.1 Introduction

The momentum of globalization is unprecedented and related to the global expansion of relationships between firms caused by production fragmentation. Recently, as part of their overall business strategy, many firms have outsourced their value-adding activities that are not based on their core competencies to other businesses either nationally or internationally. Thus, the sequence of these activities outside of the core

H. Iguchi (✉)
Research Institute of Business Administration, Waseda University, Tokyo, Japan
e-mail: igchhkr@gmail.com

T.H. Arimura
Research Institute for Environmental Economics and Management, Waseda University, Tokyo, Japan
e-mail: toshi.arimura@gmail.com

© The Author(s) 2017   **251**
E. Michida et al. (eds.), *Regulations and International Trade*,
IDE-JETRO Series, DOI 10.1007/978-3-319-55041-1_11

business, called the value chain,[1] has expanded up and downstream. In particular, the rise of offshoring[2] of intermediate inputs and assembly has had a substantial impact on the global economy. Offshoring has increased the trade flows of intermediate goods in the manufacturing sectors and has widened export markets for producers in developing countries.

Multinational enterprises (MNEs)[3] have played a prominent role in international production fragmentation because they can organize production and distribution across national boundaries. MNEs have built production bases in various locations and allocated different stages of production to different countries and regions. Thus, their value chain has expanded across the world by consigning parts of these activities to specialized external partners. Toyota, which has been expanding its globalization and localization activities, has 51 production bases in 26 different countries and regions[4] and design and R&D bases in nine locations overseas.[5]

The term "global value chain" (GVC), which reflects this trend, has attracted much attention in recent years. The concept of GVCs is important in capturing inter-firm relationships focusing on a series of flows from raw material procurement through to manufacturing and sales. This chain of activities is divided among various firms often located in various countries and regions. As value chains expand globally, final products consist of

---

[1] The idea of a value chain is closely associated with that of a supply chain. The supply chain is the network created among different companies producing, handling, and distributing a specific product. A supply chain focuses on the cost and efficiency of the supply of components and raw materials from various suppliers to the final customer, whereas a value chain incorporates the idea of value being created throughout the transactions between different companies (OECD 2013a).

[2] Offshoring refers to the purchase of intermediates from outside specialist providers abroad, which include both independent suppliers and foreign affiliates.

[3] MNE is a company that has its facilities and other assets in at least one country other than its home country. In other words, MNEs are characterized by multinationality; they are headquartered in their home country and invest in other countries. Sometimes, there are several conditions for multinationality, such as a minimum number of countries they operate in and business activities in foreign countries above a certain size. However, there are various problems with such restrictive conditions (Jones 2004).

[4] In 2014, Toyota the number of first-tier suppliers is about 5000 and that of second- or higher-tier suppliers is above 30,000 (Teikoku Databank).

[5] For further details, see Toyota HP 2017 (http://www.toyota-global.com/company/vision_philo sophy/globalizing_and_localizing_manufacturing/).

intermediates, such as components and materials, that come from a wider variety of sources because they are manufactured by various suppliers in different countries. Therefore, managing suppliers around the world is crucial for MNEs to ensure consistent quality.

However, MNEs must be cautious about various issues in expanding their international transactions. There are information asymmetries caused by cultural, geographic, and linguistic differences between developed and developing countries. Because of the information asymmetries, it is difficult to confirm the capabilities of their suppliers, especially in developing countries. International Organization for Standardization (ISO) standards can reduce these information asymmetries. For example, MNEs can decide to select firms that are ISO 9001-certified, which confirms the organizational capabilities of overseas suppliers. As a result, firms in developing countries that wish to be part of a value chain may actively seek to obtain ISO 9001 certification.

This chapter explains how the GVCs generated by the production fragmentation process affect business behavior in developing countries. Recently, various effects of globalization on developing countries have attracted much attention. We discuss whether GVCs affect the adoption of ISO 9001, focusing on Vietnam and Malaysia, which have shown rapid growth in the last few decades.

This mechanism may also apply to the adoption of ISO 14001 certification for environmental management systems. Some studies have shown that polluting industries have been migrating from developed countries to developing countries to avoid stringent environmental regulations. This is known as the pollution haven hypothesis.[6] We examine this issue from the perspective of ISO 14001. We specifically focus on product-related environmental regulations on chemicals (PRERCs), which are major environmental regulations introduced by developed economies.

This paper has the following structure. First, we discuss how Association of South East Asian Nations (ASEAN) countries became an important part

---

[6] See Grossman and Krueger (1995), Copeland and Taylor (1995), Levinson (2003) and Copeland and Taylor (2004) and Levinson (2010) for this hypothesis. The first two are classical theoretical papers.

of GVCs. Second, we review PRERCs, which were introduced in the mid-2000's in developed countries. Third, we discuss the diffusion of ISO 9001 and 14001 in ASEAN countries, especially in Malaysia and Vietnam. Then, we examine the relationship between GVCs and the diffusion of ISO 9001 and 14001 by using company survey data[7] collected in Malaysia and Vietnam. Finally, we conclude this chapter by discussing recommendations for policy makers with a possible future study.

11.2 ASEAN's role in GVCs

Southeast Asia is the region in Asia to the south of China and the east of India. Countries in this region account for almost 8% of the world's population. The region's share of the world GDP is still low, although its GDP growth rate is high, at an average of 5.4% per year in 2014 (OECD 2014). ASEAN, which is a regional cooperation organization, was established in 1967 with the signing of the Declaration of the Association of Southeast Asian Nations, also known as the Bangkok Declaration. Although ASEAN was initially more focused on regional security, its scope has expanded to include economic matters such as the establishment of a free trade area to encourage trade among ASEAN members. Consequently, economic activity in this region has developed with close links among member economies (Bower et al. 2015). ASEAN consists of 10 member states. The five founder members are Thailand, Indonesia, Singapore, Philippines, and Malaysia, followed by Brunei Darussalam, Vietnam, Laos, Myanmar, and Cambodia. These members have enjoyed rapid economic growth[8] and are now an essential part of the Asian economic miracle.

Because ASEAN countries play an important role in the global economy, these countries are being rapidly integrated into GVCs. MNEs have located some of their production processes in these countries to take advantage of lower costs and wages. Moreover, the

---

[7] For further details of these surveys, see Chapter 7.

[8] For about 25 years, from 1970 to 1995, ASEAN's GDP grew at an average annual rate of 7.0% (see ASEAN HP http://www.asean.org/asean/about-asean/history/item/economic-achievement).

expansion of the middle class has made ASEAN countries attractive to MNEs as a consumption base. Thus, as the degree of involvement in the global economy in ASEAN countries has increased through MNEs, production and exports in these countries have also increased rapidly.

Foreign direct investment (FDI) is an important tool to allow MNEs to expand into overseas markets (Oyamada and Uchida 2011). MNEs have continually rearranged their value-added activities geographically through FDI. MNEs have engaged in FDI through either acquiring existing production facilities to launch new production activities (brownfield investment) or constructing new operational facilities from the ground up (greenfield investment). Because the basic criterion of FDI is managerial control and ownership of at least 10% of the voting power, it is supposed to reflect a long-lasting commitment to the host countries. Investment criteria for MNEs include economic, institutional, political, and cultural considerations as well as the overall FDI strategy of the MNE, leading to wide variety in the structure and geographical spread of MNE activities.

ASEAN countries have tried to attract FDI in various ways, because FDI provides financial resources, links to export markets, and intangible assets that are used by MNEs to create value (Felker 2003). Extra-ASEAN FDI inflows to Southeast Asia rose by 14.7% in 2014, reaching 102 billion USD.[9] One reason for increasing investment from foreign countries is changes in the international investment environment, such as trade liberalization in ASEAN countries (Mukhopadhyay and Thomassin 2009). The establishment of the ASEAN Free Trade Area in 1992 eliminated tariff and non-tariff barriers within ASEAN countries, making the region more attractive to foreign investors. As a result, ASEAN's competitiveness as a production base in the global market was increased considerably.

In many developing countries, manufacturing activities are mainly conducted in export processing zones (EPZs). EPZs have become an integral part of the export-led development strategies of emerging and developing economies. EPZs are a policy tool used to promote economic development and export-oriented growth, and they have been used to

---

[9] ASEAN Foreign Direct Investment Statistics Database. Table 25: FDI net inflows, intra- and extra-ASEAN (http://www.asean.org/images/2015/June/FDI_tables/Table%2025.pdf).

foster manufacturing industries. Foreign investors have been attracted by EPZs with opportunities to acquire tax benefits and to facilitate import and export. The main goals of setting up EPZs are as follows: to increase foreign currency earnings by promoting non-traditional exports; to provide employment and bring income to local people; and to attract FDI, technology transfer, and information exchange with firms (Engman et al. 2007). However, setting up EPZs does not guarantee successful export expansion. The success of EPZs is more closely related to the quality of infrastructure and logistics than to low labor costs (Farole 2011). EPZs with poor governance and political instability are generally regarded as insufficient to attract foreign investors (OECD 2013b).

Since the 1970's,[10] many EPZs have been set up in ASEAN countries. Although it is difficult to pick out the effect of any single policy, EPZs in ASEAN countries have been successful in attracting FDI, in terms of accelerating exports and creating employment. For example, in Malaysia, the first EPZ was set up in 1972 in Penang. By 2015, 17 EPZs were operating in various locations.

Thus, ASEAN has attracted MNEs investments that facilitate economic growth in diverse ways. Therefore, more production activities are fragmented in Southeast Asia because of its competitive advantage, and more firms in this region are incorporated into GVCs. Because of the increase in GVCs, coordinating with suppliers is becoming more complex, especially for firms in developing countries, including ASEAN. Moreover, firms in these countries are more likely to have access to global markets if they can cooperate with leading firms of GVCs.

11.3 Coordination Through the GVC

For many MNEs, their GVCs consist of hundreds of firms with multiple tiers of suppliers, making it difficult to coordinate with suppliers across different countries and regions. However, there are cultural, geographic, and linguistic barriers between developing countries and developed countries that create information asymmetries (Potoski and Prakash 2009).

---

[10] In ASEAN countries, Malaysia set up the first EPZ near Penang's Bayan Lepas airport in 1972.

Information asymmetries cause severe problems for MNEs in developed countries. Because MNE networks for procuring, production and distribution are extended globally, it is difficult to monitor the qualifications of their suppliers and the quality of their products. If suppliers have poor management systems, this could lead to the supply of inferior quality products and unacceptable environmental performance, creating problems for downstream customer products and services (Albuquerque and Bronnenberg 2007). To confirm the quality of their suppliers, which are scattered around the world, many MNEs use international standards, specifically ISO standards such as ISO 9001. Moreover, poor management may cause poor environmental performance, which can be addressed by ISO 14001. Instead of MNEs inspecting suppliers' factories, asking suppliers to obtain ISO standards, which are certified by a third party, could reduce the burden of coordinating with suppliers for MNEs (ISO 2014).

11.3.1 ISO 9001 and 14001

When firms in developing countries are certified to these ISO standards, obstacles to international trade in GVCs are expected to decrease. In other words, these ISO standards help firms fulfill customer requirements by improving management and acting as a signal in the marketplace. In this chapter, we use "customer" to refer to manufactures purchasing products and intermediates or wholesalers, firms downstream of the value chain. Thus, firms with these certificates in developing countries have a competitive advantage in reaching the global market.

ISO 9001 was published by the ISO in 1987. It sets out the criteria for the quality management systems and specifies the requirement to prove capabilities to provide products that consistently meet customer and regulatory requirements (ISO 2002). An accredited third party completes the audit to ensure that a firm's management system meets the ISO requirements. Firms need to be audited by an ISO-approved third party every three years to maintain their certification status. Organizations with ISO 9001 certificates must meet the following requirements. First, they must define their environmental policy. Second, they must have project planning (plan). Then, they have to implement and operate (do) their policy as planned. Finally, they must check (check) and take corrective action (act). After this, they must conduct a management review. Organizations are expected to follow this plan–do–check–act (PDCA) cycle. The latest edition of ISO 9001 was published in 2015 and it focuses more on the management of processes and less on documentation, thereby easing the burden of bureaucratic activities in daily operations.

Since its initial publication, ISO 9001 has become popular among developed countries, especially in Europe and East Asia and the Pacific. As of 2014, the number of certified organizations in these two regions accounts for 84.3% of all certificates issued worldwide (Fig. 11.1). China has the highest number of ISO 9001 certified organizations, followed by Italy. The ISO 9001 standard is increasingly used worldwide. By 2014, this standard had been adopted by firms in more than 160 countries and 1,138,155 organizations were certified around the world. The widespread ISO 9001 certification has resulted from the extension of the certification

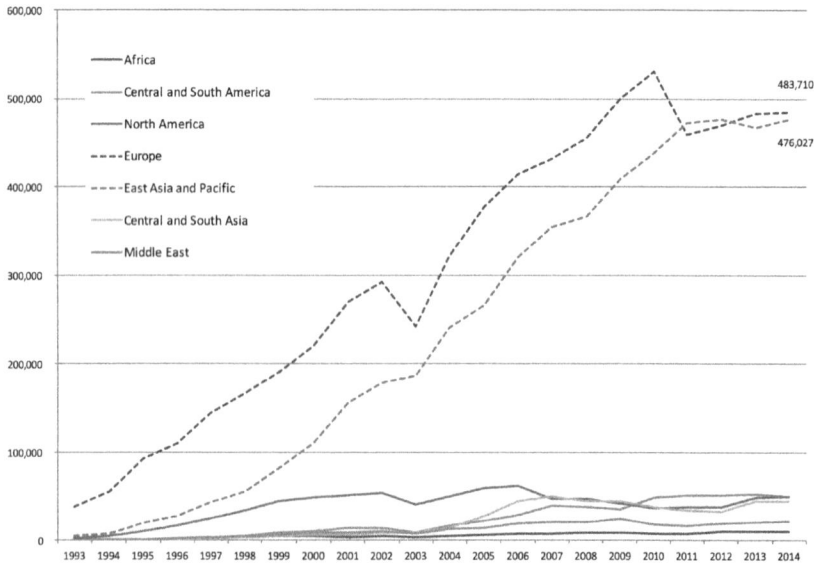

Fig. 11.1 The number of ISO 9001 certifications worldwide

Source: ISO survey (ISO 2014)

to a wide variety of industrial sectors, products, and services. Lead firms in GVCs have strongly recommended certification, also contributing to the diffusion of this standard (Heras et al. 2001).

ISO 14001, which was published in 1996, is an international standard for environmental management systems that is closely related to ISO 9001. The ISO 14001 standard is a useful tool for organizations to reduce the impact of their operations on the environment; to comply with the applicable domestic laws, regulations, and other environmentally oriented requirements; and to improve continually through the PDCA cycle. Thus, ISO 14001 is similar to ISO 9001 because it involves this management cycle. Therefore, firms with ISO 9001 certification can acquire ISO 14001 certification more easily than firms without ISO 9001.

Organizations in Europe and East Asia and Pacific have actively sought to obtain ISO 14001 certification. As of 2014, the organizations in these regions accounted for 89.5% of the certificates worldwide (Fig. 11.2). Similar to the adoption of ISO 9001, organizations in

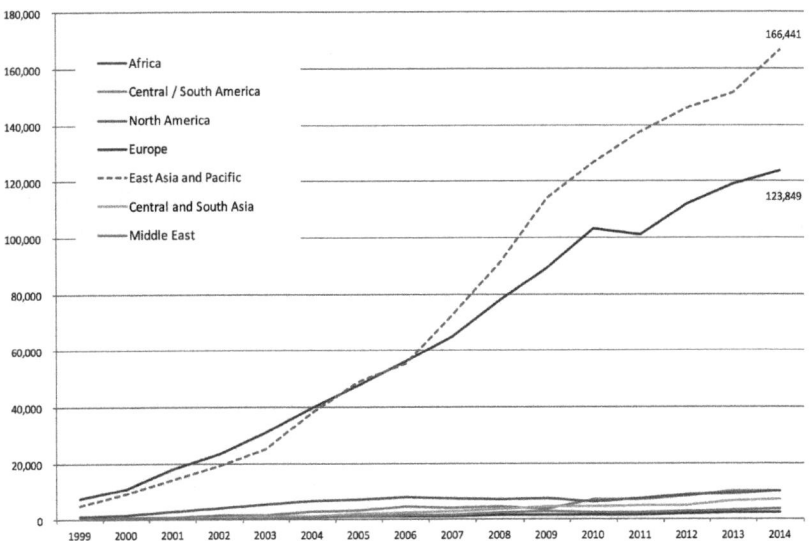

Fig. 11.2 The number of ISO 14001 certifications

Source: ISO survey (ISO 2014)

China have promoted ISO 14001 certification proactively. Japan has led the world in terms of the number of certified organizations and held the largest number of certificates until China became the top-ranked country in 2007. Though ISO 14001 is expected to improve the environmental performance of organizations, firms with this certificate do not necessarily have make improvements. Consequently, there is some doubt about its effectiveness, although numerous studies have confirmed the effectiveness of ISO 14001 in improving environmental performance. Potoski and Prakash (2005) found that ISO 14001 was effective in the US. Moreover, Arimura et al. (2008) examined the effects of ISO 14001 on the reduction of solid waste generation, depletion of natural resources, and levels of wastewater effluent. They confirmed that ISO 14001 certification led to great improvements. Thus, the effectiveness of ISO 14001 certification to protect the environment is supported by various studies, at least in developed countries (Potoski and Prakash 2005; Russo 2009; Gomez and Rodriguez 2011).

Most existing literature relating to ISO 9001 and 14001 certification has focused on developed countries or some developing countries such as China. The number of ISO-certified firms is increasing gradually in developing countries, especially in ASEAN countries. However, the number of studies of ISO certification in developing countries has been limited. Tambunlertchai et al. (2013) conducted a seminal study on ISO 14001 certification in developing countries with a large survey data set that examined the factors promoting ISO 14001 in the food and beverage, textile and apparel, and electronics and electrical appliance industries in Thailand. However, little is known about the effectiveness or incentives of ISO 9001 and 14001 adoption in developing countries.

11.3.2 ISO Certificates in Vietnam and Malaysia

In ASEAN countries, the number of ISO 9001 certificates has increased in the last 10 years. Among ASEAN countries, Vietnam ranks fifth in ISO 9001 certification, accounting for approximately 9.6% of all certificates held by these countries in 2014 (ISO 2014). Because ISO 9001 certification can reduce the overall cost of ISO 14001 certification, firms with ISO 9001 certification can obtain ISO 14001 certification more easily than firms without ISO 9001 certification (Arimura et al. 2014). However, fewer firms in Vietnam have ISO 14001 certification; Vietnam ranks fifth in terms of ISO 14001 certification in this region, with 830 certificates (Fig. 11.3).

Malaysia ranks first among the ASEAN countries for ISO 9001 certification and held 29.0% of all certificates worldwide in 2014. There are fewer ISO 14001 certificates than ISO 9001 certificates in Malaysia, as expected. Malaysia ranks second in this region with 2284 certifications (ISO 2014) (Fig. 11.4).

Next, we examine the tabulation of ISO 9001 and 14001. We use the survey conducted by the Institute of Developing Economies, Japan External Trade Organization (IDE-JETRO) in Malaysia and Vietnam in 2012 and 2011. The details of the survey are provided in Chapter 7. Table 11.1 indicates that the sample characteristics of our survey are similar to those of the ISO survey. In total, 8.5% of firms have adopted ISO 14001, whereas 24.7% have adopted ISO 9001. Furthermore, 17.7% have adopted only

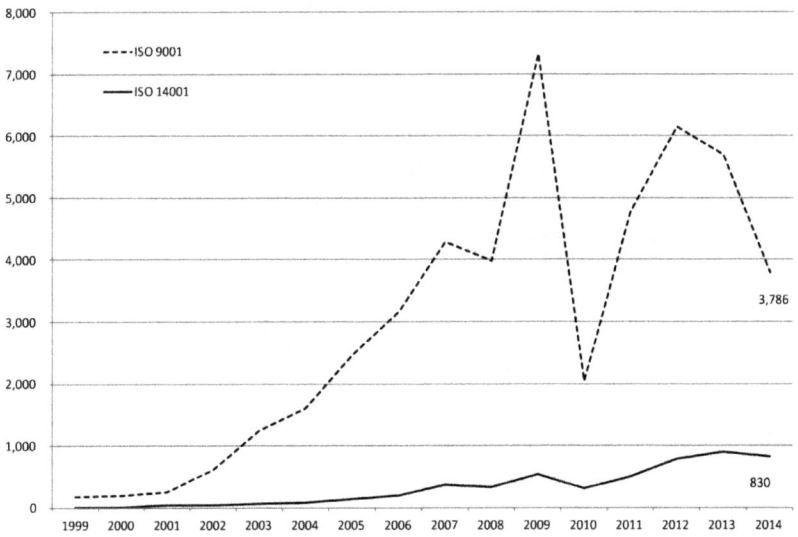

Fig. 11.3 The number of ISO 9001 and 14001 certifications in Vietnam
Source: ISO survey (ISO 2014)

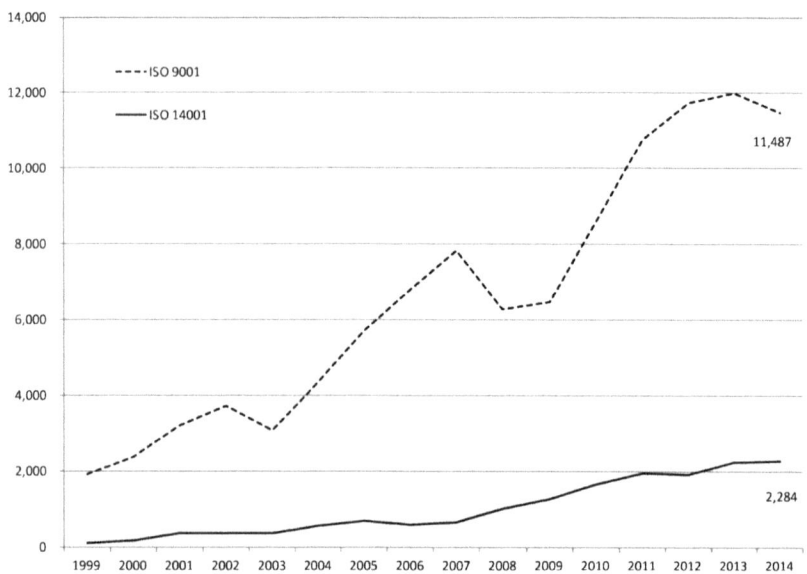

Fig. 11.4 The number of ISO 9001 and 14001 certifications in Malaysia
Source: ISO survey (ISO 2014)

ISO 9001, whereas 7.0% have adopted both ISO 14001 and 9001. These results indicate that firms in Vietnam that adopt ISO 9001 do not necessarily adopt ISO 14001. Because the number of ISO 14001 certificates has increased recently, it is important to examine whether ISO 9001 adoption also promotes ISO 14001 adoption in developing countries.[11]

Table 11.1 ISO 9001/14001 adoption in Vietnamese firms (n=1,055)

	Adopt ISO 9001	Not Adopt ISO 9001	Total
Adopt ISO 14001	7.0%	1.5%	8.5%
Not Adopt ISO 14001	17.7%	73.7%	91.5%
Total	24.7%	75.3%	

Source: IDE-JETRO survey

---

[11] Another interpretation is that ISO 9001 is a precursor to ISO 14001 because about 90% of the ISO 14,001 adopters also have ISO 9001.

Table 11.2 ISO 9001/14001 adoption in Malaysian firms (n=178)

	Adopt ISO 9001	Not Adopt ISO 9001	Total
Adopt ISO 14001	35.4%	0.6%	36.0%
Not adopt ISO 14001	48.3%	15.7%	64.0%
Total	83.7%	16.3%	

Source: IDE-JETRO survey

Table 11.2 also shows that our sample has characteristics similar to the ISO survey among Malaysian firms; 36.0% of the firms adopted ISO 14001, whereas 83.7% adopted ISO 9001. Furthermore, 48.3% adopted only ISO 9001, whereas 35.4 % of the firms adopted both ISO 14001 and 9001. This indicates that firms that adopted ISO 9001 do not necessarily adopt ISO 14001 in Malaysia, similar to Vietnamese firms at this stage.[12]

11.4 Effects of PRERCs on ISO Adoption in Malaysian and Vietnamese Firms

Recently, the importance of supply chain management has increased because of the various environmental regulations of final products in important markets such as the European Union (EU), United States of America, and other countries (Michida 2014). To comply with these PRERCs, MNEs must coordinate with their suppliers through the GVCs, because a single supplier's failure to meet the regulations in a single component could result in lack of compliance for the entire final product.

11.4.1 Product-Related Environmental Regulations

PRERCs have been introduced in many countries, and both the number and variety of PRERCs have increased worldwide (Michida 2014). Among PRERCs, the EU's Restriction of Hazardous

---

[12] From another viewpoint, however, the decision to ISO 14001 certification is not dependent upon ISO 9001, companies with 14001 certification would have adopted ISO 9001 previously.

Substances (RoHS) directive and Registration, Evaluation, Authorisation and Restriction of Chemicals (REACH) regulation are typical examples. The RoHS directive, implemented in 2006, requires hazardous substances[13] in electronic and electrical equipment to be phased out and replaced with safer substances. The REACH regulation, introduced in 2007, regulates chemical substances and articles that contain chemical substances. Because chemicals are used extensively in many products, such as clothes, furniture, and electrical and electronic equipment, PRERCs affect not only the chemical industry but also industries that rely on ingredients and materials that contain chemical substances.

One of the most important characteristics of PRERCs is that they affect the behavior of firms in developing countries (Arimura et al. 2014). If regulated chemicals are contained in final products above the permissible level, the product materials, parts, and components may need to be redesigned, monitored, tested, and approved to meet the chemical thresholds (Michida 2014). Because GVC's extend globally, PRERCs, such as RoHS and REACH, affect firms within and outside the regulated area, and MNEs need to manage suppliers across borders. The concerns about PRERCs are particularly relevant to countries in Southeast Asia, which has been a center of global manufacturing for decades and has many suppliers of parts and components to global assemblers.

It is difficult to capture the effect of a single environmental regulation, because firms are generally affected by many environmental regulations simultaneously. However, for PRERCs, it is essential to manage chemical substances throughout entire value chains. Therefore, MNEs that extend their value chain globally may request their suppliers to meet PRERCs. Such requests may transmit the information and requirements for PRERCs through the value chain, and change the business behavior in developing countries with regard to product quality and environmental performance.

---

[13] The prohibited substances are heavy metals, such as lead, mercury, cadmium, and hexavalent chromium, and flame retardants such as polybrominated biphenyls and polybrominated diphenyl ethers.

11.4.2 Requests from Customers Through GVCs

Because of PRERCs, firms that export their products to regulated markets need to manage chemical substances that are used in their products. Thus, these firms must ask their suppliers to comply with these chemical substance regulations. In particular, MNEs may need to manage product quality and environmental performance of their suppliers in developing countries. We asked several questions in the survey to reveal how PRERCs affect the behavior of firms in developing countries. First, we asked "Why did you think you needed to meet the chemical regulations/private requirements?" The responses from both Vietnamese and Malaysian firms are similar. The respondents in both countries answered that avoiding rejection of products by customers or buyers was the most important reason (Table 11.3). This indicates that PRERCs affect trading patterns of firms in developing countries. Moreover, being fully compliant with domestic regulations and requirements is also an important reason why firms meet the chemical regulations. In both countries, about 60% of firms cited these two factors as reasons for compliance.

Given the nature of ISO 9001 and 14001, firms in developing countries that have customers who require them to comply with chemical substance regulations may adopt both standards. To capture the

Table 11.3 Why did you think you needed to meet the chemical regulations/private requirements?(%)

	Vietnam (n=337)	Malaysia (n=227)
To avoid rejection of your products by customs or buyers	41.3	44.9
To be in full compliances with domestic regulations/requirement	24.9	23.4
To increase export	11.9	2.6
To improve the brand image	5.9	4.0
To keep the current transaction relationship	5.3	6.2
To increase domestic sales	5.3	0.4
To develop new transaction relationship	3.0	1.8
To attain higher sales price	1.2	0.9
Others	1.2	15.9

Source: IDE-JETRO survey

Table 11.4 Who required/recommended you to take measures about chemicals in your product? (%)

	Vietnam (n=439)	Malaysia (n=229)
Customers	59.7	72.9
Voluntary/self-initiate	29.4	8.7
Competent authority	9.6	5.2
Supplier	0.5	35.4
Industrial associations	0.2	6.6

Source: IDE-JETRO survey

effects of PRERCs, we asked the following questions. First, we asked "Have you ever needed or been asked to take measures to address chemical substances in your products after 2000?" Second, we asked, "Who required you to take measures to address chemicals in your products?" Table 11.4 shows that 59.7% of firms received requests from their customers. However, some firms take measures to address chemical substances in their product voluntarily.

Next, we examine whether requests about the usage of chemical substances from customers influences the adoption of ISO 9001 in each country. Table 11.5 shows the relationship between ISO 9001 adoption and requests about chemical substances from customers. The chi-square test reveals that there is a strong correlation between ISO 9001 adoptions and requests about chemical substances from customers

Table 11.5 The relationship between ISO 9001 certification and request from customer about chemical in Vietnam and Malaysia (%)

ISO 9001		Request from customer about Chemical			
		Vietnam		Malaysia	
		Yes	No	Yes	No
	Yes	68.0	32.0	80.1	19.9
	No	34.7	65.3	52.8	47.2
	Total	43.1	56.9	75.4	24.6
		Pearson chi2(1)=78.0 Pr=0.000		Pearson chi2(1)=12.0 Pr=0.001	

Table 11.6 The relationship between ISO 14001 adoption and request from customer about chemical in Vietnam and Malaysia (%)

ISO 14001		Request from customer about chemical			
		Vietnam		Malaysia	
		Yes	No	Yes	No
	Yes	75.0	25.0	76.8	23.2
	No	39.3	60.7	73.6	26.4
	Total	42.8	57.2	74.8	25.3
		Pearson chi2(1)=39.5		Pearson chi2(1)=0.2	
		Pr=0.000		Pr=0.625	

in both countries. This table indicates that firms in both countries may respond to requests about chemicals from customers by adopting ISO 9001. Alternatively, firms that have customers who are concerned about chemical substances and related regulations are larger and more able to adopt ISO 9001. However, about half the uncertified firms receive requests about chemicals from their customers.

The cross tabulation in Table 11.6 shows ISO 14001 adoption and requests about chemical substances from customers in Vietnam and Malaysia. The chi-square test reveals that there is a correlation between ISO 14001 adoptions and requests from customers in Vietnam,[14] whereas there is no correlation in Malaysia.

These results from Tables 11.5 and 11.6 indicate that PRERCs may promote the ISO 9001 and 14001 adoption by Vietnamese firms. For Malaysian firms, PRERCs only affected ISO 9001 adoption. However, if the effect of ISO 9001 adoption on facilitating ISO 14001 adoption is confirmed, it is possible that PRERCs facilitate ISO 14001 adoption, and consequently environmental improvement. This is an example of a regulatory race to the top. ISO 9001 certification could help firms to comply with the PRERCs because it can improve the quality of the products by

---

[14] Because only 8.5% of the sample from Vietnam was ISO 14001-certified, in absolute numbers, 6.4% of the "total" sample was ISO 14001 certified and received requests about chemicals from their customers.

improving production processes, and improve the control of chemical substances.

This result has important implications for the pollution haven hypothesis. It hints that PRERCs may improve environmental performance in developing countries if adopting ISO 14001 leads to better environmental performance, as in developed countries (Arimura et al. 2008).

11.4.3 Export and Trade

It is difficult for MNEs to monitor the product quality of suppliers in developing countries. However, ISO 9001 and 14001 certification can provide signaling that indicates that firms with these standards can meet their customers' quality and environmental expectations. In other words, with these standards, firms' unobservable characteristics can be made visible to the public. Therefore, these ISO certifications may play a large role in signaling unobservable characteristics and increasing a firm's legitimacy and trustworthiness (Zucker 1986). As a result, this certification helps firms in developing countries gain entry to the global market. Export firms in ASEAN countries are also expected to be more likely to adopt ISO 9001 or 14001 to increase their exports.

To construct the variables that capture the export status, we asked the following questions. First, we asked, "Is your main product exported?" If they responded "yes," then we categorized them as exporters. The share of exporters in our sample was 74.1% among Vietnamese firms and 76.2% among Malaysian firms. Table 11.7 shows the relationship between ISO 9001 adoption and exporters. The value of Pearson's chi-square is 20.3 in Vietnamese firms and 13.3 in Malaysian firms. Thus, we can reject the null hypotheses and conclude that the export status of the firm is related to ISO 9001 adoption in both countries. For ISO 14001, there is a significant correlation between the standard certification and exporters only for Malaysian firms (Table 11.8). These results suggest that exporters are more likely to be ISO 9001 certified in both countries. This may be because customers require their

Table 11.7 The relationship between ISO 9001 and whether exporters or not (%)

		Export			
		Vietnam		Malaysia	
		Yes	No	Yes	No
ISO 9001	Yes	84.4	15.6	89.1	10.9
	No	68.2	31.9	70.8	29.2
	Total	72.6	27.4	85.0	15.0
		Pearson chi2(1)=20.3		Pearson chi2(1)=13.3	
		Pr=0.000		Pr=0.000	

Table 11.8 The relationship between ISO 14001 and whether exporters or not (%)

		Export			
		Vietnam		Malaysia	
		Yes	No	Yes	No
ISO 14001	Yes	79.2	20.8	92.6	7.4
	No	72.8	27.2	81.9	18.1
	Total	73.3	26.7	85.0	15.0
		Pearson chi2(1)=1.3		Pearson chi2(1)=5.2	
		Pr=0.242		Pr=0.023	

suppliers in developing countries to prove the quality of their production process, which is the basis of the quality of their products. Another possibility is that manufactures in these two countries adopt ISO 9001 so that they gain a competitive advantage in quality when they try to enter global markets. In either case, ISO 9001 serves as a gateway to international markets.

11.5 Conclusion

This chapter examined the diffusion of quality management standard, ISO 9001, and environmental management standard, ISO 14001, in Vietnam and Malaysia. PRERCs in importing countries and the number of exporters to global markets may be positively related to the ISO 9001 certification. Thus, ISO 9001 certification may serve as a signal to importers. This relationship may lead to policy recommendations to governments in developing economies. For firms in developing economies to be part of GVCs, it is important that they can indicate that the quality of their products is high enough for GVCs. Our study suggests that ISO 9001 certification serves this function. Thus, if governments in developing economies want to expand exports, they should help firms to acquire ISO 19001 certificates through assistance programs[15] such as information provision and technical assistance.

The diffusion of ISO 14001 follows a similar pattern, although the relationship is not as clear as for ISO 9001. In general, the diffusion of ISO 14001 is assisted by that of ISO 9001. Thus, PRERCs or export motives may promote ISO 14001 certification through the diffusion of ISO 9001. If this is the case, PRERCs or the motivation of exports indirectly assists the diffusion of ISO 14001.

This link may have important implications for the pollution haven hypothesis. A typical argument of the hypothesis is that globalization promotes pollution in developing economies because MNEs move their production facilities to developing countries where the environmental regulations are less stringent than in developed countries. If the indirect link between PRERCs and ISO 14001 is valid, then PRERCs may be promoting better environmental performances in developing economies, assuming that ISO 14001 improves environmental performance. This argument hinges on the assumption that ISO 14001 improves environmental performance in developing economies; this assumption should be empirically examined in future work.

Our findings are also relevant to recent development of trade agreements. For example, major economies around the Pacific Ocean agreed the Trans-Pacific Partnership (TPP). If TPP is ratified, then we expect more foreign investment by MNEs and more international trade in goods and services among ratified members. If so, we expect more

---

[15] For example, Arimura and Yamamoto (2014) list the assistance programs provided by Japanese local governments to promote the adoption of ISO 14001 certificates.

investment in ASEAN, which will lead to the expansion of GVCs in the regions. Consequently, we would expect an increase in the adoption of ISO 9001 and 14001.

References

Albuquerque, P., & Bronnenberg, B. (2007). A spatiotemporal analysis of the global diffusion of ISO 9000 and ISO 14000 certification. *Management Science, 53*(3), 451–468. 10.1287/mnsc.1060.0633.

Arimura, T. H., Hibiki, A., & Katayama, H. (2008). Is a voluntary approach an effective environmental policy instrument? *Journal of Environmental Economics and Management, 55*(3), 281–295. 10.1016/j.jeem.2007.09.002.

Arimura, T. H., Iguchi, H., & Michida, E. (2014). Product-related environmental regulation and voluntary environmental actions: Impacts of RoHS and REACH in Malaysia. *IDE Discussion Papers, 454*, 1–29. Retrieved from http://ir.ide.go.jp/dspace/bitstream/2344/1317/1/ARRIDE_Discussion_No.454_arimura.pdf.

Arimura, T. H., & Yamamoto, Y. (2014). The role of local government in the voluntary approach to environmental policy: A case study of policy mix and multilevel governance aimed at sustainable development in Japan. In H. Niizawa & T. Morotomi (Eds.), *Governing low-carbon development and the economy* (pp. 132–146). Tokyo: United Nations University Press.

Bower, E. Z., Hiebert, M., Nguyen, P., & Poling, G. B. (2015). *Southeast Asia's geopolitical centrality and the US–Japan alliance*. Retrieved from https://csis-prod.s3.amazonaws.com/s3fs-public/legacy_files/files/publication/150609_Bower_SoutheastAsiaCentrality_Web.pdf.

Copeland, B. R., & Taylor, M. S. (1995). Trade and transboundary pollution. *The American Economic Review, 85*(4), 716–737, Retrieved from http://www.jstor.org/stable/2118228.

Copeland, B. R., & Taylor, M. S. (2004). Trade, growth, and the environment. *Journal of Economic Literature, 42*(1), 7–71, Retrieved from http://www.jstor.org/stable/3217036.

Engman, M., Onodera, O., & Pinali, E. (2007). *Export processing zones: Past and future role in trade and development.* OECD Trade Policy Papers, No. 53. Paris: OECD Publishing. doi: 10.1787/035168776831.

Farole, T. (2011). Special economic zones: What have we learned? *World Bank-Economic Premise.* No. 64. Retrieved from Washington DC: World Bank.

http://documents.worldbank.org/curated/en/275691468204537118/pdf/644300NEWS0Eco000PUBLIC00BOX361537B.pdf.

Felker, G. B. (2003). Southeast Asian industrialisation and the changing global production system. *Third World Quarterly*, *24*(2), 255–282. 10.1080/0143659032000074583.

Gomez, A., & Rodriguez, M. A. (2011). The effect of ISO 14001 certification on toxic emissions: An analysis of industrial facilities in the north of Spain. *Journal of Cleaner Production*, *19*(9–10), 1091–1195. 10.1016/j.jclepro.2011.01.012.

Grossman, G., & Krueger, A. (1995). Economic growth and the environment. *The Quarterly Journal of Economics*, *110*(2), 353–377. 10.2307/2118443.

Heras, I., Casadesús, M., & Ochoa, C. (2001). *Effects of ISO 9000 certification on companies' profitability: An empirical study*. Retrieved from http://www.sc.ehu.es/oewhesai/02-02%20AYR.pdf.

International Organization for Standardization. (2014). *ISO Survey*. Retrieved from http://www.iso.org/iso/iso-survey_2014.zip.

Jones, G.. (2004). *Multinationals and Global Capitalism: From the nineteenth to the twenty-first century*. Oxford: Oxford University Press.

Levinson, A. (2003). Environmental regulatory competition: A status report and some new evidence. *National Tax Journal*, *56*(1), 91–106. 10.17310/ntj.2003.1.06.

Levinson, A. (2010). Offshoring pollution: Is the United States increasingly importing polluting goods? *Review of Environmental Economics and Policy*, *4*(1), 63–83. 10.1093/reep/rep017.

Michida, E. (2014). The policy impact of product-related environmental regulations in Asia. *IDE Discussion Paper*, *451*, 1–21. Retrieved from http://ir.ide.go.jp/dspace/bitstream/2344/1314/1/ARRIDE_Discussion_No.451_michida.pdf.

Mukhopadhyay, K., & Thomassin, P. J. (2009). *Economic and environmental impact of free trade in East and South East Asia*. New York: Springer Science & Business Media.

OECD. (2013a). *Interconnected economies: benefiting from global value chains*. Paris: OECD Publishing. 10.1787/9789264189560-en.

OECD. (2013b). *Economic outlook for Southeast Asia, China and India 2014: Beyond the middle-income trap*. Paris: OECD Publishing. 10.1787/saeo-2014-en.

OECD. (2014), *Southeast Asia Investment Policy Perspectives*, Retrieved from Paris: OECD Publishing. http://www.oecd.org/daf/inv/investment-pol icy/Southeast-Asia-Investment-Policy-Perspectives-2014.pdf.

Oyamada, K., & Uchida, Y. (2011). Domestic, vertical, and horizontal multinationals: A general equilibrium approach using the "knowledge capital model". *IDE Discussion Paper, 290*, 1–35. Retrieved from http://ir.ide.go. jp/dspace/bitstream/2344/1074/1/ARRIDE_Discussion_No.290_oya mada.pdf.

Potoski, M., & Prakash, A. (2005). Green clubs and voluntary governance: ISO 14001 and firms' regulatory compliance. *American Journal of Political Science, 49*(2), 235–248. 10.1111/j.0092-5853.2005.00120.x.

Potoski, M., & Prakash, A. (2009). Information asymmetries as trade barriers: ISO 9000 increases international commerce. *Journal of Policy Analysis and Management, 28*(2), 221–238. 10.1002/pam.20424.

Russo, M. V. (2009). Explaining the impact of ISO 14001 on emission performance: A dynamic capabilities perspective on process and learning. *Business Strategy and the Environment, 18*(5), 307–319. 10.1002/ bse.587.

Tambunlertchai, K., Kontoleon, A., & Khanna, M. (2013). Assessing participation in voluntary environmental programmes in the developing world: The role of FDI and export orientation on ISO14001 adoption in Thailand. *Applied Economics, 45*(15), 2039–2048. 10.1080/ 00036846.2011.648320.

Toyota HP. (2017) *Globalizing and localizing manufacturing*. Retrieved from http://www.toyota-global.com/company/vision_philosophy/globalizing_ and_localizing_manufacturing/.

Zucker, L. G. (1986). Production of trust: Institutional sources of economic structure, 1840–1920. *Research in Organizational Behavior, 8*, 53–111.

Hakaru Iguchi is a Research Associate at Research Institute of Business Administration, Waseda University, Japan. Before joining Waseda University, he was Assistant Professor at Atomi University from 2012 to 2016. He currently teaches Environmental Management and Statistics at the undergraduate level. He obtained Master of Management at Sophia University, Japan. His recent research focuses on Green Supply Chain Management, the spillover effects of firms' voluntary environmental practices and internationalization of SMEs.

Toshi H. Arimura is a Professor of environmental economics in the Faculty of Political Science and Economics at Waseda University, Tokyo, Japan. He also serves as the director of the Research Institute for Environmental Economics and Management.His research interests encompass climate change policies, corporate environmental actions, and the innovation of environmental technology. His publication includes his coauthored book," An Evaluation of Japanese Environmental Regulation: A Quantitative Approach from Environmental Economics" from Springer. Professor Arimura received a B.A. from Tokyo University, an M.S. in Environmental Sciences from Tsukuba University, and a Ph.D. in economics from the University of Minnesota.

12

Challenges of EU Chemical Regulations: The Case of Thai Firms

Nudjarin Ramungul

12.1 Introduction

The European Union is well known among Thai producers for its environmental regulations based on the extended producer responsibility (EPR) principle and its risk-based chemical safety regulations. Examples of EPR-based regulations that have a high impact on Thai producers are the Restriction of Certain Hazardous Substances in Electrical and Electronic

This paper summarizes efforts made by the National Metal and Materials Technology Center (MTEC) and its partners to support Thai industries to adapt to products' environmental and chemical safety legislations during 2002–2012. However, the views and opinions expressed in this paper are strictly those of the author and should not be purported to represent the views of MTEC.

N. Ramungul (✉)
National Metal and Materials Technology Center, National Science and Technology Development Agency, Pathum Thani, Thailand
e-mail: nudjarr@mtec.or.th

© The Author(s) 2017 **275**
E. Michida et al. (eds.), *Regulations and International Trade*,
IDE-JETRO Series, DOI 10.1007/978-3-319-55041-1_12

Equipment (RoHS) Directive (European Parliament 2003, 2011), the End-of-Life Vehicles (ELV) Directive (European Parliament 2000), and the Packaging and Packaging Waste Directive (PPWD) (European Parliament 1994, 2004). The risk-based chemical safety regulation that imposes a high burden in Thailand is the law concerning the Registration, Evaluation, Authorization and Restriction of Chemicals regulation (European Parliament 2006), also known as the REACH regulation.

Both EPR-based regulations and the REACH regulation concern chemical substances within products that will be placed on the EU market. However, the subjects to be controlled by the two regulations are different. Subjects for EPR-based regulation or RoHS-like regulation are specific to particular products (EEE for RoHS, automotive for ELV, and packaging for PPWD), but non-specific in terms of controlled or restricted substances. For example, the RoHS restriction on lead (Pb) covers lead in any form. The directive places a limit for the total concentration of Pb in homogeneous materials. PbO and Pb_3O_4 make no difference under RoHS-like regulations. Subjects for the REACH regulation are specific to chemical substances, but not the product. Under the REACH regulation, PbO and Pb_3O_4, for example, are two different substances that have to be traced and reported separately, regardless of the type of article they are contained in. Nevertheless, both REACH and RoHS-like regulations require that relevant producers have full knowledge of possible contents of the concerned substances in materials/parts they deliver to the market and ensure that their products comply with both regulations.

During the EU's first introductions of RoHS and REACH, both EPR and risk-based chemicals control concepts were new for both Thai producers and authorities. To produce a compliant part/product, producers needed to survey all of their material inputs; remove non-compliant materials from production lines; evaluate the performances and reliabilities of substitute materials while ensuring technology compatibility with downstream processes; as well as evaluate and install new equipment to accommodate new materials technology (such as Pb-free soldering technology), if necessary. Clearly, this adjustment process could not be accomplished without the collaboration and commitment of all firms throughout the supply chain.

EEE and automotive industries in Thailand operate in a system of highly integrated supply chains. Most factories (>90%) in Thailand are parts and components makers who supply their products along local and global supply chains to finished products companies. Thai firms, therefore, were in the middle section of the worldwide supply-chain adjustment process. They had a large number of supply-chain and end-product customers who wanted confirmation along with reliable proof of compliance from them. They also sourced materials from multiple suppliers both locally and from the global market. They too had to confirm and obtain proof for all materials they used to produce their products. It is important to note that there was very little infrastructure[1] in place to facilitate firms during their transition period. It is, therefore, interesting to learn how Thai firms adjusted their practices under these complex circumstances.

This chapter discusses responses of Thai firms during their transition to bring their products into compliance with EU environmental and chemical safety (ECS) regulations through a study of survey results conducted in the period 2010–2012, along with notes of actions taken by the National Metal and Materials Technology Center (MTEC) and its ThaiRoHS Alliance partners. The discussion will focus on reactions of firms in different levels along the supply chain, namely upstream firms who produce chemicals and raw materials, middle-stream firms who transform materials into parts and components, downstream firms who produce finished parts and products and place their products on the consumer market, and packaging firms who provide packaging to all firms. Where the available data provide, this chapter will also explore the contrast of actions taken between firms in high-tech businesses [electrical and electronics (EEE) and automotive and automotive parts (Auto)] and firms in less sophisticated sectors (furniture, packaging, textiles, and food), who also faced similar challenges.

MTEC is a national research center specializing in materials technology. MTEC has played the role of providing technical assistants to help Thai

---

[1] This infrastructure includes standard test methods, reference materials to verify the reliability of test results, recognized materials testing laboratories, testing equipment, and standard procedures for verifying product compliance that all parties, especially the enforcement authority, accept, etc.

industries adjust their practice to eliminate hazardous substances from their products/processes in a more sustainable manner. ThaiRoHS Alliance, formed in 2004, is an informal group of representatives from manufacturers, research institutes, testing laboratories, equipment providers, and private and government organizations, who came forward and shared their knowledge and expertise to help establish the necessary supportive platform to improve industry's ability to handle new market regulations. During the period 2005-2012, MTEC implemented various capacity-building activities through ThaiRoHS Alliance. It also conducted timely surveys on ThaiRoHS members who attended its activities. The aims of these surveys were to assess the state of demand for ECS compliant products and the state of the target group at the time, and to gain a better understanding of factors that hinder development in order to direct more appropriate assistance.

The objective of this chapter is to learn how Thai firms realigned themselves under this complex situation. Particularly, it hopes to explore:

1. How the reactions of Thai firms evolved before the regulation and after the regulation had been introduced for some years.
2. How measures were taken by Thai firms in different supply chain levels.
3. How the position of firms in the supply chain affected the measures or reactions for regulation.
4. What barriers there are for adoption of ECS regulations.

Lessons learned from this study could help to inform relevant agencies who wish to develop appropriate support to cope with RoHS/REACH-like regulations.

12.2 Data Sources

Data sources for this chapter comprise three consecutive survey results conducted by MTEC on firms attending its training courses and seminars during the period 2010–2012. Attendants for all MTEC activities in this period were limited to ThaiRoHS.org members. Subscriptions to ThaiRoHS.org membership and MTEC activities were free of charge and open to all interested parties who agreed to share their experiences according to ThaiRoHS Alliance conduct.

The numbers of complete responses for the dataset used in this study are 122, 333, and 222 for the year 2010, 2011, and 2012 data sets, respectively. The respondent profiles, sectors served, their level in the supply chain, the number of employees, and company location, for these data sets are summarized in Fig. 12.1. Note that some respondents (e.g., plastic resins providers, metal plating providers) served multiple sectors. Therefore, the sum of frequencies in Fig. 12.1(a) may be greater than 100%.

12.3 Changes Over Time

In 2002, when Thailand took its first assessment on the state of Thai EEE industries in relation to the final draft of the RoHS directive, the implications of RoHS were not fully understood (Vossenaar et al. 2006). Out of 100 companies the government contacted, 69 answered the questionnaire and granted factory visits and management interviews. The main reasons for relative lack of response were that their emissions were within the limits of the law and they did not contain RoHS's six restricted substances. Responses from the questionnaire also followed the same track. These responses clearly indicated a lack of understanding of the implications of the EPR-based regulation. The idea of controlling the environmental performance of the products, particularly constituent substances in the manufactured products, was relatively new at the time. Since then, a number of government capacity-building efforts have been initiated.

In January 2003, the European Union officially published directive 2002/95/EC, also known as the RoHS directive. The directive granted member states 20 months to transpose the directive into national law, and 42 months for the electrical and electronic industry to eliminate the six restricted substances; namely lead (Pb), cadmium (Cd), mercury (Hg), hexavalent chromium (Cr(VI)), polybrominated diphenyl

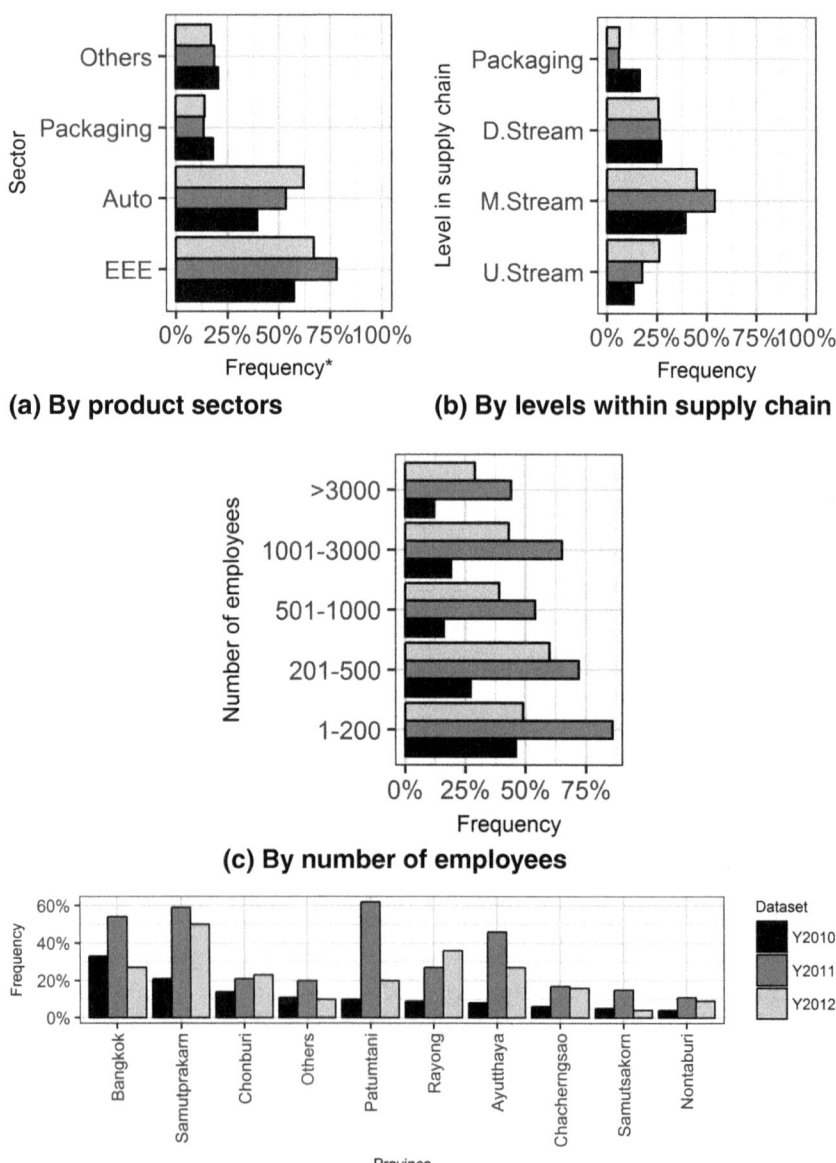

(a) By product sectors

(b) By levels within supply chain

(c) By number of employees

(d) By location within the country

Fig. 12.1   Respondent profile for Y2010–2012 surveys

(PBB), and polybrominated diphenyl ethers (PBDE), from their products. Directive 2002/95/EC did not specify any technical details. Specifically, it did not specify the maximum concentration values (MCV) it would allow; standard test methods it would recognize; and the approach it would use to verify producers' declaration of conformity. Without these critical criteria, it would depend on each member state to interpret the directive and enforce the law as they saw fit in their circumstances. Since RoHS is a single market directive, products for which non-compliance was found by any member state would be removed from the entire EU market. This put the EEE industry in a highly uncertain situation as their products would have to meet every member state's interpretation.

During the same period, a variety of "green initiatives" from multinational corporations (MNCs) began to emerge among the Thai supplychains. The majority of these initiatives included ambitious policies to impose a corporate ban on certain hazardous substances within a certain time frame. The MNCs' green initiatives were usually supported with well-organized action plans and guidelines for relevant parties within their supply chain to follow.

Although target substances for these initiatives were RoHS-like, they were not limited to RoHS restricted substances. Specific mentions of the keyword "RoHS" in these initiatives were initially low. Frequent words found in corporate green initiatives include "Pb-free" for the absence of lead, "SOC" for the absence of the automotive industry's substances of concern, "Halogen-free" for the absence of halogenated substances – a large family of chemical substances to which PBBs and PBDEs belong. Furthermore, since RoHS in its original version did not specify maximum concentration limits and there were no standard test methods available at the time, each MNC specified different limits and acceptable test methods as they saw fit in their circumstances. MNCs with high brand values to guard tended to impose more stringent limits than others. Some MNCs also required that analytical tests be performed by a designated testing laboratory.

It was not until late 2005–2006 when the word "RoHS,""SOC-4" (a word frequently used in the automotive sector, presumably referring to the ELV four restricted substances), and "SOC-6" (for the extension of ELV to cover PBB and certain types of PBDE, but not as stringent as RoHS) began to replace corporate-specific keywords, while other words: Japan J-MOSS, China-RoHS, Korea-RoHS, and California RoHS, began to appear as special versions of EU-RoHS. In this period, the European Commission finally published its MCVs for the six restricted substances in the Commission decision 2005/618/EC (European Commission 2005), while EU RoHS Enforcement Authorities Informal Network published its first non-binding document on RoHS enforcement guidance (EU RoHS Enforcement Authorities Informal Network 2005). The Commission decision helped to clarify the acceptable limits for the restricted substances, but introduced a new basis for their evaluation. Specifically, it specified maximum concentration values based on the weight of "homogeneous materials." This placed new challenges on the industry. First, this word was not clearly understood by all concerned parties and there was no official explanation for it. Second, it would render previous test reports that were conducted on a different basis useless and neither laboratories nor industries had any idea how to take samples of each "homogeneous material" out from products so that they could be tested for compliance. Fortunately, the non-binding RoHS enforcement guidance issued shortly after Commission decision 2005/618/EC shed some light in some areas.

Figure 12.2 shows results from MTEC's survey on factors that firms took into consideration when making decisions to adjust their practices in 2007. The results clearly indicate that the initial movement was driven by multinational firms through their early corporate green initiatives. To comply with headquarters' mandates, subsidiary firms relayed the demands to their suppliers, which created customer demand. Since the movement was driven by specific mandates from MNCs, the context of the market regulation was not as strong as the customers' mandate.

In 2007, firms appeared to be in a defensive mode. New market opportunities for RoHS compliant products were not given high priority at the time. It is also interesting to note that making cleaner products was the last factor that firms took into consideration.

In December 2006, the EU published yet another high-impact regulation, known as REACH (European Parliament 2006). This 849-page long regulation is highly complex, but the majority of the provisions are obligations for chemical substances and mixtures manufacturers.

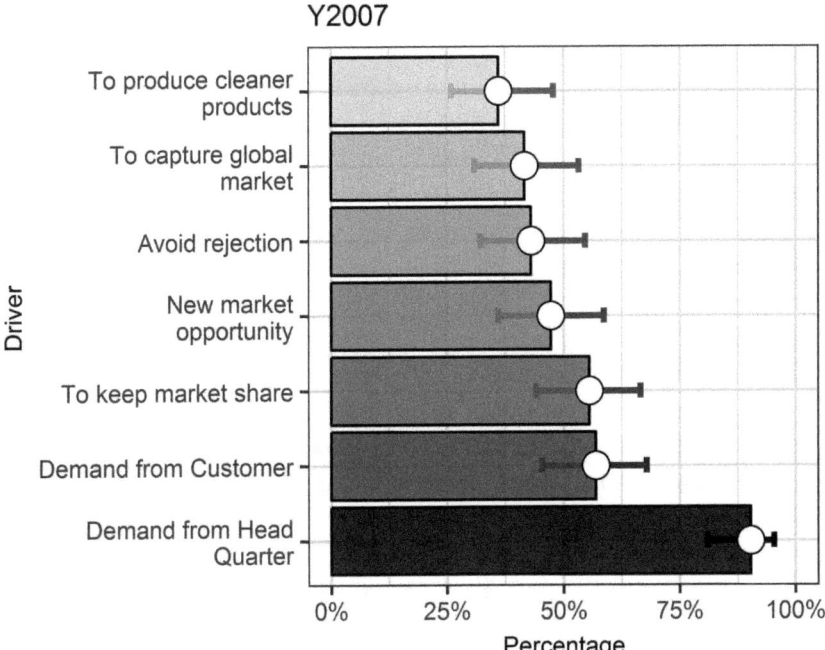

Fig. 12.2 Factors that effect firms decision to make actions in 2007

Producers of articles, on the other hand, are expected to fulfill their obligations in two areas; one related to a group of substances that are listed in the so-called Candidate List of substances of very high concern (SVHC), and the other related to substances whose uses are restricted. Particularly, suppliers of articles are obligated to provide the recipient of articles (ROA) with sufficient information if the article contains a Candidate List substance above 0.1% by weight of each article,[2] and producers or importers of articles are obligated to notify the European Chemical Agency (ECHA) if the article contains a Candidate List substance above 0.1% by weight of each article and the substance is present in quantities totaling over 1 ton per producer/importer per year. The duty to communicate information on

---

[2] Based on the ruling by the European Court of Justice (ECJ) on Case C-106/14 given on September 10, 2015.

substances in articles is applied the moment the substance is included in the Candidate List and posted on the ECHA Candidate List website,[3] while the duty to notify the agency must be fulfilled within six months after the inclusion of the substance in the Candidate List.

Although both the REACH regulation and RoHS-like directives involve chemical substances in products, obligations for relevant actors under the REACH regulation and requirements for products under RoHS-like directives are two different subjects that require different approaches for compliance. Substances under RoHS are restricted, while SVHCs in the REACH Candidate List are not. The list of substances under RoHS is quite rigid, while the REACH Candidate List of SVHCs are "living lists" that will be updated (more substances added) every six months. RoHS requires that producers take action to ensure that their products are free of the restricted substances, while REACH requirements are applied only to article producers whose products contain the listed substances above the threshold. REACH also has many other obligations and timelines that are not applied to producers of articles. Nevertheless, since the REACH regulation is so complex, not all customers, both local and international, fully understood their roles.

In October 2008, ECHA published its first Candidate List of 15 substances of very high concern. This was a huge jump from RoHS's six restricted substances if firms mistakenly thought that they were the same and attempted to use the same approach to respond.

Beginning from 2009, requests related to REACH-SVHC started to emerge in Thai supply-chain markets. To assess the state of market demand, we asked firms three questions on an ordinal scale of 1–5:

1. What ratio of customers (based on proportion of overall sales volume) require ECS-compliant products? (1: almost none, 3: 50%, 5: almost all)
2. What is the trend for the number of customers who made requests during the past three years? (1: sharply decreased, 3: steady, 5: sharply increased)

---

[3] http://echa.europa.eu/web/guest/candidate-list-table.

3. Judging by the number of substances requested, maximum concentration limits, and degree of complexity of the requests, what is the trend in terms of level of difficulty of customer requirements? (1: sharply decreased, 3: steady, 5: sharply increased)

Figure 12.3 shows diverging staked bar charts for the ratio of customers (in proportion to overall sales volume) who requested ECS-compliant products during the period 2010–2012. The percentages of respondents whose products had been requested to comply with ECS regulations that were more than 50% of their sale volumes are shown on the right side of the zero line along with the sums of the positive percentages (above a 50% share) on the right-hand side; the percentages of those with less than 50% of sale volumes are shown on the left along with percentages of their sums; and those with about 50% are shown in the middle.

In this period, the overall number of respondents whose ECS-compliant products had become the majority of their products increased. ECS-compliant products had become the majority products for about 60% of the respondents (57%, 75%, 66% for year 2010, 2011, and 2012, respectively). However, proportions of the demands for ECS-compliant products were not uniform across the supply chain. From Fig. 12.4, it appears that middle–stream firms were driven ahead of others. For most of the respondents who produced parts and components in the middle of the supply chain, ECS-compliant products had become their main products. A large percentage of firms in this level produced only ECS-compliant products. For packaging firms, while ECS compliance became the mainstream for products, percentages of firms who produced only ECS-compliant products was less than in other sectors. This may be because packaging firms supplied products to a broad range of market sectors. Sectors that did not require ECS compliance, for example local markets, still exist in an undeniable volume.

Compared to middle-stream firms, the ECS-compliant product shares for respondents in the downstream level were smaller. This may be because downstream firms had more freedom to market their products and the markets for non-ECS-compliant products were still sizable.

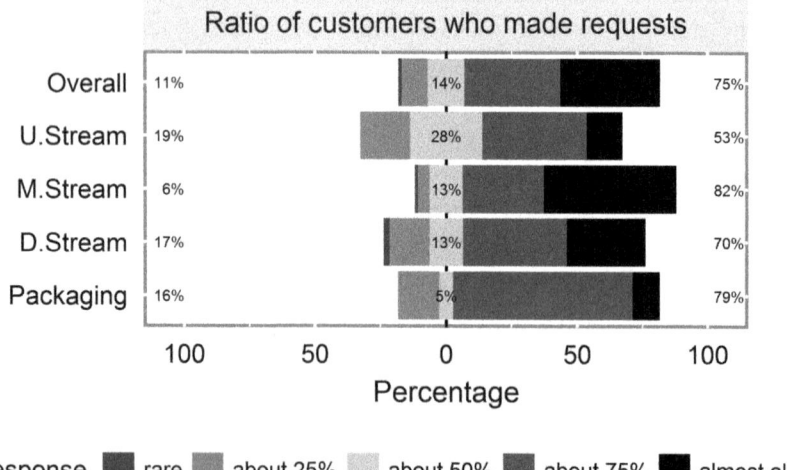

(a) Responses from firms at different level along supply chain

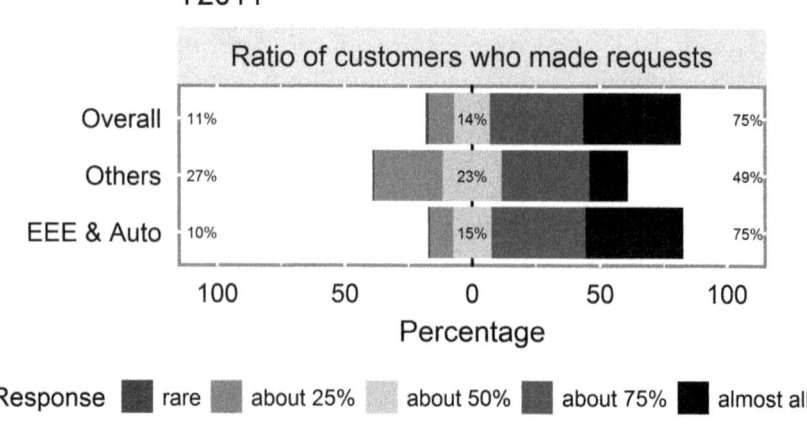

(b) Responses from firms in different sectors

Fig. 12.3 Ratio of customers who requested ECS compliance products to overall products in 2011

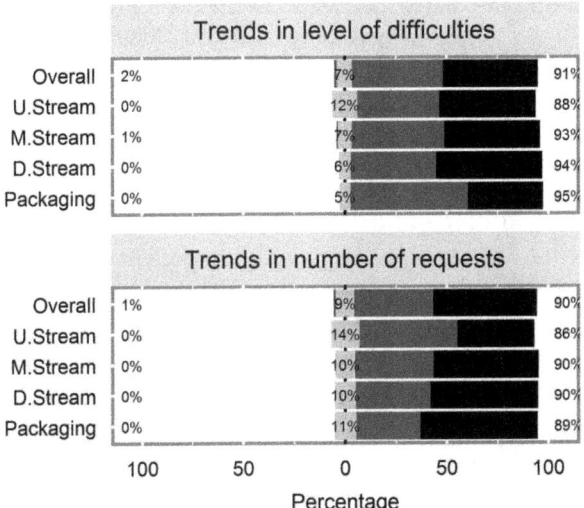

(a) **Responses from firms at different level along supply chain**

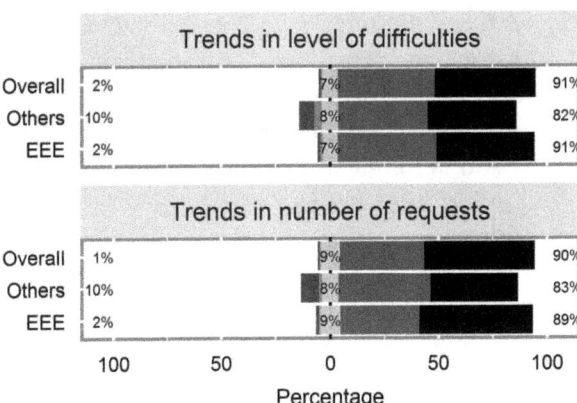

(b) **Responses from firms in different sectors**

Fig. 12.4 Trends in customers' RoHS/REACH-related requests in the past three years in 2011

Producing multiple-standard products could lead to extra management costs and redundant parts/materials inventories. However, the cost for producing ECS-compliant products in this early stage was also reportedly higher than that for non-ECS-compliant products. Since markets that did not have ECS controls in place were usually cost-sensitive markets, this result could indicate that the dedicated production of ECS-compliant products was not yet as cost-effective as producing products with multiple standards.

Firms in the upstream levels may also experience the same multiple standards situation, as the percentage of respondents who supplied mainly ECS-compliant products was relatively low. Markets for upstream products are more diverse, both in terms of their possible applications in different product sectors and in terms of the destination of the end products. The same material, for example plastics, can be used to produce high-tech, export-oriented products or simple products for the domestic/regional market. Since non-ECS-compliant markets were still wide open for upstream firms, percentages of firms who committed to supplying mainly ECS-compliant products was smaller.

When viewing the ECS-compliant product share across product sectors, Fig. 12.3(b) shows that demand also exists in product sectors other than the EEE and automotive sectors (packaging, toys, furniture, and textiles). However, the percentages of respondents who committed to producing predominantly ECS-compliant products were far smaller. These results were inline with their respective market focuses: global markets for EEE and automotive firms and domestic/regional markets for firms in less sophisticated product sectors.

From the overall picture, it appeared that the market for EEE and automotive sectors, especially those in the supply-chain middle stream, began to tip toward RoHS/REACH-compliant products as the ratio of customers who requested these products became a majority.

Regardless of the difference in ECS market proportions across product sectors and levels along the supply chain, in terms of trends in the number of requests and level of difficulty in customer requests that firms experienced in the past three years, Fig. 12.4 clearly shows that firms across supply chains shared common experiences. This is because these responses were received while firms were in the early stage of implementing REACH-SVHC actions. Unlike RoHS-like directives, REACH affects almost every firm regardless of the size of their business, especially those who produce products mainly for export.

Under most circumstances, article producers/importers need to obtain information about substances from suppliers along the supply chain to fulfill their obligations as required by the REACH regulation. However, this is only limited to the substances that were listed in the Candidate List, and only when they exist in the articles above the threshold limits. Unfortunately, at the beginning, not every firm or customer truly understood their obligations, but felt the importance of compliance. Customer requests that were irrelevant to article producers' obligations (such as requests that direct suppliers to register their products, the mandate to use only materials that have been registered under REACH registration procedures, etc.) were not uncommon during this period.

By the end of 2012, substances published in the REACH SVHC Candidate List had escalated to 138. This was a sudden jump if firms compared this list to RoHS, which had remained constant at six restricted substances since 2006. Firms would feel even stronger pressure if their customers attempted to control all the substances in the list in the same manner as they did for RoHS.

Figure 12.5 further confirms the arrival of REACH. As seen from the figure, RoHS and ELV were still the majority for most respondents, while requests for REACH-SVHC and REACH-restricted substances were picking up during this period. Requests for compliance with the packaging waste directive (PPWD) were relatively low as this directive only applied to packaging firms and those who placed their products on the market with packaging waste-related regulations in place. Likewise, requests related to the emission of volatile organic compounds (VOC) from products were limited only to the automotive, toys, and furniture sectors that have VOC mandates in place. The VOC mandate in the automotive sector is a voluntary initiative, mainly among Japanese car makers, to limit emissions of certain VOCs inside the passenger room.

During the period 2007–2012, a large number of capacity-building programs were implemented in Thailand by both local and international

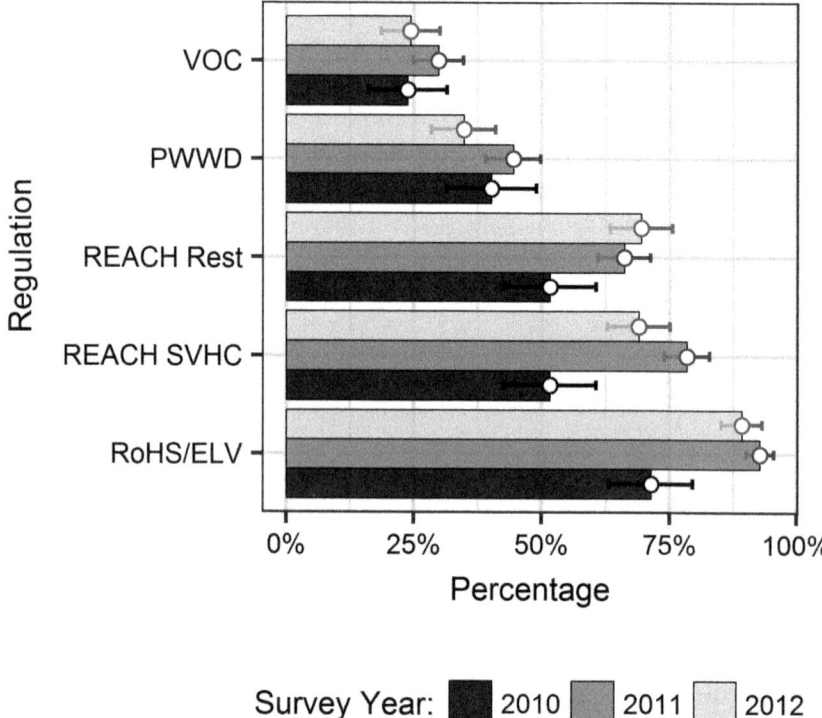

Fig. 12.5 Most frequent regulations that customers requested during 2010–2012

agencies. Important infrastructure needed to facilitate supply-chain realignment was also picking up. Particularly, the International Electrotechnical Commission (IEC) formed a technical committee, TC-111, for environmental standardization of electrical and electronic products and systems. Among the many standards, IEC TC-111 published standards that helped to relieve supply-chain firms from multiple customer-specific mandates; particularly, standard procedures for the determination of the restricted substances in 2008 (IEC 62321:2008 2008), guidance for the evaluation of products with respect to substance-use restrictions in electrical and electronic products in 2010 (IEC TR62476:2010 2010), and standards for materials declaration in 2012 (IEC 62474: 2012 2012).

In 2010, we asked firms the same questions as in 2007 about factors that firms took into consideration when they made the decision to become ECS-compliant products producers. Figure 12.6 summarizes the responses. Comparing with results from the 2007 survey, it appeared that firms had gained a better understanding of the context of EU-RoHS/REACH regulations. Overwhelmed with the number of substances of concern and the complexity of the regulation, firms appeared to accept the fact that product-related environmental and chemicals safety regulations were becoming the new norm in the global market, and hence made decisions based on demands from markets and regulations. Firms also began to take new market opportunities into consideration. Again,

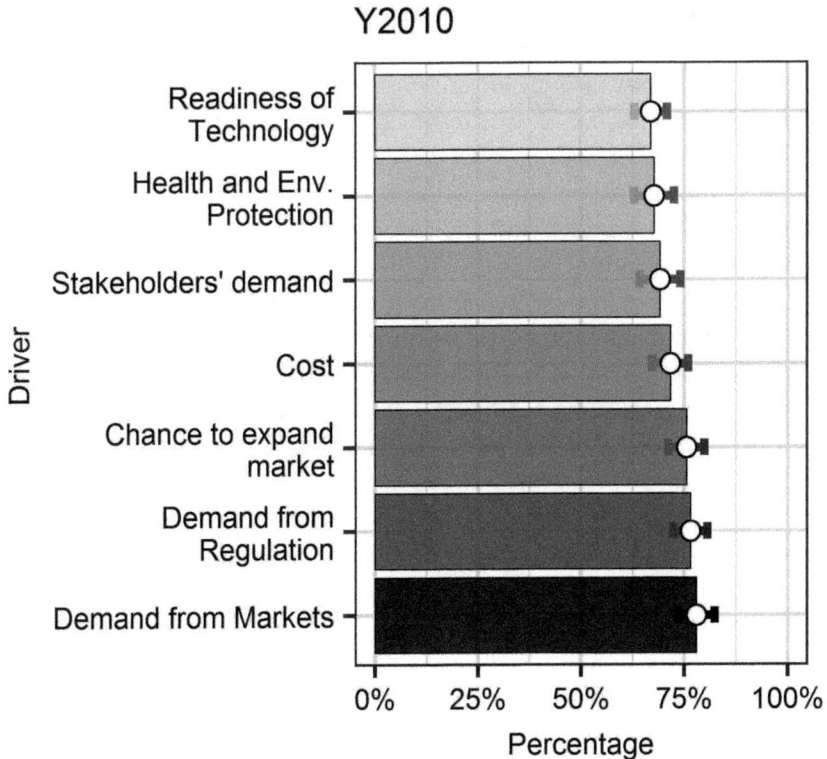

Fig. 12.6 Factors that affect firms decision to make actions in 2010

although by complying with RoHS/REACH their products should have become safer for consumers and for the environment, health, and environmental protection were not given high priority.

12.4 Measures and Costs

Once firms decided to produce RoHS/REACH-compliant products, they needed to make appropriate adjustments. Figure 12.7 shows that a large percentage of the respondents had started their actions and the percentage of those who took action increased every year.

Based on the 2010 survey, more firms in the middle stream started their actions earlier than others. This may appear to contradict with previous results that indicated firms' actions were driven by MNCs and end-product producers. Most middle-stream firms in Thailand are integral parts of EEE and the automotive supply chain. They feed their products to both local and global customers. Downstream firms, on the other hand, are more diverse, in terms of both product diversity and market destinations. From Fig. 12.7, we can see the similarity between responses from middle stream-firms and those in EEE and the automotive sector. These sectors were driven ahead of others by RoHS/ELV directives. Nevertheless, by 2012, the percentages of firms who had made their adjustment across the supply chain were not significantly different. Firms outside EEE and the automotive sectors, and upstream firms were slightly behind because there was still demand for non-ECS products, as mentioned earlier.

It became possible to elaborate specific measures taken by firms when we asked firms to select every action item that they took in the 2010 and 2011 questionnaires. The results are shown in Fig. 12.8.

At first glance, it appears that firms took a variety of measures to bring their products to compliance. Requesting certificates from suppliers was the most popular action for both years. These initial responses may cause some concern as product certification processes are costly. Beside, with the large number of substances in play, no analytical laboratory can reliably certify a product by just testing samples supplied by customers. However, respondents also took other actions that may be relevant to this context. Particularly, in 2011, management policy was catching up with the

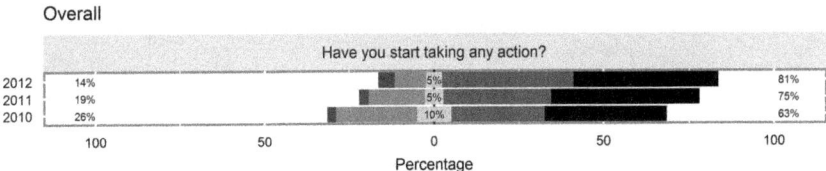

(a) Overall responses

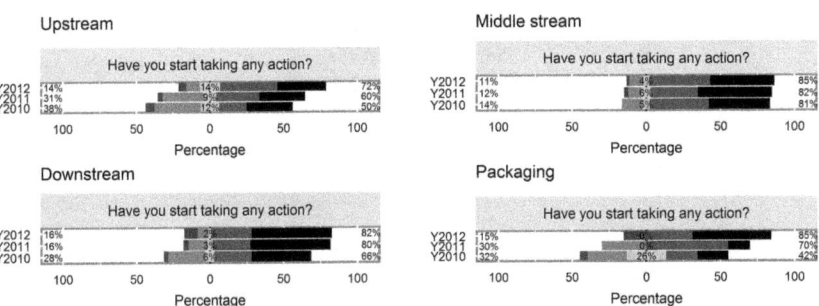

(b) Responses from firms at different levels along supply chain

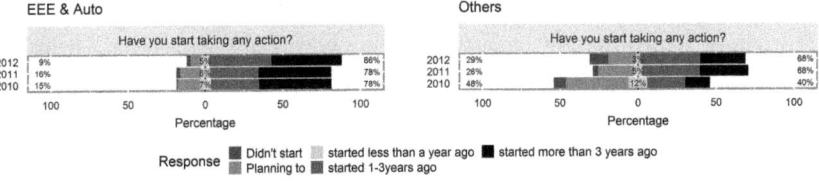

(c) Responses from firms in different product sectors

Fig. 12.7   Comparison of movements to ensure products compliance by firms along supply chain and by firms in different product sectors

certificates while the monitoring system was also gaining high attention. Results from 2010 and 2011 also displayed different patterns, but these are hard to distinguish at this stage.

To gain more understanding of the underlying pattern of the responses, we performed a cluster analysis that hierarchically groups items with similar characteristics. Particularly, we employed item cluster analysis (ICLUST), an algorithm that hierarchically clusters items to form composite scales, to identify homogeneous groups of items that share similar characteristics and combine them. Hierarchical cluster analysis is a useful data reduction

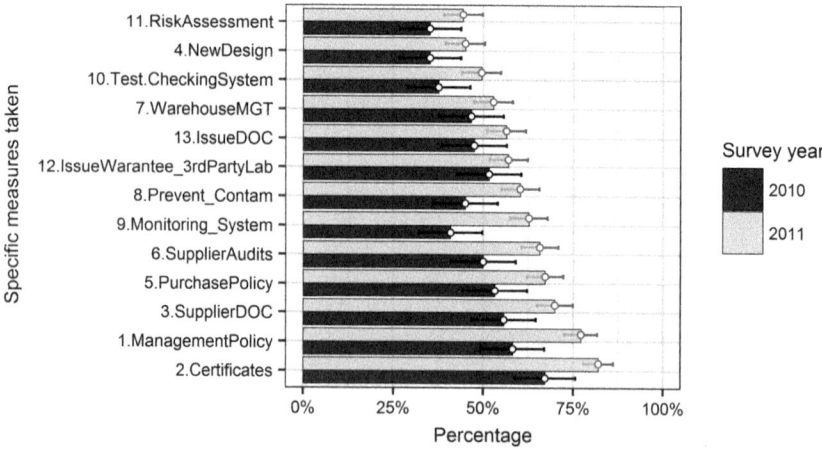

Fig. 12.8 Specific measures taken by respondents during 2010–2011

technique that finds uses in many data mining fields such as computational biology and bioinformatics, customer segmentation in marketing. It can be thought of as an alternative to factor analysis with a simpler model. The main objective of this process is to group items into clusters so that items within the same cluster have high similarity but are dissimilar to other clusters. After identifying the most similar pair of items, the ICLUST algorithm combine these items to form a new cluster and find the similarity of this cluster to all other items and clusters until one of the two measures of internal consistency; Cronbach's alpha (mean split half reliability) and Revelle's beta (the worst or minimum split half reliability) (R Documentation (n.d.); Revelle 1978, 2011; Cooksey and Soutar 2006) fails to increase.

Figure 12.9 illustrated the results from ICLUST for measure items with 2 cluster model. The goodness of fit index (cluster fit) for this cluster model of 0.94 (0 is a very poor fit, 1 is a perfect fit). In addition to connected structure of the clusters Fig. 12.9 also provided with three statistic results: Cronbach's alphas (α), Revelle's betas (β), and the correlation of the new cluster with two subclusters. Ideally, higher values of Cronbach's alpha are more desirable (preferably higher than 0.7) as they imply that items measure the same construct. Additionally, there should not be large discrepancy between α and β (preferably not more than 0.2).

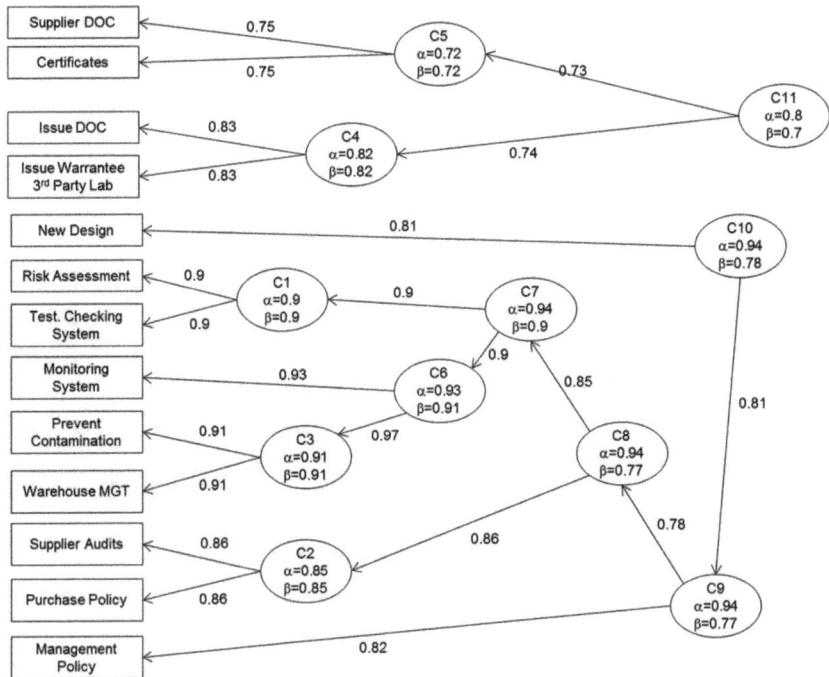

Fig. 12.9 Cluster diagram of measure items (2 clusters model)

Considering the measured items that form two homogeneous clusters in Fig. 12.9, items in cluster C10 are core components of a quality management system such as ISO 9001 (ISO 9001 2008), while items in cluster C11 are different types of documents used to accommodate the supplied products along a supply chain. These two clusters appear to indicate adjustment approaches. Thus, we called cluster C10 the "Pro-system" approach and C11 the "Pro-document" approach. Interestingly, these approaches are inline with advice given by the EU RoHS Enforcement Network in their 2006 guidance document (IEC 62321: 2008 2008) and the concept for product evaluation given by IEC TR62476:2010 (2010). These guidance documents acknowledged the complexity and diversity of EEE products and production practice and addressed the complexity and the deficiency of the compliance approach that relied heavily on certificates based on analytical results. For products with only a few parts, the recommended "Route B" that accepts suppliers' warranties/certificates and/or analysis reports for homogeneous materials in parts/components may be the optimum choice as long as producers can provide evidence that they had assessed all the documents and, hence, proved that they can be trusted. For complex products or for producers who produce multiple products, typically with many common parts and materials, it was recommended that "Route A" should be followed. Under this route, it was recommended that a compliance assurance system (CAS) should be established and integrated within the company's quality and management systems. Furthermore, evidence of active control of CAS, such as results of internal and supplier audits, evidence that the CAS system has been followed, results of product-specific conformance assessment, etc., should be available upon request.

Of course, recommendations in this period were meant for RoHS-like regulation only. With REACH-SVHC coming into play, these two approaches may need to be modified to accommodate the transfer of the required safety information along a supply chain.

Figure 12.10 shows results after combining the measured items into two clusters. Although the "pro-document" approach is dominant, Fig. 12.10 shows that firms also took the "system approach," that is, adjusting the production management system, to transform their products. Results from 2011 also suggest that the system approach had gained popularity, as seen by the fact that the rate of increase from 2010 was greater than actions in the documentation side.

The adoption of the system approach to control chemical substances in products requires an awareness of the content of high-risk substances in the incoming materials as well as management practices on the supplier side. Table 12.1 and Table 12.2 reveal some hints about actions that were taking place along the supply chain. First, most respondents had implemented control systems that required an approved vendor list (AVL). This process required that suppliers passed the customers' qualifying process before being granted a chance to supply their products. Most systems also required a re-evaluation procedure. Based on this process, a large proportion of the respondents were forced to find new suppliers for RoHS/REACH non-compliance reasons. Furthermore, around 10% of the respondents reported that their products had been rejected by customers. It was

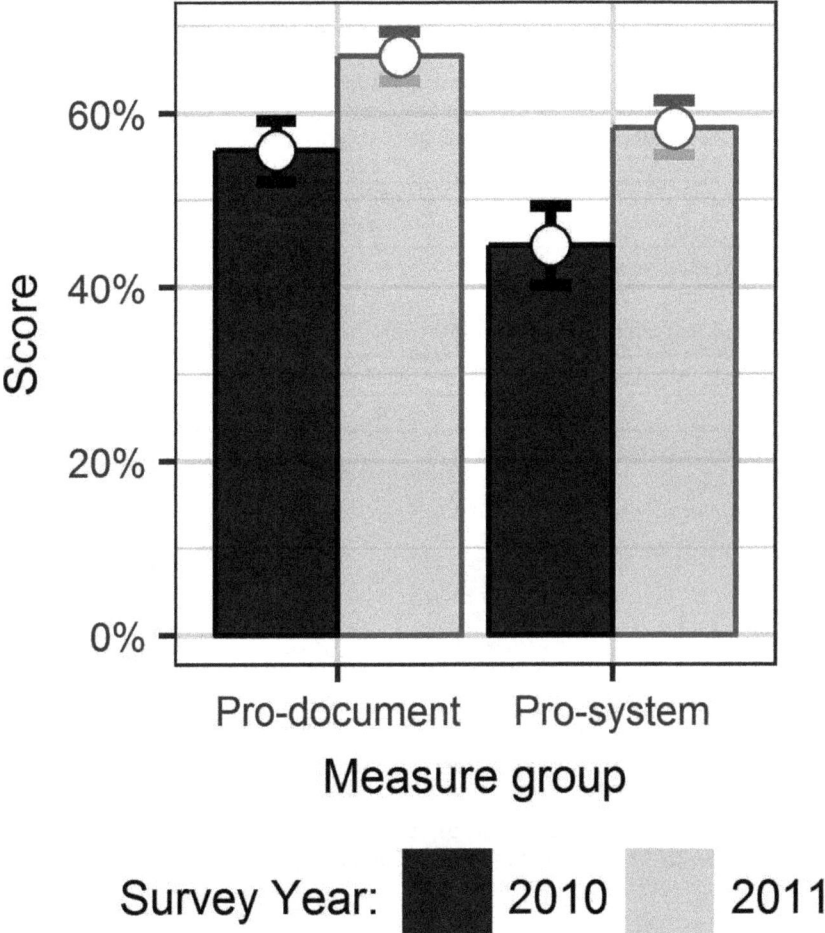

Fig. 12.10 Group of measures taken by respondents during 2010–2011

unavoidable that those who could not adjust their processes on time would be eliminated from the supply chain. Sudden supply-chain redirection always causes concerns to most developing countries. Fortunately, as seen in Figs. 12.7 and 12.11, by 2012 a majority of respondents were able to complete their adjustment processes. Most changes in materials sourcing, therefore, were bounded within the country (see Table 12.2).

Table 12.1 Supply chain-specific actions (%)

Dataset	Have approved vendor list (AVL)	Have to find new supplier for non-compliance reasons	Have been rejected from non-compliance reasons	Have seek out new markets that do not require RoHS/REACH
2011	87.1	63.1	11.1	19.8
2012	93.7	47.7	12.6	16.2

Source: Author created

Table 12.2 Supplier re-alignment direction (%)

Data set	Local-to-Local	Local-to-Import	Import-to-Import
2012	37.4	10.4	5.4

Source: Author created

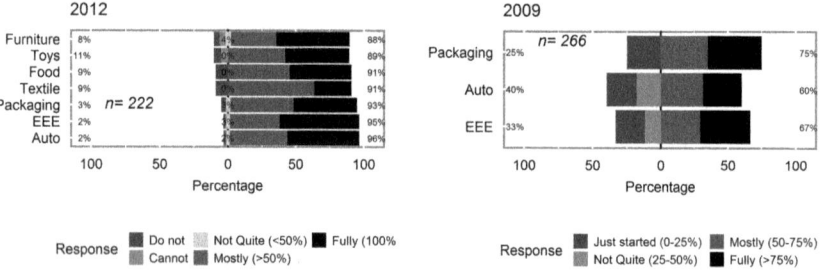

Fig. 12.11 Compare firms levels of confidence in their ability to meet customers RoHS/REACH-related requests in 2009 and 2012

Figure 12.11 compares firms' levels of confidence in their ability to meet customer demand in 2009 and 2012, respectively. With years of making the transformation together with the type of thorough actions being implemented, respondents in 2012 were mostly confident that their products could meet the customers' requirements. This is in contrast with the confidence level in 2009, when firms were still busy aligning their practices to cope with RoHS/ELV and the new demands from REACH-SVHC came along.

With appropriate measures in place and firms highly confident of their products, it is interesting to see the outcome of their efforts. Figure 12.12

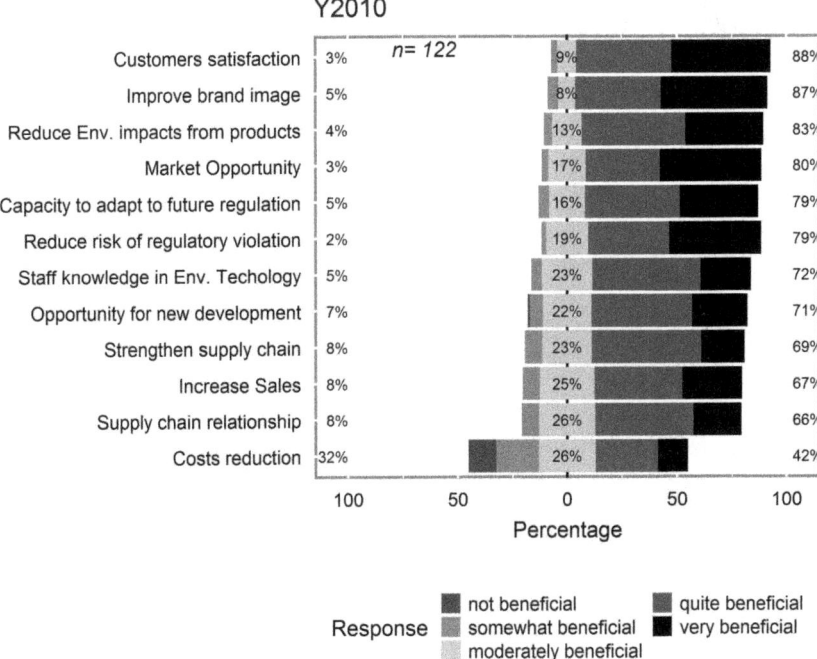

Fig. 12.12 Outcome of the adjustment in 2010

summarizes results from the 2010 survey. The first prominent outcome, customer satisfaction, appears to be inline with the force that drove firms in this direction (see Fig. 12.6). Among the outcomes reported, cost reductions were separated from others. It appears that respondents had mixed feelings about costs. Based on the measures firms had taken, this result is understandable. Most firms had to bear extra costs, especially for materials/products certifications and supplier requalification. Since cost reductions were not the main objective of these activities, benefits in this area would arise either by chance or from secondary knowledge gained from a better management system being put in place.

Apart from cost reductions, outcome items, as shown in Fig. 12.12, are rather hard to interpret. By employing item cluster analysis with an ICLUST algorithm, the outcome items could be modeled with four clusters, as shown in Fig. 12.13, with goodness of fit index of 0.96.

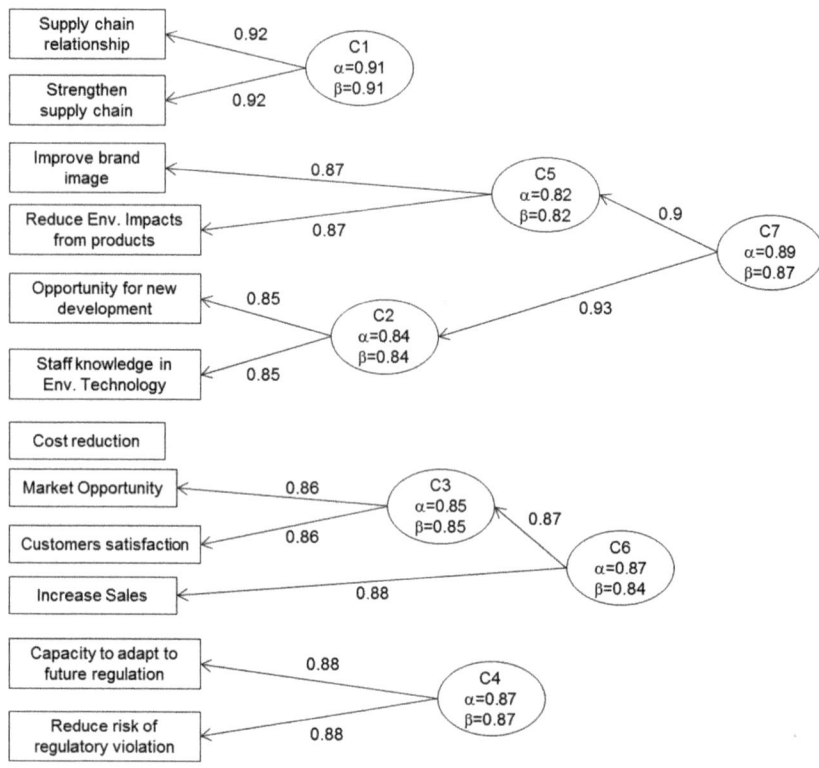

Fig. 12.13 Cluster diagram of outcome items (4 clusters model)

The four outcome clusters plus one isolated item (cost reduction), as shown in Fig. 12.13, bear some similarities to Esty and Winston's green strategy framework (Esty and Winston 2009) and MITSloan's findings in their retailers' survey (MIT Sloan Management, n.d.). Particularly, Esty and Winston found that leading companies' green strategies can be mapped in two dimensions, the motivation dimension and the goal dimension. The motivations are either "upside" for gaining competitive advantage or "downside" for avoiding harm. The goals or the types of benefit are short-term/tangible benefits and long-term/intangible benefits. When mapped in two dimensions, the two upside strategies are strategies that lead to tangible outcomes, such as revenues, and intangible outcomes, such as brand image and corporate reputation, etc. Similarly, the two downside strategies are

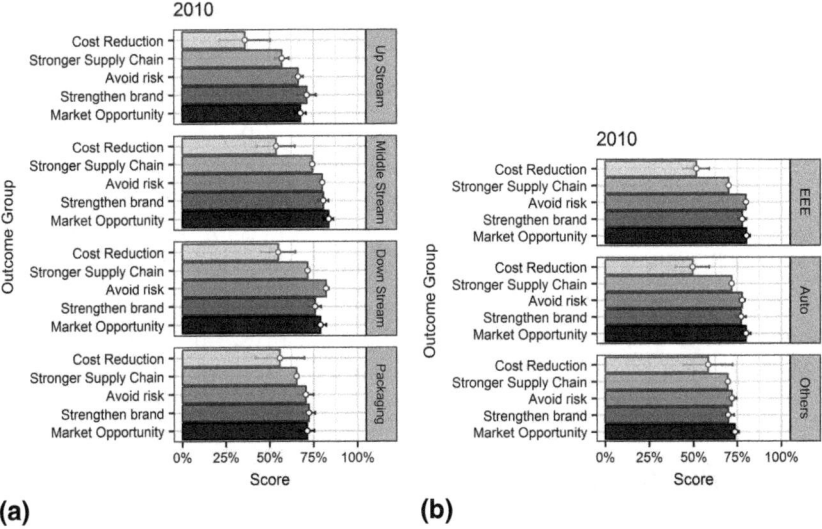

Fig. 12.14   Groups of outcomes in 2010

tangible outcomes, such as cost reduction, and intangible outcomes, such as risk avoidance.

To consider the outcome clusters from this perspective, we assigned cluster C1 the name "Stronger supply chain," cluster C4 "Avoid risk," cluster C6 "Market opportunity" and cluster C7 "Strengthen brand." Finally, cost reduction, the only outcome item that stoodout from other clusters, can be viewed as a short-term benefit from the downside perspective.

Figure 12.14 shows the results after combining the outcome responses into four clusters and one isolated item as described above. Most respondents felt positive impacts in terms of market opportunity (customer satisfaction, increase sales, and open market opportunities), strengthening brand (brand image, reduce impacts, opportunity for improvement, and staff competency) and avoiding risk (risk of violation and capacity to adapt to future regulations). Firms at all levels along the supply chain and across product sectors gave similar responses for these three outcome groups, except for firms in the downstream level, who favored avoiding risk over the other two benefits. This may be because firms at this level were held liable for products they put on the market.

Most respondents, on the other hand, rated stronger supply chain significantly lower than the first three outcome groups. Among respondents along the supply chain, upstream-level firms rated benefits in this area the lowest. These results may reflect the intense situation along a supply chain during the transition period. Note also that respondents in the upstream level tended to rate strengthen brand higher than other benefits. As seen from the previous section, markets for non-ECS products were still open for upstream firms. Thus avoiding harm might not be a strong motive for these firms. This result may imply that upstream respondents did not need to adjust their practices, but wanted to transform themselves to capture long-term benefits from the green markets.

12.5 Barriers to Change

During the transition, firms faced multiple obstacles that might be beyond their control. Some of these obstacles can be captured through the survey results in 2010, as shown in Fig. 12.15. Testing and product certification costs appeared to be the most prominent barrier that the respondents sensed. This problem is inline with the requirement for test certificates, which was the most popular action seen in Fig. 12.8. However, from the previous section we learned that respondents also took other actions. These actions might also be costly and Fig. 12.15 appears to capture these costs in the consecutive obstacle items.

To gain more understanding about the type of obstacles that hindered the adjustment process, we employed ICLUST to identify groups of obstacles that share similar characteristics. Figure 12.16 summarizes the results with a four-cluster model with a goodness of fit of 0.87.

Considering the cluster diagram in Fig. 12.16, items in cluster C1 are a combination of product pricing and switching costs. These items are fundamental factors for products/processes adjustment decisions in the industry. We called this cluster "Prices/Costs prospects." High switching costs with insufficient price leverage could hinder management decisions to implement more radical actions.

Items in cluster C8 are difficulties related to the complexity and technicality of the regulation/requirements. We attributed this cluster to

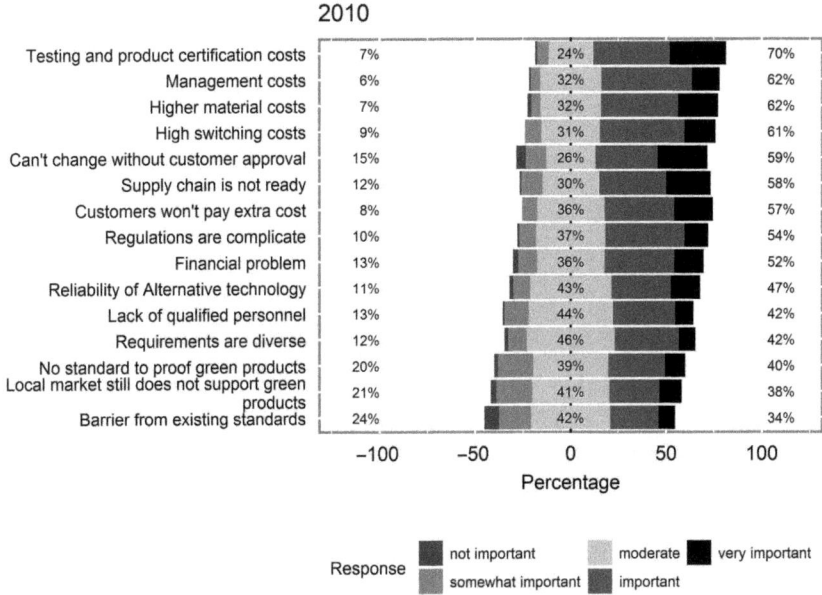

Fig. 12.15 Obstacles during the adjustment

"Regulations." On the other hand, items in cluster C11 reflect the level of confidence of relevant stakeholders in the alternative/greener products, so we called this cluster "Confidence in new materials/products."

Items in cluster C10 are not straightforward to characterize. Material costs, testing and certification costs, and management costs can be attributed to "compliance costs." These items depend on the levels of readiness of supply-chain companies. With competent suppliers, these costs can be reduced. Lack of access to necessary funding could also slow down firms' adjustment processes and create extra costs.[4] Since all these items are associated with the costs firms had to bear to bring their products to compliance, we attributed this cluster to "compliance costs."

---

[4] For example, firms who could not allocate a dedicated machine for RoHS & Non-RoHS products may have to implement extra operations, such as switching of production lines and equipment clean-ups to reduce the risk of cross-contamination.

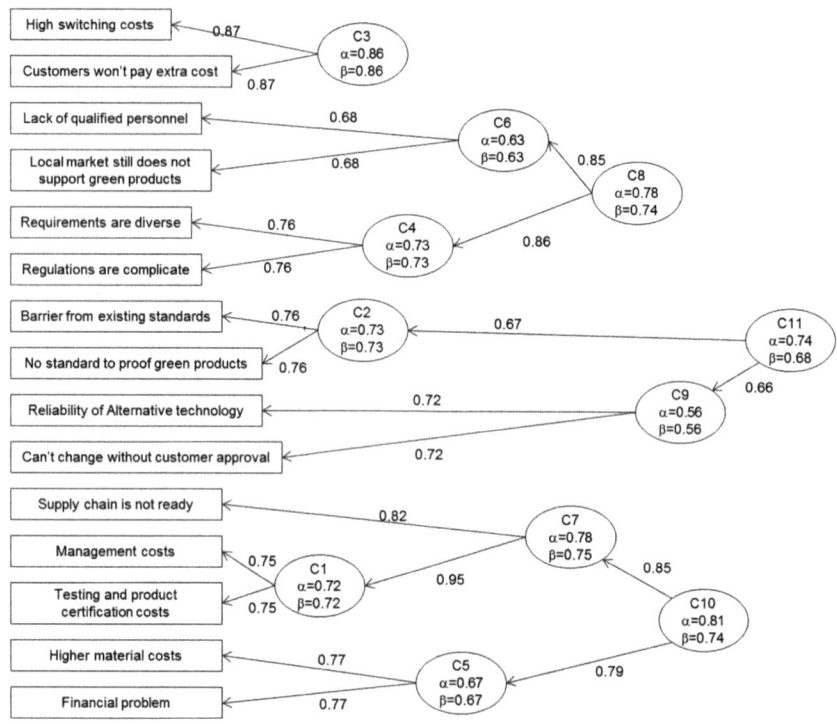

Fig. 12.16 Cluster diagram for obstacles for the adjustment (4 clusters model)

The combined results based on the four-cluster model for the years 2010 and 2011 surveys for firms along a supply chain and across products sectors are shown in Fig. 12.17. In 2010, Prices/Costs prospects and compliance costs were key barriers for firms in the middle- and downstream of the supply chain regardless of the product sectors. However, in 2011, barriers from compliance costs appeared to have decreased while barriers related to the complexities of regulations/requirements were gaining importance, exceeding compliance costs for most respondent groups except packaging firms.

These responses are inline with the escalating number of substances incorporated into the REACH-SVHC Candidate List and the first deadline for articles producers to fulfill their obligations. These include the obligation to communicate safety information along the supply chain and to notify EU authorities of the existence of any substances of concern in

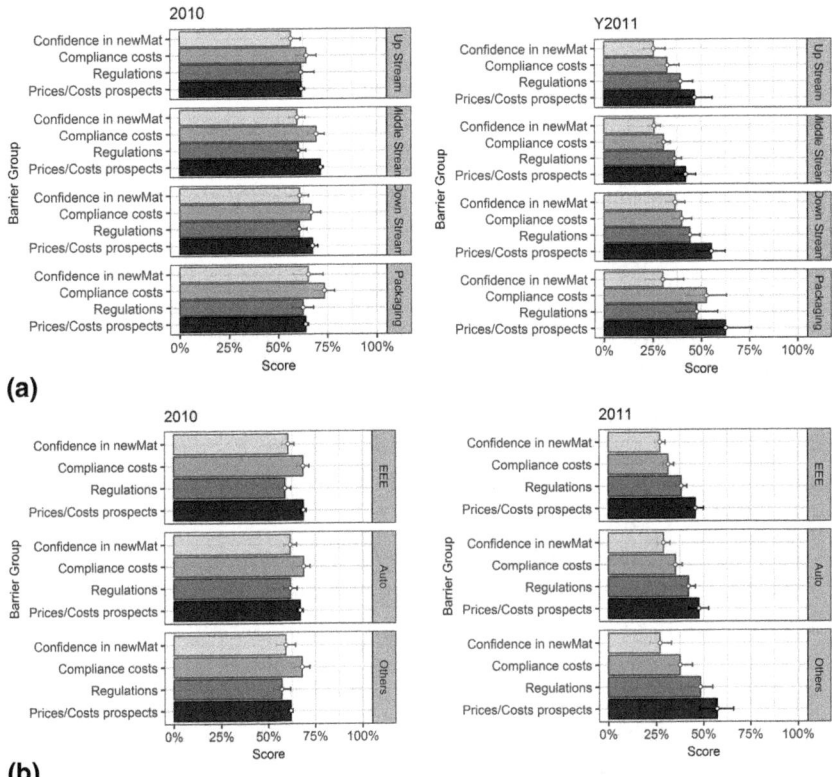

(a)

(b)

Fig. 12.17 Groups of factors that hindered RoHS/REACH compliance development process along supply chain and across sectors in 2010 and 2011

their articles above the trigger limits. Obligations related to SVHC in the Candidate List for different article producers along the supply chain are not straightforward but depend on several risk factors. Substances in the Candidate List are also causes of concern. Although the list of substances in the REACH-SVHC Candidate List are overwhelming, a specific substance only impacts specific firms who use it. In theory, this should bear no consequence for those outside the "use-group." In practice, firms along the supply chain had little knowledge of these substances, their possible incorporation in the incoming materials, and the possibility of substance formation/transformation within their production processes. It would be a huge burden for a firm to apprehend all the substances in the rapidly growing list. With the obligation and deadline in hand, downstream producers had no choice but to relay the whole list of substances along the supply chain and wait for information feedback from upstream firms. Unlike RoHS/ELV, where restricted substances were actually used in the EEE/automotive sectors and each player could develop their knowledge-base to help identify high-risk items, most substances in the SVHC Candidate List were unfamiliar to most firms except those who used/produced them. Downstream firms, those requesting the information, were in no position to explain their requests to the suppliers. It is important to note that this burden is not sharedby firms within the European Union because REACH mandates the flow of relevant information to the recipient of articles (ROA). In this complex situation, it is no surprise that barriers related to regulations escalated over compliance costs for most firms along the supply chain.

It is also possible that firms had gained more understanding on the outlook of the situation and had put in place appropriate management systems (as seen in Section 11.3) that helped eliminate unnecessary actions, such as redundant and irrelevant analytical testing. The improved readiness level of suppliers and the increasing number of suppliers who could supply compliant products over the years would also help bring compliance costs down.

Figure 12.18 shows results from the 2012 survey for the same questions as in 2010 and 2011. However, unlike the previous years, this survey asked respondents to choose only three prominent barriers. As seen in the figure, the response patterns were similar, but this survey method made it possible to differentiate prominent barriers better than in the previous years. From this figure, we can clearly see the importance of barriers from prices/costs prospects over the rest of the barriers, particularly for firms who produce products that still had sizable markets for non-ECS-compliant products. As seen in Section 11.2, there were smaller percentages of firms in the upstream level of the supply chain, in packaging business, and in less sophisticated product sectors who committed to supplying ECS-compliant products. Here, these groups also rated the prices/costs prospects barrier higher than other respondents.

Prices/costs prospects can be a very difficult barrier for firms to cross. Esty and Winston (2009) warned that firms should not expect a price

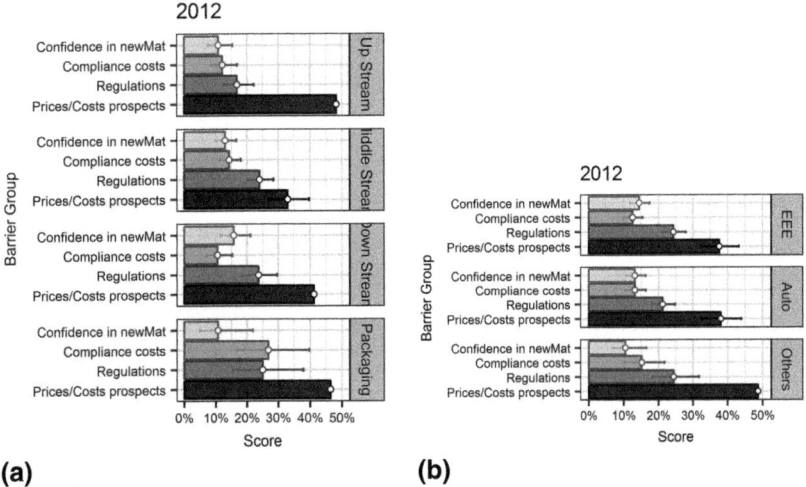

(a)   **(b)**

Fig. 12.18 Groups of factors that hindered RoHS/REACH compliance development process (a) along supply chain and (b) across product sector in 2012

premium for greener products. Based on our results, it appeared that the difference between firms who experienced less stress from the prices/costs prospects and committed to producing ECS products and those who did not was the risk of punishment from customers/markets.

Notice that respondents at the downstream level appeared to have higher concerns related to the confidence of alternative materials/products than others. But these responses were still too diverse to discriminate this concern over the rest of the barrier groups at a high confidence level.

12.6 Suggested Capacity-Building Areas

Firms were asked for their recommendations on assets Thai producers should have in order to cope with RoHS/REACH-like regulations in a more efficient manner. Figure 12.19 summarizes the results from the 2010 survey. Interestingly, awareness of market context change in the green economy and awareness of the pressing environmental problems received the highest recommendations. Nevertheless, it appears that the respondents sensed the importance of other assets as well, making it hard to select any

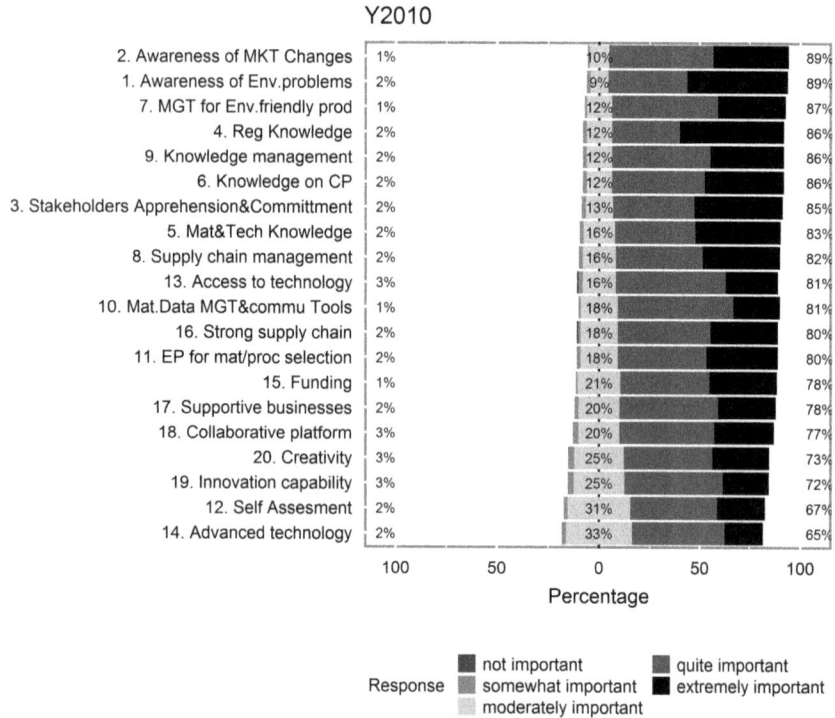

Fig. 12.19 Firms recommendations in 2010 on assets a producer should have in order to cope with RoHS/REACH-like regulations

asset over another. Thus, again, we employed ICLUST to help us group items that share similar characteristics together. Results from the items cluster analysis suggested five clusters with a goodness of fit index of 0.96, as shown in Fig. 12.20.

Clusters of asset items in Fig. 12.20 can be considered as competency areas the respondents thought Thai firms should have or suggestions for capacity-building areas that would help Thai firms to cope with ECS regulations. Items in cluster C1 are both awareness, one on the global market shift and the other on environmental problems. We labeled this cluster "Awareness of global green markets." Items in cluster C3 are related to the supplychain, and thus we called this cluster "Supply chain management." Cluster C10, called "Capitals," is related to capital investment.

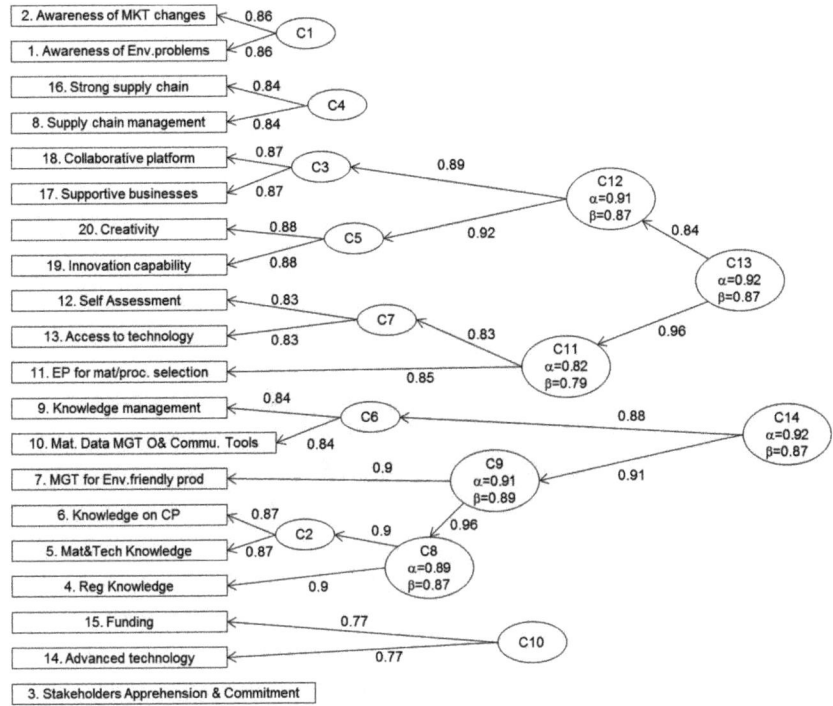

Fig. 12.20 Cluster diagram of assets items (5 clusters model)

Items in cluster C13 and C14 appeared to be competency areas for two different development objectives. Assets in cluster C14 are mostly knowledge that can be useful in helping firms develop their products/processes with the aim of avoiding punishment from customers/markets. We called this cluster "Technical knowledge and management." On the other hand, assets in cluster C13 will be useful if firms aim to capture the upside of green markets by developing greener products beyond regulatory requirements. We gave this cluster the attribution "Green products development capability."

Figure 12.21 summarizes capacity-building areas hinted by items cluster analysis, as described above. For the 2010 survey data, every capacity item appears to be equally important. On the other hand, survey results in 2011 suggested that awareness of global green markets, supply chain management, and technical knowledge, consecutively, were more important than others.

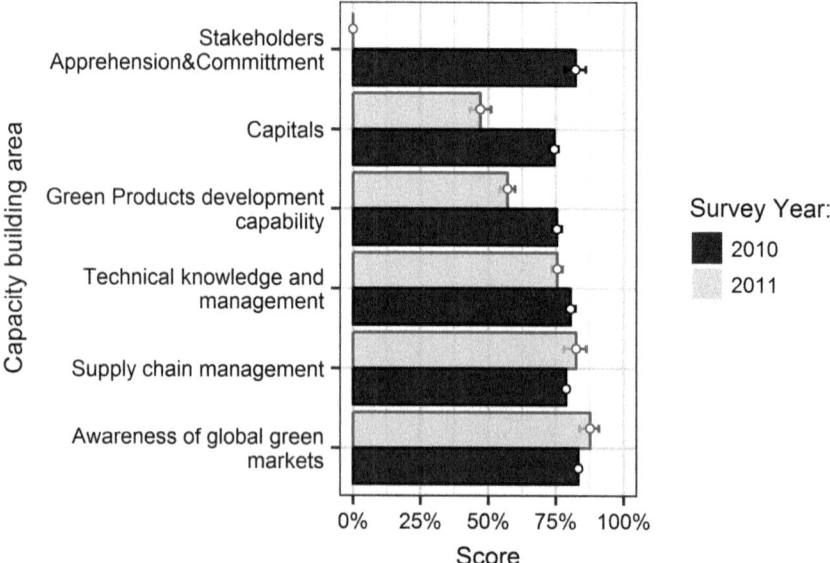

Fig. 12.21 Area of competency recommended for the adjustment

Green product development capacity and capital, on the other hand, are not as desirable as tools to help firms cope with RoHS/REACH-like regulations.

These patterns were further confirmed by looking at survey results for 2011 and 2012 for firms along the supply chain and across product sectors, as shown in Fig. 12.22.

In addition to the awareness of the global market shifting toward green markets that all respondents rated as the most important competency area that Thai firms should have, supply chain management and technical knowledge and management were also important. These capacity-building areas could be considered as core competency areas that would help firms to direct their measures in the right direction. As with other results we have learned thus far, respondents at the downstream and middle-stream levels rated supply chain management higher than other firms. These results reflected the pressing difficulties these firms faced and also suggested capacity-building areas that we should consider.

These results help to remind us about the different contexts in which each firm operates, hence requiring different supporting tools. Downstream

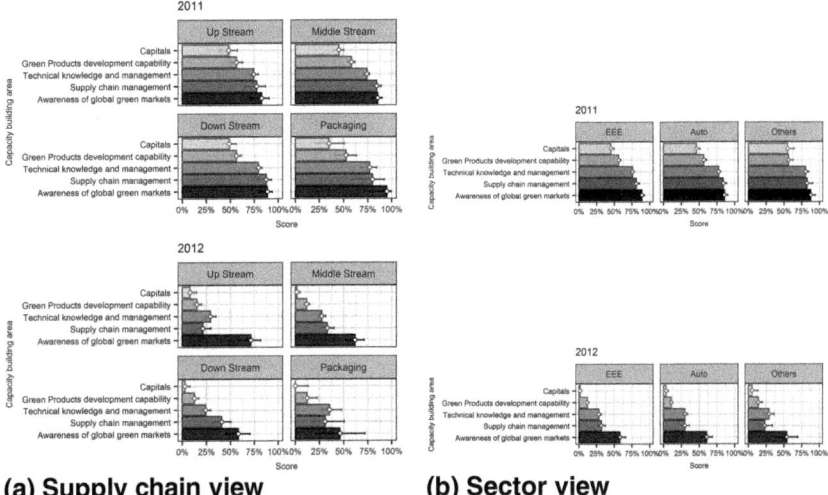

(a) Supply chain view   **(b) Sector view**

Fig. 12.22   Capacity building area extracted from firms recommendations in 2011 and 2012

producers are the first actors who bear responsibility for product compliance, and they need not only compliant products/materials but information on the contents of controlled substances from their suppliers as well. Middle-stream producers also needed supports from the supply chain to fulfill their obligations. Upstream firms, on the other hand, do not have to rely on suppliers to fulfill their role, and hence did not see this item as important. It will be harder for middle-stream and down-stream firms to push upstream firms to realign in their direction when upstream firms still have other non-ECS markets wide open. Figure 12.23 illustrates an example of parts that are widely used in construction and aluminum frames businesses. Demand from the EEE sector was not large enough to get producer's collaboration to ensure products' free of restricted substances.

Packaging firms were also in an interesting situation. Firms in this sector were mostly SMEs. They fed their products to different product sectors that faced different requirements. Customer requirements that passed along the supply chain also reached packaging firms. Very often, these firms were forced to provide compliance reports for product-oriented regulations, such as RoHS/ELV, that were not relevant to them. This

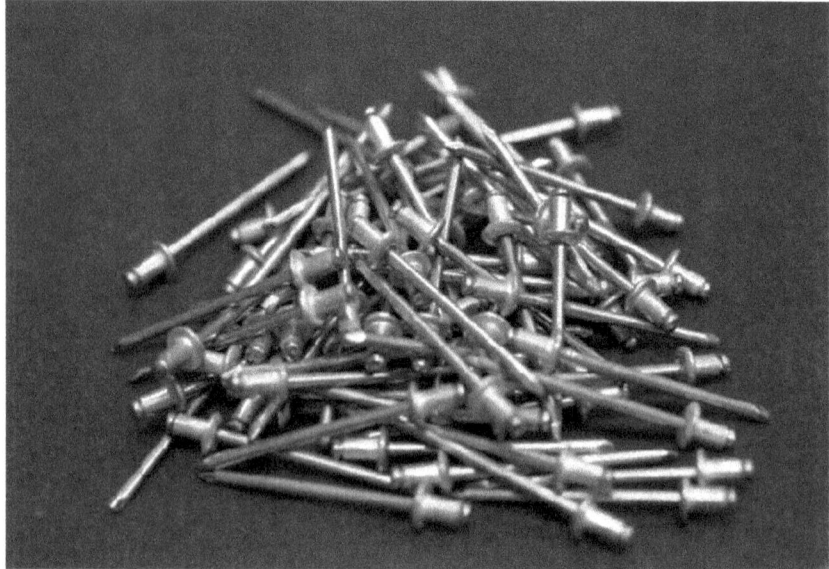

Fig. 12.23 Case example

type of requirement created unnecessary burdens, and it was usually the packaging firms' job to clarify the fact to customers until they were satisfied. Packaging was also the first product consumers notice when an item is placed on the market. Respondents from packaging firms, therefore, rated highly on technical knowledge, which included up-to-date knowledge on regulations and substances of concern.

Unlike capacity that would help firms to avoid harm, most respondents also sensed the importance of green product development capability, but this appeared to be a area for the second stage of development, when firms are ready to move forward in a more efficient manner to capture the upside of the green markets.

12.7 Lessons Learned

Based on information gained from the survey results, we learned the following lessons:

Lesson 1: ECS compliance is driven by customers/markets

It is undeniable that EU has set new standards for ECS products. However, these new requirements are not directly impact Thai firms who, in most parts, supply materials and parts to satisfy customers' requirements. Based on our results in the early stage of the adjustment, firms did not make movement until their customers, particularly MNCs, made their move through their green products initiatives. EU ECS products regulations, nevertheless, helped reduce the prices/costs prospects barrier making it easier for firms in EEE and automotive industries to make their decisions.

Lesson 2: ECS compliance could be easier if it had clear rules and supportive infrastructures

In practice, supplying firms followed customers' mandates, not EU regulations. Unclear regulations, for example as in RoHS version 1, created uncertainties that pushed brand owners to set individual standards. Multiple standards created confusion and made it harder for supply chain firms to adjust their practices to conform every customer's requirement.

With clear rules and accompanying standards, for example as in RoHS version 2, relevant stakeholders could apprehend their duties and made more appropriate plans for the adjustment.

Lesson 3: ECS needs a strong supply chain to be successful

It is important to realize the fact that different actors operate in different contexts, and hence have different motivations. Downstream firms took actions to avoid harm to their businesses. Middle-stream firms initially took actions to avoid rejection, and then moved forward to capture new market opportunities. Upstream firms and firms in less sophisticated product sectors took action to strengthen their businesses. When firms along the supply chain gained control of their materials/processes and were ready to supply ECS products with high confidence, barrier from compliance costs went down and firms started exploring new opportunities from ECS markets.

Lesson 4: Middle-stream firms cannot be greener than customers/markets

Firms needed clear market prospects to make their adjustment. For firms in the middle stream to become a leader in greener products market, not only that they need prior approval from their customers but also supports from their upstream suppliers. This burden is too heavy for any Thai middle-stream firm to act alone.

Lesson 5: The most prominent barrier for greener products is also customers/markets

In the initial stage of the transition, there were several barriers for firms to cross. These barriers can be clustered into four groups; high compliance costs, low confidence in new materials/technologies, complexity of the new regulations, and unfavorable prices/costs prospects. Most of the barriers were lowered as the transition proceeded; compliance costs decreased with a stronger supply chain, confidence in new materials/technologies increased with experience and records from the field, barrier due to difficult/complex regulations could be lowered by many means, such as technical standards, simplified texts, e.g., guidance & guidelines, technical training, and appropriate tools. Prices/costs prospects, however, needed convincing messages from markets to persuade firms to make their adjustment.

Lesson 6: Suggested capacity-building areas

Different firms have different developmental goals, hence requiring different capacity-building programs. To help firms cope with ECS-like regulations, first we need to raise awareness to get relevant parties on board, then provide the industry with appropriate tools (standards, guidelines, etc.) to ease the transition and strengthen the supply chain, as well as equip firms with technical knowledge to enable them to solve practical problems. To support firm who intent to capture the upside of the green market, means to collect technical data to identify "hot spots" for improvement, training programs to improve green innovation capability, and supportive platforms to share burdens and resources were suggested.

References

Cooksey, R. W., & Soutar, G. N. (2006). Coefficient beta and hierarchical item clustering an analytical procedure for establishing and displaying the dimensionality and homogeneity of summated scales. *Organizational Research Methods, 9*(1), 78–98. 10.1177/1094428105283939.

Esty, D., & Winston, A. (2009). *Green to gold: How smart companies use environmental strategy to innovate, create value, and build competitive advantage.* Hoboken, NJ: John Wiley & Sons.

EU RoHS Enforcement Authorities Informal Network. (2005). RoHS Enforcement Guidance Document, Version 1. Retrieved from https://www.epa.ie/pubs/advice/waste/rohs/RoHS%20Enforcement%20Guidance%20Document%20-%20v%201%20May%2020061.pdf.

European Commission. (2005). Commission Decision of 18 August 2005 amending Directive 2002/95/EC of the European Parliament and of the Council for the purpose of establishing the maximum concentration values for certain hazardous substances in electrical and electronic equipment. Retrieved from http://eur-lex.europa.eu/legal-content/EN/TXT/PDF/?uri=CELEX:32005D0618&from=EN.

European Parliament. (1994). Directive 94/62/EC on packaging and packaging waste. Retrieved from http://eur-lex.europa.eu/legal-content/EN/TXT/PDF/?uri=CELEX:31994L0062&from=en.

European Parliament. (2000). Directive 2000/53/EC of the European Parliament and of the Council on end-of life vehicles. Retrieved from http://eur-lex.europa.eu/LexUriServ/LexUriServ.do?uri=CONSLEG:2000L0053:20050701:EN:PDF.

European Parliament. (2003). Directive 2002/95/EC of the European Parliament and of the Council on the Restriction of the Use of Certain Hazardous Substances in Electrical and Electronic Equipment. Retrieved from http://eur-lex.europa.eu/legal-content/EN/TXT/PDF/?uri=CELEX:32002L0095&from=EN.

European Parliament. (2004). Directive 2004/12/EC of the European Parliament and of the Council amending Directive 94/62/EC on packaging and packaging waste. Retrieved from http://eur-lex.europa.eu/resource.html?uri=cellar:f8128bcf-ee21-4b9c-b506-e0eaf56868e6.0004.02/DOC_1&format=PDF.

European Parliament. (2006). Regulation (EC) No 1907/2006 of the European Parliament and of the Council of 18 December 2006 concerning the Registration, Evaluation, Authorization and Restriction of Chemicals (REACH). Retrieved from http://eur-lex.europa.eu/legalcontent/EN/TXT/PDF/?uri=CELEX:02006R1907-20140410&from=EN.

European Parliament. (2011). Directive 2011/65/EU of the European Parliament and of the Council on the restriction of the use of certain hazardous substances in electrical and electronic equipment. Retrieved from http://eur-lex.europa.eu/legal-content/EN/TXT/PDF/?uri=CELEX:32011L0065&from=en.

IEC 62321: 2008. (2008). Electrotechnical products – Determination of levels of six regulated substances (lead, mercury, cadmium, hexavalent chromium, polybrominated biphenyls, polybrominated diphenyl ethers), International Electrotechnical Commission.

IEC 62474: 2012. (2012). Material declaration for products of and for the electrotechnical industry. International Electrotechnical Commission.

IEC TR62476:2010. (2010). Guidance for evaluation of product with respect to substance-use restrictions in electrical and electronic products. International Electrotechnical Commission.

ISO 9001:2008. (2008). Quality management systems. ISO.

MIT Sloan Management. (n.d.). *Improving sustainable supply chain efforts among retail leaders*. Retrieved from http://mitsloan.mit.edu/actionlearn ing/media/documents/s-lab-projects/RILA-report.pdf.

R Documentation, iclust: Item Cluster Analysis. (n.d.). *Hierarchical cluster analysis using psychometric principles*. Retrieved from http://personality-pro ject.org/r/html/ICLUST.html.

Revelle, W. (1978). ICLUST: A cluster analytic approach to exploratory and confirmatory scale construction. *Behavior Research Methods, 10*(5), 739–742. 10.3758/BF03205389.

Revelle, W. (2011). An overview of the psych package. Retrieved from http:// personality-project.org/r/book/overview.pdf.

Vossenaar, R., Santucci, L., & Ramungul, N. (2006). Environmental require-ments and market access for developing countries: the case of electrical and electronic equipment. *Trade and Environment Review 2006*. New York and Geneva: United Nations. Retrieved from http://unctad.org/en/docs/ ditcted200512_en.pdf.

Nudjarin Ramungul is a Research Specialist and the Director of Environment Research Unit at National Metal and Materials Technology Center, Thailand. She received her Ph.D degree in Electrical Engineering from Rensselaer Polytechnic Institute, NY, USA, in 1998. She started working on WEEE and RoHS directives since 2002. She initiated several research projects aimed to gain in-depth understanding of Thai firms and to provide them with appro-priate technical supports. Her works led to the initiation of ThaiRoHS alliance and the subsequent multi-stakeholders collaborative works that helped Thai EEE and automotive firms cope with global waves of substances in products regulations.

Index

© The Author(s) 2017
E. Michida et al. (eds.), *Regulations and International Trade*,
IDE-JETRO Series, DOI 10.1007/978-3-319-55041-1

CPI Antony Rowe
Chippenham, UK
2017-09-08 17:11